Creating Mixed Communities through Housing Policies

This book focuses on socially mixed (e.g., by income, tenure, ethnicity, or any other characteristic) communities developed through housing renewal and critically examines the policies and practices in view of the growing urban inequality. The volume expands the discussion to the second phase of social mix – "social mix version 2.0" and offers constructive reflections on how social mix can "be better conceived and delivered, with fewer negative side effects".

The chapters in this book cover diverse national contexts and policy backgrounds, and represent the perspectives of many key stakeholders, including national and local governments, services and NGOs, developers and, most importantly, residents. Chapters present diverse case studies from Europe, the Middle East, Africa, India, Australia, and the United States and discuss projects that range in scale from small housing initiatives to neighborhoods and to whole districts. They focus on diverse experiences of social mix: between university students and young professionals and low-income social housing tenants; between older, low-income residents and younger, middle-class residents; between diverse ethnic and social class groups sharing a neighborhood; and between private and public housing residents. Chapters also vary on the tools used to create social mix, from local non-for-profit initiatives, a national policy intervention, and urban policies that aim to enhance social mix. Lastly, the book shows the range of analytical tools researchers have used to understand the diverse appearances of social mix, its underlying goals, and its consequent outcomes. These include comparative analyses of social mix in diverse national and political settings, including the Global East, an evaluation of social mix from the perspective of social justice, a historical analysis of the development of an urban district, and a design analysis of urban renewal projects.

The chapters in this book were originally published as a special issue of *Journal of Urban Affairs*.

Anna Maria Santiago is an Administrator, Researcher, Professor, and Community Practitioner at Michigan State University, USA, whose interests focus on how housing and social welfare policies and programs can be used to reduce the social and economic disparities experienced by vulnerable, minoritized families and children residing in urban areas.

Iris Levin is an Architect, Urban Planner, Lecturer, and Researcher at RMIT University, Australia, whose interests focus on housing, social mix, social planning, migration, and social diversity in cities. She is passionate about working with diverse communities and understanding the effects of migration on the built environment.

Kathy Arthurson holds Full Academic Status at Flinders University of South Australia since 2017. Her research primarily focuses on the interdisciplinary field of housing, incorporating scholarship in the disciplines of urban planning, public health, and social policy.

Creating Mixed Communities through Housing Policies

Global Perspectives

**Edited by
Anna Maria Santiago, Iris Levin
and Kathy Arthurson**

LONDON AND NEW YORK

First published 2024
by Routledge
4 Park Square, Milton Park, Abingdon, Oxon OX14 4RN

and by Routledge
605 Third Avenue, New York, NY 10158

Routledge is an imprint of the Taylor & Francis Group, an informa business

© 2024 Urban Affairs Association

All rights reserved. No part of this book may be reprinted or reproduced or utilised in any form or by any electronic, mechanical, or other means, now known or hereafter invented, including photocopying and recording, or in any information storage or retrieval system, without permission in writing from the publishers.

Trademark notice: Product or corporate names may be trademarks or registered trademarks, and are used only for identification and explanation without intent to infringe.

British Library Cataloguing in Publication Data
A catalogue record for this book is available from the British Library

ISBN13: 978-1-032-62530-0 (hbk)
ISBN13: 978-1-032-62531-7 (pbk)
ISBN13: 978-1-032-62533-1 (ebk)

DOI: 10.4324/9781032625331

Typeset in Minion Pro
by Newgen Publishing UK

Publisher's Note
The publisher accepts responsibility for any inconsistencies that may have arisen during the conversion of this book from journal articles to book chapters, namely the inclusion of journal terminology.

Disclaimer
Every effort has been made to contact copyright holders for their permission to reprint material in this book. The publishers would be grateful to hear from any copyright holder who is not here acknowledged and will undertake to rectify any errors or omissions in future editions of this book.

Contents

Citation Information vi
Notes on Contributors viii

Introduction—Creating mixed communities through housing policies: Global perspectives 1
Iris Levin, Anna Maria Santiago, and Kathy Arthurson

1 Promoting a geography of opportunity in Accra, Ghana: Applying lessons from mixed-income development successes and shortcomings 15
 Mark L. Joseph, Isaac K. Arthur, and Edmund Kwame Botchway

2 Low-income housing development in India: Strategies for income mixing and inclusive urban planning 35
 Naganika Sanga

3 In the name of "social mixing": The privatization of public housing to non-governmental organizations 53
 Yael Shmaryahu-Yeshurun

4 Social mix in context: Comparing housing regeneration programs in Australia and Israel 71
 Iris Levin, Nava Kainer Persov, Kathy Arthurson, and Anna Ziersch

5 Re-scaling social mix: Public housing renewal in Melbourne 90
 Ruby Capp, Libby Porter, and David Kelly

6 Housing motivated youth in low-income neighborhoods: How practitioners shape conditions for encounters across diversity in 'intentional' social mix programs in Milan and Paris 107
 Igor Costarelli and Talia Melic

7 Does pre-purchase counseling help low-income buyers choose and sustain homeownership in socially mixed destination neighborhoods? 126
 Anna Maria Santiago and Joffré Leroux

Index 149

Citation Information

The chapters in this book were originally published in the *Journal of Urban Affairs* (https://www.tandfonline.com/journals/ujua20) volume 44, issue 3 (2022). When citing this material, please use the original page numbering for each article, as follows:

Introduction
Creating mixed communities through housing policies: Global perspectives
Iris Levin, Anna Maria Santiago and Kathy Arthurson
Journal of Urban Affairs, volume 44, issue 3 (2022), pp. 291–304

Chapter 1
Promoting a geography of opportunity in Accra, Ghana: Applying lessons from mixed-income development successes and shortcomings
Mark L. Joseph, Isaac K. Arthur and Edmund Kwame Botchway
Journal of Urban Affairs, volume 44, issue 3 (2022), pp. 305–324

Chapter 2
Low-income housing development in India: Strategies for income mixing and inclusive urban planning
Naganika Sanga
Journal of Urban Affairs, volume 44, issue 3 (2022), pp. 325–342

Chapter 3
In the name of "social mixing": The privatization of public housing to non-governmental organizations
Yael Shmaryahu-Yeshurun
Journal of Urban Affairs, volume 44, issue 3 (2022), pp. 343–360

Chapter 4
Social mix in context: Comparing housing regeneration programs in Australia and Israel
Iris Levin, Nava Kainer Persov, Kathy Arthurson and Anna Ziersch
Journal of Urban Affairs, volume 44, issue 3 (2022), pp. 361–379

Chapter 5
Re-scaling social mix: Public housing renewal in Melbourne
Ruby Capp, Libby Porter and David Kelly
Journal of Urban Affairs, volume 44, issue 3 (2022), pp. 380–396

Chapter 6
Housing motivated youth in low-income neighborhoods: How practitioners shape conditions for encounters across diversity in 'intentional' social mix programs in Milan and Paris
Igor Costarelli and Talia Melic
Journal of Urban Affairs, volume 44, issue 3 (2022), pp. 397–415

Chapter 7
Does pre-purchase counseling help low-income buyers choose and sustain homeownership in socially mixed destination neighborhoods?
Anna Maria Santiago and Joffré Leroux
Journal of Urban Affairs, volume 44, issue 3 (2022), pp. 416–438

For any permission-related enquiries please visit:
www.tandfonline.com/page/help/permissions

Notes on Contributors

Isaac K. Arthur is Senior Lecturer of Human Geography at the Department of Geography and Resource Development and the Director for the Centre for Urban Management Studies, University of Ghana, Ghana. He is an interdisciplinary researcher and has conducted research in the areas of urban studies, planning and development, the experience economy, migration, and innovation and entrepreneurship in food-related rural enterprises. He is a member of the Regional Studies Association, UK, and editorial board member of the *African Journal for Housing and Sustainable Development*.

Kathy Arthurson holds Full Academic Status at Flinders University of South Australia since 2017. Her research primarily focuses on the interdisciplinary field of housing, incorporating scholarship in the disciplines of urban planning, public health, and social policy.

Nava Kainer Persov is Lecturer at the Faculty of Architecture and Town Planning at the Technion – Israel Institute of Technology and Postdoctoral Fellow at the Remote Sensing and GIS Lab at University of Haifa. Nava's research interests include urban regeneration strategies, housing policy, social-spatial equity, urban design, planning in dialogue with the community, social mix, affordable housing, and urban networks that promote urban resilience.

Edmund Kwame Botchway is Director of Community Impact and Innovation at Cleveland Neighborhood Progress, a community development funding intermediary in Cleveland, Ohio, USA. Botchway is an urban development specialist with research and work experience focused on inclusive and equitable development practices, creating social impact, and evaluation and monitoring. His areas of expertise include affordable and mixed-income housing development, sustainability, community, and economic development, and racial equity and inclusion, and nonprofit management. He is an executive committee member of the Cleveland branch of the NAACP, serving as Chair of International Affairs.

Ruby Capp is Senior Policy Adviser – Infrastructure, Planning and Major Projects at the Department of Premier and Cabinet, Melbourne, Australia. Her research interests include transit-oriented development and social and affordable housing.

Igor Costarelli is Post-Doc Fellow at the Department of Sociology and Social Research, University of Milan-Bicocca, Italy. His research focuses on social mix, residential segregation, social housing management, housing, and urban renewal policy.

Mark L. Joseph is the Leona Bevis and Marguerite Haynam Professor of Community Development at the Jack, Joseph and Morton Mandel School of Applied Social Sciences at Case Western Reserve University, USA. His research focuses on promoting urban equity and inclusion. He is the coauthor of *Integrating the Inner City: The Promise and Perils of Mixed Income Public Housing Transformation* and co-editor of *What Works to Promote Inclusive, Equitable Mixed-Income Communities*. He is the Founding Director of the National Initiative on Mixed-Income Communities and serves on the Governing Board of the Urban Affairs Association.

David Kelly is a cultural geographer who explores the spatial and affective life of policy in relation to Aboriginal homelands, low-income urban housing, inclusivity for people with disability, and urban renewal.

Joffré Leroux is a PhD candidate in economics at Michigan State University, USA. His research interests are in public and labor economics. His publications revolve around home ownership and the impact of self-sufficiency on human beings.

Iris Levin is an Architect, Urban Planner, Lecturer, and Researcher at RMIT University, Australia, whose interests focus on housing, social mix, social planning, migration, and social diversity in cities. She is passionate about working with diverse communities and understanding the effects of migration on the built environment.

Talia Melic is a PhD candidate in Urban Geography with the University of Melbourne, Australia, in co-tutorship with Université Paris-Est, France. She is a member of the ARC Life Course Centre and Laboratoire Lab'urba, Gustave Eiffel University, France. Her research focuses on mixed-income housing, urban encounters, housing theory and policy, and urban social relations.

Libby Porter is a Professor at the Centre for Urban Research, RMIT University, Australia. Porter's research interests include the relationship between urbanization, dispossession, and displacement in contemporary cities.

Naganika Sanga is a social science research monitoring associate at Abt Associates, USA. She studies housing policies in the United States and India, focusing on the influence of multilevel governance systems and diverse actors on local policy decisions. Her research and work experience also include community engagement, advocacy, land policies, and strategic planning.

Anna Maria Santiago is an Administrator, Researcher, Professor, and Community Practitioner at Michigan State University, USA, whose interests focus on how housing and social welfare policies and programs can be used to reduce the social and economic disparities experienced by vulnerable, minoritized families and children residing in urban areas.

Yael Shmaryahu-Yeshurun is a lecturer in urban studies and planning at UC-San Diego, USA. Yael's research interests focus on spatial policy, urban communities, and spatial relations between different ethno-national, class, and religious groups. Her research combines theories, concepts, and methods from public policy, political science, urban sociology, and geography.

Anna Ziersch is an Associate Professor (Research) at the Southgate Institute for Health, Society and Equity/Flinders Health and Medical Research Institute at Flinders University, Australia. Anna's research focuses on the social determinants of health and health equity, with a particular focus on migrant and refugee health. She has a strong commitment to applied multidisciplinary research and participatory methodologies. She is a co-convenor of the Migration and Refugee Research Network.

Introduction—Creating mixed communities through housing policies: Global perspectives

Iris Levin, Anna Maria Santiago, and Kathy Arthurson

ABSTRACT
This introductory review essay examines some of the key concepts and approaches framing the ongoing debate around mixed communities and housing regeneration policies around the world. This review summarizes past positive and negative side effects of social mix reported in the extant international literature. It then describes social mix housing policies in the Global East and the Global South, including China, Japan, South Korea, sub-Saharan Africa, and Singapore. In moving forward, the review essay adopts Galster and Friedrichs's challenge to think about the progressive reformation of a "social mix version 2.0"—what it might look like, and what the policy implications of such an improved version of social mix might be. Three policy implications are discussed: intentionality of social mix; mixed-income housing transit-oriented design; and learning from the Global East and Global South.

Introduction

In this introductory review essay, we examine some of the key concepts and approaches from the ongoing debate around mixed-income communities[1] and housing regeneration policies. We first provide a summary of the current literature to identify the positive and negative side effects of social mix before presenting social mix housing policies in the Global East and the Global South. In this review, we take up Galster and Friedrichs's challenge to think about the progressive reformation of a "social mix version 2.0" (Galster & Friedrichs, 2015, p. 178), what it might look like, and what the policy implications of such an improved version of social mix might be.

The idea of social mix in planning and housing policy has existed since the mid-19th century in England and the United States (Arthurson, 2012; Sarkissian, 1976). Historically, creating mixed communities was considered as a means for improving the social position and health of disadvantaged communities in society; a rationale for clearing slums to eliminate pestilence; raising the esthetic diversity of residential neighborhoods; encouraging cultural cross-fertilization; increasing equal opportunity; and promoting social cohesion by reducing racial tensions, among other objectives (Sarkissian, 1976). This partial list of objectives clearly reflects the main goal of social mix: "enhancing the social diversity of residential environments" (Galster, 2007, p. 19) or creating a "balanced community" (Cole & Goodchild, 2001, p. 351), although "diversity" and "balanced" have been defined differently in different contexts. Through this main goal, it is claimed that social mix can create several mechanisms to improve the lives of disadvantaged communities (Galster & Friedrichs, 2015).

One mechanism is the promotion of social capital and social interaction among residents, leading to improved employment opportunities and better sustainable communities. Other mechanisms can be role modeling, better access to higher quality public and private services and institutions, better access to housing, decreased exposure to violence, and reduced area-based stigma (Galster &

Friedrichs, 2015). As Galster and Friedrichs (2015) note, social mix has been considered from diverse perspectives, including as a planning theory, a socioeconomic condition, urban strategies, and has even been appropriated by both right- and left-wing political views. Similarly, Arthurson et al. (2015a) have argued that social mix has been understood from two main perspectives: on the one hand, it has been viewed as a social inclusion project that aims to advance disadvantaged communities (e.g., Arthurson, 2010; Chaskin et al., 2012; Curley, 2010), and on the other, it has been criticized as a state-led gentrification project that in practice displaces residents of disadvantaged communities (e.g., Davidson, 2010; Lees, 2008; Slater, 2008). Galster and Friedrichs (2015, p. 176) view social mix as a "mezzo-level" construct, a condition of urban space involving the composition of the resident population. They define it as "a combination of diverse shares of social groups in a neighbourhood." In practice, socially mixed communities (or mixed-income communities as they are known in the United States) can take many forms. The point of diversity or mix can vary according to income, housing tenure, ethnicity, nativity, household composition, age, visa status or a combination of these factors. Additionally, the spatial scale of mix can vary between a large district, a neighborhood, a street, a smaller estate, or subdivision.

Although the approach has been around for almost 2 centuries, the use of social mix has witnessed a revival during the past 3 decades in urban policy settings in developed countries, such as the United Kingdom, the United States, Canada, Australia and in Western Europe nations. Since the late 1980s, with the neo-liberalization of governments, privatization trends, and the withdrawal from government spending, social mix has been employed as a major policy objective to justify urban renewal projects in prime locations in cities through different financial mechanisms, often involving private sector funds.

A review of the extensive scholarship on social mix reveals the diverse uses of the approach and the variety of ways it has emerged in different Western contexts. The plethora of literature on social mix in its different forms and contexts encompasses numerous research articles, special editions of journals (e.g., Bolt & van Kempen, 2013; Bond et al., 2011; Fraser et al., 2013; Galster & Friedrichs, 2015; Sautkina et al., 2012) and books devoted to the topic (Arthurson, 2012; Bridge et al., 2012; Varady, 2005). Nevertheless, these scholarly works have focused on specific aspects of mixed communities, such as the neighborhood effects of mixing social groups (Baily et al., 2012; Bolt et al., 2010; Bolt & van Kempen, 2013; Van Ham & Manley, 2010); community participation in public housing redevelopment projects (Arthurson et al., 2015b; Chaskin et al., 2012); and relocation outcomes for public housing residents moving to other neighborhoods (Goetz, 2013; Kleinhans & Kearns, 2013; Kleit & Galvez, 2011; Levin et al., 2018; Oakley & Burchfield, 2009; Popkin et al., 2009). However, demolition of public housing and relocation of tenants is not the only way to achieve social mix. Few studies have focused on the various ways housing development and renewal in general (i.e., at a broader focus beyond public housing renewal) have been used to create social mix, especially where it has evolved inadvertently (i.e., without explicit policies aiming at achieving it). As Bridge et al. (2014) contend, little attention has been given to social mix in the gentrification literature. There also is a lack of nuanced understanding of how social mix operates in diverse contexts (Galster & Friedrichs, 2015) or comparatively beyond a focus on Western countries to new emerging regions.

What have been the past positive and negative side effects of social mix?

There is considerable debate in previous special journal issues about whether social mix initiatives meet their anticipated objectives for disadvantaged communities, such as: improved employment opportunities; building sustainable communities; providing access to better quality services and housing; and an improved quality of life. In the main, earlier studies sought to identify the positive effects of social mix for public housing tenants and whether (or not) different socioeconomic or tenure groups interacted with each other (August, 2014; Bacqué et al., 2011; Bond et al., 2011; Joseph, 2008; Sautkina et al., 2012; Varady et al., 2005). The latter aspect is an important precursor to ascertain the perceived benefits of social mix. Following this line of inquiry, as the research showed little evidence of social interaction, investigations turned to questioning how to support social interaction in mixed communities and whether there are negative consequences of implementing social mix in practice (Fraser et al., 2013). Nevertheless, it is possible that middle-class residents will attract more public sector attention and investment to the neighborhood regardless of whether there is social interaction, although some activities can be beyond reach for poorer residents (Arthurson, 2012).

Previous research identified several mediating factors that facilitate the effects of social mix on social interaction. These include the residential trajectories of the residents (which correlate with familiarity with the neighborhood); residents' lifestyle (and especially those with busy lifestyles who have little time for mixing); the scale of implementation (with a recommended scale of neighborhood rather than the building or housing cluster); the spatial layout and physical arrangement of the neighborhood, and the stigma attached to social housing. Moreover, to encourage social interaction, there needs to be a hierarchy of spaces from private to semi-private to semi-public, to public spaces, to allow for social interaction to occur (Lelévrier, 2013; Levin et al., 2014).

More to the point, the initial tendency of studies to target identifying the benefits of social mix means there has been less of a focus on unraveling the realities of the negative effects from social mix policies, such as diminished sense of community (Sautkina et al. (2012, p. 776). Perhaps as suggested by Bond et al. (2011), this situation has occurred through ongoing efforts to support an evidence base for policymakers. In a systematic review of other reviews of the literature (UK between 1995 and 2009), Bond et al. (2011, p. 23) found that these reviews overemphasized the positive effects of social mix. Little or no evidence was often interpreted as "success" or at the least doing "no harm," and the same studies were often interpreted differently. Bond et al. (2011) concluded that in this case much of the exploration of "evidence" was fraught with methodological issues making it difficult to draw firm conclusions. In effect, while there is a large literature on mixed tenure, policymakers are likely to rely on reviews and summaries of the evidence rather than primary studies. Nevertheless, although there is some evidence for improved neighborhood satisfaction and improvements to local environment and amenities, the latter reflect indirect changes associated with physical renewal rather than social mix per se.

Other studies have identified negative effects, such as physical and social disruption and constraints on housing choices (especially in wholesale neighborhood demolition projects) and the potential disruption to community kinship networks from regeneration efforts (Fraser et al., 2013). The latter aspect has been known since the earliest community studies conducted in the 1950s and 1960s (e.g., Gans, 1962; Jacobs, 1961). Bridge et al. (2014) argued that we need to look at power relations existing between different groups involved in the social mix. They concluded that in gentrified neighborhoods, which result in a revised social mix through middle-income residents moving into previously working-class areas, there is a reassertion of class power by the middle classes through controlling community agendas and public events.

In their special journal issue on social mix, Bolt and van Kempen (2013) focused on desegregation policies in different national contexts. They concluded that although there are a variety of policy initiatives across Europe, these initiatives have not succeeded in reducing the level of ethnic and class concentration in urban settings. Similarly, in their special edition, Galster and Friedrichs (2015) focused on the question of whether social mix has an impact on improving the wellbeing of lower-income residents living at concentrated disadvantage. They concluded that there is adequate evidence (at least in the Western European and United States contexts) to support the equity goals of social mix on grounds of improving the wellbeing of low-income residents. They cautioned, however, that past programs focusing on restructuring large public housing estates and forced displacement of communities have caused significant harm and proposed that social mix can be achieved by strategies that attract low-income households to voluntarily settle in stronger communities over the longer-term and avoid the negative side effects of past programs. Galster and Friedrichs concluded that "[s]ocial mix can be achieved in principle by more voluntary, gradualist, housing option-enhancing strategies" (Galster & Friedrichs, 2015, p. 183).

Social mix housing policies in the Global East and Global South

As the world's population continues to urbanize, how might social mix housing policies serve as tools to support the United Nations's Sustainable Development Goal 11 which "commits to making cities inclusive, safe, resilient and sustainable" (United Nations, 2019, p. 3) while accommodating a burgeoning urban population? Current population projections suggest that an additional 2.5 billion people will reside in the world's cities by 2050 with 90% of this new growth occurring in Asia and Africa (United Nations, 2019, p. 3). Since the late 1990s, there has been growing attention to rapid urbanization trends in the Global East[2] and Global South (see, for example, Wang & Murie, 2000; McTarnaghan et al., 2016; Yap, 2016; Abubakar & Doan, 2017; Cho et al., 2017; King et al., 2017; Mishra & Mohanty, 2017; Steel et al., 2017; Phang, 2018;; Ramanathan & Gandhi, 2018; Coelho et al., 2020). Nonetheless, there is still limited research on how social mix housing policies have been or might be implemented as strategies to mitigate the effects of rapid growth especially for the most disadvantaged city dwellers, while supporting sustainable urban development (Satterthwaite & Mitlin, 2014).

Although prior studies of social mix housing policies have focused primarily on Australia, Western Europe, North America and the United Kingdom, there is an emerging literature on social mix in the Global East and Global South, particularly in China (Chu et al., 2019; Tian et al., 2007); Japan (Hsiao, 2021; Mizuuchi & Jeon, 2010; Ronald & Hirayama, 2007); Singapore (Ho & Chua, 2018; Kumar, 2020; Phang, 2018; Weder di Mauro, 2018); South Korea (Ronald & Lee, 2012; Yang et al., 2018); Taiwan (Chen, 2011); and South Africa (Mosselson, 2017; Sinxadi et al., 2019). Except for Singapore, the use of social mix policies in these regions is a relatively recent phenomenon occurring within the past 10–15 years. To date, most of the applications of social mix housing policies in the Global East and Global South have focused on income mixing, particularly in government subsidized housing for low-income or worker families. However, there are some interesting illustrations of other types of social mix at play: the need to consider age mixing in subsidized housing in a rapidly aging population in Japan (Hsiao, 2021) or the deliberate use of racial/ethnic mixing strategies in Singapore (Kumar, 2020; Weder di Mauro, 2018). Further, the substantial role of governments in supporting housing creation or regeneration including social mix, particularly in the Global East, stands in sharp contrast to the shrinking role of governments in Europe, the United Kingdom, and North America (Hsiao, 2021; Weder di Mauro, 2018).

Social mix in China

After decades of operating state-controlled housing for workers, China introduced housing reform in the 1980s geared toward the growing privatization of housing through homeownership and support of the private rental market (Wang & Murie, 2000). By the 2010s, 90% of Chinese households owned their own homes (Clark et al., 2019), leaving low-income households on the margins. In the pre-reform era, housing was tied to employment with workers residing in buildings located near their workplaces and occupying flats of different sizes reflective of their occupational positions. During the past decade or so, the Chinese government has fostered mixed habitation complexes or communities to address concerns for providing adequate shelter for China's low-income population. The government has encouraged the development of residential communities that include mixes of low-income households and households from other income groups. Tian et al. (2007) found that residential segregation was maintained through the physical design of these communities. However, they report that the social distance between income groups diminished between those who resided in these mixed communities relative to households that resided in more economically homogeneous housing communities. Chu et al. (2019) report that China has begun developing public-rental housing in privately owned housing complexes to generate income mix and mitigate the concentration of poverty and residential segregation in Chinese cities. Their study, which examines the extent to which physical and social integration is occurring in these mixed habitation complexes, found that the physical configurations of these complexes maintained spatial segregation by income groups. Further, the physical layout of these complexes limited opportunities for social interaction between residents because many public spaces were constructed in ways that restricted traffic flow or access to communal space.

Social mix in Japan

A key feature of the Japanese housing system has been the provision by larger corporations of company housing, rental subsidies, and mortgages for home purchases to their employees (Ronald & Hirayama, 2007), which effectively created occupationally and economically mixed communities tied to places of employment. More recently, housing policies in Japan have been used to integrate social and ethnic minority populations in Japan's urban areas (Hsiao, 2021; Mizuuchi & Jeon, 2010). Given the rapidly aging population of Japan, however, current housing policies at both the state and municipality levels have focused on maximizing the use of the existing subsidized housing stock for use primarily by lower-income households and those headed by vulnerable elders. As Hsiao (2021) notes, population trends in Japan run counter to social mix efforts as poor and elderly households become more concentrated within public housing estates.

Social mix in South Korea

During the late 2000s, the South Korean government adopted legislation mandating the incorporation of affordable housing in every new residential or redevelopment project (Ronald & Lee, 2012; Yang et al., 2018). One of the key features of the expansion of affordable housing was the extension of such housing to households in the lowest 50% of the income distribution (Ronald & Lee, 2012). While recent housing policies prohibited discrimination against the exclusion of affordable rental housing in developments, they did not "provide guidelines for achieving social mix at the neighbourhood level" (p. 811). In a study examining the impact of social mix on social capital formation, Yang et al. (2018) report that residing in a socially mixed neighborhood had positive effects on social norms but was negatively associated with trust and the development of social networks between low- and higher-income groups.

Social mix in Sub-Saharan Africa

To date, limited research has focused on the use of social mix housing policies in sub-Saharan African cities (see Joseph, Arthur and Botchway in this special issue). As Abubakar and Doan (2017) note, relatively few of the emerging capital and satellite cities in Africa have been deliberately planned as fully integrated cities with mixed residential areas. They argue that Gaborone, Botswana, provides one exception. Instead, they note that zoning regulations and high housing construction standards in these newer cities are contributing to heightened spatial exclusion and social inequality as new spaces become increasingly privatized. Moreover, the flight of residents to these new urban centers is exacerbating poverty for those who are left behind in the older cities. Additionally, severe spatial and social inequalities fostered by colonialism and segregationist policies, like apartheid in South Africa, continue to hamper poverty alleviation efforts on the continent (Mosselson, 2017). Mosselson notes that although inner-city, post-apartheid Johannesburg reflects a mix of poor to middle-class households, it is a city that is highly segregated and fragmented. However, recent initiatives have emerged to foster integration. In a preliminary study examining the effects of mixed income housing policies on reducing spatial and social inequalities, Sinxadi et al. (2019) report that the community stakeholders they interviewed recognized the potential of using social mix policies to curb poverty in urban areas through spatial restructuring. Nonetheless, respondents noted that current activities providing a variety of tenure options seem to be more effective in resolving spatial inequalities but not social inequalities.

Singapore—A unique adoption of social mix housing policy

As an independent city-state that emerged from racial conflict and a colonial past in the 1960s, Singapore provides a unique case study of successful implementation of social mix housing policy. The cornerstones of government policy in Singapore are social inclusion and the absence of racial segregation (Kumar, 2020). In addition, Singapore's government mandates that there are no disadvantaged neighborhoods within the city-state (see discussion in Weder di Mauro, 2018). In order to achieve these policy goals, Singapore created the state-funded Housing Development Board in the late 1960s to generate well built, attractive subsidized housing and high-quality neighborhood social infrastructure with playgrounds, markets, community centers, and schools (Ho & Chua, 2018) and used them as vehicles to promote income and racial/ethnic residential integration. Flats of different sizes are deliberately mixed in every apartment building to foster income integration. Quotas for each of the main ethnic groups—Chinese, Malay and Indian—apply to each apartment block and neighborhood in order to maximize racial integration and minimize racial conflict (see Weder di Mauro, 2018).

Today, more than eight out of 10 Singaporeans reside in state-subsidized housing; only wealthy individuals and foreigners are excluded. Additionally, citizens and permanent residents can purchase their apartments; more than 90% of them do (Ho & Chua, 2018). These purchases, however, are highly regulated by the Housing Development Bank—only purchases that remain within established ethnic quotas are approved. As a result, Singapore is characterized by very low levels of racial residential segregation (Weder di Mauro, 2018). Further, the design of these neighborhoods and apartment blocks have generated opportunities for multi-ethnic neighboring as well as wider consciousness and consensus for multiculturalism (Ho & Chua, 2018).

Social Mix Version 2.0

Our recognition of the negative side effects of social mix policies and the policy experience in countries in the Global East and the Global South has led us to consider how to improve future social mix policy and move to an updated "Social Mix Version 2.0" (as explicated further below). As we have seen, previous special journal editions on social mix have reached confident, albeit conflicting conclusions regarding the success or failure of social mix. In summary, the key issues in the field are:

(1) Policy evaluations on social mix produced by organizations outside of academe tend to be uncritical and have often focused on identifying the anticipated positive effects of social mix and the related strategy of how to enhance mixing across different socioeconomic or tenure groups. In contrast, while the academic literature is often critical of social mix, separate strands across housing renewal and gentrification studies have emerged within this literature (see, for example, Watt & Smets, 2017).
(2) There is little understanding of social mix approaches in different contexts beyond developed countries.
(3) Our understanding of how to facilitate social mix beyond demolition and relocation of public housing tenants is limited.

To address these gaps, this special issue focuses on social mix achieved through the re-creation of housing communities beyond public housing renewal. We embrace Galster and Friedrichs's suggestion (Galster & Friedrichs, 2015) to expand the discussion to the second phase of social mix—what they term "social mix version 2.0"—and offer constructive reflections on how social mix can "be better conceived and delivered, with fewer negative side effects" (p. 178). Like them, we agree that there is a need to move beyond "a one size fits all" approach without deflecting attention away from the real causes of urban social and spatial inequality.

Yet, the claimed benefits of social mix as a policy tool seem overstated. Disadvantaged communities are often portrayed as problematic in the public discourse (Darcy, 2010; Doney et al., 2013), so the policy tool is to "dilute" the community and mix it with other, "stronger" (middle income) communities. This is a distorted assumption because urban and social disadvantage is a result of complex structural processes related to housing policy, renewal policy, education policy, labor markets and more (Darcy, 2010). One of the main underlying ideas of social mix is about design or environmental determinism, so regeneration and various forms of manipulation of the built environment are perceived to be adequate solutions. In the United States and elsewhere, this appears as the physical transformation of large public housing developments or estates, which is also strongly linked to the neoliberal turn of the 1980s and the withdrawal of the state regarding policy making of public housing (Goetz, 2012). Therefore, a simplistic idea of design determinism is assumed to solve complex structural issues, which are much broader than housing renewal, hence its attraction to policymakers.

What might Social Mix Version 2.0 look like?

Existing evidence suggests that social mix programs alleviate the physical spatial inequality experienced in disadvantaged communities (Goetz & Chapple, 2010; Jourdan et al., 2013; Kearns et al., 2013). This aspect of social mix is also mentioned by Capp, Porter and Kelly, Levin, Kainer Persov, Arthurson and Ziersch, and Santiago and Leroux in this special issue. Regeneration housing programs that replace old, dilapidated housing estates have improved the physical housing stock and neighborhood conditions and amenities for most residents who previously lived in them, although not all (Bond et al., 2011; Curley, 2010).

Nonetheless, the evidence is inconclusive regarding any reductions in the levels of social inequality within such communities. Further, there is no certainty of social interactions between social groups, or if it is taking place at all, that such interactions are meaningful (Curley, 2009; Goetz & Chapple, 2010). Indeed, there is conflicting evidence regarding a whole raft of anticipated benefits: the improvement of the self-sufficiency of disadvantaged communities (Curley, 2010; Goetz & Chapple, 2010); improvement to children's schooling (Goetz & Chapple, 2010); mental health (Jackson et al., 2009; Goetz & Chapple, 2010; Kearns et al., 2013); safety (Goetz & Chapple, 2010); and other community wellbeing indicators. Moreover, as noted earlier, the existing evidence is fraught with methodological problems (Bond et al., 2011).

We have identified three essential issues for the development of social mix version 2.0: (1) the question of intentionality; (2) socially mixed transit-oriented development; and (3) learnings from the Global East and South. Each of these is discussed in more detail below.

The question of intentionality

One of the concerns identified by Levin et al. and others in this special issue centers on the question of intentionality. Is social mix an intentional outcome of planning and housing programs or merely an unexpected consequence? Should intentions for social mix always be fully explicated? How should related planning and community development work be funded to facilitate successful social mix? One pertinent example is in the case of housing vouchers aimed at moving residents to rental properties in more affluent neighborhoods. Previous research found that residents provided with vouchers in the United States tend to concentrate in poorer neighborhoods (e.g., Oakley & Burchfield, 2009). Providing vouchers for disadvantaged residents to move to rental market properties in "better" neighborhoods without community development work and sustainable social planning of the community, does not allow for a mixed income community to flourish and for the expected benefits of mixed communities to be achieved. Therefore, policymakers must consider how to sustain mixed communities for the benefit of disadvantaged community residents. Potential ways that this can be achieved are through the creative use of public and private funds, tax incentives, and housing option-enhancing strategies (Galster & Friedrichs, 2015).

We believe that housing regeneration programs, whether they focus on public or private housing developments or any other housing that may become a mixed community, need to consider all the intended and unintended outcomes of these programs. If a socially mixed community is created without planning for and recognizing it, different aspects that might promote physical and social integration (Chaskin & Joseph, 2010; Levin et al., 2014) may be overlooked and the benefits of social mix may not be achieved. If social mix is not planned for (and even where it is), it can have negative consequences for disadvantaged communities. These include displacement and dislocation (Lees, 2008); increased stigma based on housing tenure (Arthurson, 2013; Ruiz-Tagle, 2017); and even alienation between social groups if social cohesion is not intentionally encouraged (Chaskin & Joseph, 2010).

Mixed-income housing transit-oriented design

Since the beginning of the 21st century, transit-oriented design (TOD) has emerged as an important tool for urban planning. In North America and Australia, principles of mixed income housing development have been enfolded into transit-oriented designs (Belzer et al., 2007; Center for Transit Oriented Development, 2017; Edmonds, 2018) based on the premise that mixed income TOD holds great potential for connecting lower-income households to both place-based opportunities and regional opportunities. Indeed, the Center for Transit Oriented Development (2017, p. 5), suggests that when mixed income housing is coupled with access to transportation nodes, these combined efforts yield truly affordable housing by reducing both housing and transportation costs, increasing ridership on public transit, reducing traffic congestion and pollution while encouraging health promotion and healthy lifestyle activities such as more walking and biking. Moreover, mixed income neighborhoods situated along transit zones are more likely to support higher levels of racial/ethnic and income diversity than the average neighborhood (Belzer et al., 2007).

One of the communities in the United States with a 20-year history of engaging in mixed-income housing transit-oriented development is Denver, Colorado. To date, the Housing Authority of the City and County of Denver (n.d.) has served as the lead agency in the redevelopment or retention of low-income housing in five districts situated along light rail lines in the city. These projects created affordable and market-rate housing units as well as supported commercial and neighborhood retail development. Embedded in the development plans was extensive community engagement with neighborhood residents and other stakeholders. Additionally, each of the development plans included provisions for community centers, childcare centers, health clinics, charter schools, community gardens and fresh food markets (see Edmonds, 2018). Central to these projects are the intentional decisions made to "preserve opportunities for low-income and affordable housing near transit stops." (Housing Authority of the City and County of Denver, n.d., para 2). The redevelopment of the Mariposa Arts District at South Lincoln Park and Sun Valley Eco District are two examples of how such intentionality is helping to create sustainable communities. Funding to finance these developments included support from the Denver Regional TOD fund, the use of Low-Income Housing Tax Credits (LIHTC), and support from other public and private entities (Edmonds, 2018; Enterprise Community Partners, 2020).

Evidence to date suggests that these projects have produced affordable housing units for diverse working- and middle-class families in Denver because of financing mechanisms that support this type of development as well as local regulations that seek to preserve social mix (Mueller et al., 2018; Pollack et al., 2010). Recent studies also suggest, however, neighborhoods near Denver's light rail stations that are the core of its transit-oriented design have attracted an increase in White, more affluent, and better-educated residents (Baker & Lee, 2019). Nonetheless, evidence about the degree of subsequent gentrification in these areas is mixed (see Padeiro et al., 2019).

Learnings from the Global East and Global South

Our review of policies of social mix through housing policies in the Global East and Global South has shown that governments in countries beyond the Global North have demonstrated a willingness and ability to invest in and expand social mix policies. In contrast to the diminishing role of governments in housing creation in the Western Europe, the United Kingdom, and North America, governments in the Global East seem to support housing regeneration including the creation of socially mixed communities (Hsiao, 2021; Weder di Mauro, 2018).

One such example is that of Singapore. As Weder di Mauro (2018, p. 7) notes, it is highly unlikely that other countries or locations could reproduce the nearly universal state-subsidized housing provision that is available in Singapore. Previous work has identified four best practices from Singapore that have the potential for adoption elsewhere and indeed, the first two have been utilized in other mixed income developments. First, the use of different apartment sizes to foster income mix could be employed elsewhere. Second, ensuring that mixed communities are well maintained and regularly updated would avoid deterioration and obsolescence as well as being smart and sustainable business practices. Third, mixed communities elsewhere would also benefit from the same level of careful attention to the public amenities and services offered to residents in Singapore with the goal of providing only those of the highest quality. Finally, the "no neighborhood left behind" ethos that permeates state policy in Singapore is something that could be replicated in places that recognize that such investments are good for both the families involved as well as the larger society. This last practice of no "neighborhood left behind" was used in the City of Ottawa between 2005 and 2017 to foster community development, enhance safety and improve health and quality of life (see South-East Ottawa Community Health Centre, n.d.). Adoption of several of these principles by communities outside of the Singaporean context suggests that local strategies where community development is focused on collaboration, coordination, community participation and resource leveraging, are feasible at smaller scales.

This special issue

In February 2020, the guest editors for this special issue announced a call for contributions that examined the influence of social mix policies utilizing housing as a way of creating mixed communities in different countries and contexts. When reviewing the abstracts and full papers that were submitted, the criteria employed to ensure coherence of the special issue focused on the range of geographical coverage, social mix models employed, scale of policy or program implementation, type and rigor of empirical methodologies employed, key stakeholder involvement, and contribution to the literature. The articles in this special issue deal with the reshaping of communities through policy interventions in housing development. They cover diverse national contexts and policy backgrounds, and represent the perspectives of many key stakeholders, including national and local governments, services and NGOs, developers and, most importantly, low-income residents. The articles present diverse case studies from Western Europe, North America, Australia, the Middle East, Africa, and South Asia. They discuss projects that range in scale from small housing initiatives (Costarelli & Melic; Shmaryahu-Yeshurun), to housing estates and neighborhoods (Capp et al., Levin et al.; Sanga), to city-wide programs and strategies (Santiago & Leroux). They focus on diverse experiences of social mix: between university students and young professionals and low-income social housing tenants (Costarelli & Melic), between older, low-income residents and younger, middle-class residents (Levin et al.), between diverse ethnic and social class groups sharing a neighborhood (Santiago & Leroux; Sanga), and between private and public housing residents (Capp et al., Levin et al.). The articles also vary by the tools used to create social mix, from local non-for-profit initiatives (Costarelli & Melic; Shmaryahu-Yeshurun), inclusionary planning laws (Sanga), public-private partnerships (Capp et al.; Levin et al.; Sanga), and a program to encourage homeownership (Santiago & Leroux). Finally, the articles present different analytical tools used by researchers to understand the diverse appearances of social mix, its underlying goals and its consequent outcomes. These include qualitative examinations using discourse and content analyses (Capp et al., Sanga); in-depth interviews and observations (Levin et al., Shmaryahu-Yeshurun); quantitative examinations using surveys and administrative datasets (Santiago & Leroux); comparative analysis of social mix in diverse national and political settings (Levin et al.); and a conceptual framework developed to better understand perceptions of social mix or advance urban development (Joseph et al.).

Notes

1. The term *community* is used throughout the article to indicate a non-spatial entity. We have referred to the term as other authors use it when referencing their specific contributions to the literature in our article. When we refer to mixed community, we mean a community that is made up of two or more diverse social groups that is often the result of housing regeneration programs.
2. The Global East is the eastern region of Asia, which is defined in geographical, ethno-cultural and developmental terms. The modern states of East Asia include China (People's Republic of China), Hong Kong (SAR of PRC), Japan, Macau (SAR of PRC), Mongolia, North Korea (Democratic People's Republic of Korea), South Korea (Republic of Korea) and Taiwan (Republic of China); see special issue of Urban Studies on Global East and introduction by Shin et al. (2016).

Acknowledgments

We wish to thank the three anonymous reviewers whose comments strengthened this review essay as well as all the reviewers who commented on the papers included in this special issue.

Disclosure statement

No potential conflict of interest was reported by the author(s).

ORCID

Iris Levin http://orcid.org/0000-0002-5176-4903
Anna Maria Santiago http://orcid.org/0000-0003-1983-3937

References

Abubakar, I. R., & Doan, P. R. (2017). Building new capital cities in Africa: Lessons for new satellite towns in developing countries. *African Studies*, 76(4), 1–20. https://doi.org/10.1080/00020184.2017.1376850

Arthurson, K., Levin, I., & Ziersch, A. (2015a). Social mix, '[A] very, very good idea in a vacuum but you have to do it properly!' Exploring social mix in a right to the city framework. *International Journal of Housing Policy*, 15(4), 418–435. https://doi.org/10.1080/14616718.2015.1093748

Arthurson, K., Levin, I., & Ziersch, A. (2015b). What is the meaning of 'social mix'? Shifting perspectives in planning and implementing public housing estate redevelopment. *Australian Geographer*, 46(4), 491–505. https://doi.org/10.1080/00049182.2015.1075270

Arthurson, K. (2010). Questioning the rhetoric of social mix as a tool for planning social inclusion. *Urban Policy and Research*, 28(2), 225–231. https://doi.org/10.1080/08111141003693117

Arthurson, K. (2012). *Social mix and the city: Challenging the mixed communities consensus in housing and urban planning policies*. CSIRO Publishing.

Arthurson, K. (2013). Mixed tenure communities and the effects on neighbourhood reputation and stigma: Residents' experiences from within. *Cities*, 35, 432–438. http://dx.doi.org/10.1016/j.cities.2013.03.007

August, M. (2014). Negotiating social mix in Toronto's first public housing redevelopment: Power, space and social control in Don Mount Court. *International Journal of Urban and Regional Research*, 38(4), 1160–1180. https://doi.org/10.1111/1468-2427.12127

Bacqué, M.-H., Fijalkow, Y., Launay, L., & Vermeersch, S. (2011). Social mix policies in Paris: Discourses, policies and social effects. *International Journal of Urban and Regional Research*, 35(2), 256–273. http://dx.doi.org/10.1111/j.1468-2427.2010.00995.x

Baily, N., Kearns, A., & Livingston, M. (2012). Place attachment in deprived neighbourhoods: The impacts of population turnover and social mix. *Housing Studies*, 27(2), 208–231. https://doi.org/10.1080/02673037.2012.632620

Baker, D. M., & Lee, B. (2019). How does light rail transit (LRT) impact gentrification? Evidence from fourteen US urbanized areas. *Journal of Planning Education and Research*, 39(1), 35–49. https://doi.org/10.1177/0739456X17713619

Belzer, D., Hickey, R., Lawson, W., Poticha, S., & Wood, J. (2007). *The case for mixed income transit-oriented development in the Denver region*. Center for Transit Oriented Development and Reconnecting America. https://urbanlandc.org/wp-content/uploads/2011/10/Case-for-Mixed-Income-TOD1.pdf#:~:text=The%20Case%20for%20Mixed-Income%20Transit-Oriented%20Development%20in%20the,region%20will%20be%20unaffordable%20to%20lower%20income%20households. www.reconnectingamerica.org/assets/Uploads/enterprise.pdf

Bolt, G., Phillips, D., & van Kempen, R. (2010). Housing policy, (de)segregation and social mixing: An international perspective. *Housing Studies*, 25(2), 129–135. https://doi.org/10.1080/02673030903564838

Bolt, G., & van Kempen, R. (2013). Introduction special issue: Mixing neighbourhoods: Success or failure? *Cities*, 35, 391–396. http://dx.doi.org/10.1016/j.cities.2013.04.006

Bond, L., Sautkina, E., & Kearns, A. (2011). Mixed messages about mixed tenure: Do reviews tell the real story? *Housing Studies*, 26(1), 69–94. https://doi.org/10.1080/02673037.2010.512752

Bridge, G., Butler, T., & Le Galès, P. (2014). Power relations and social mix in metropolitan neighbourhoods in North America and Europe: Moving beyond gentrification? *International Journal of Urban and Regional Research*, 38(4), 1133–1141. https://doi.org/10.1111/1468-2427.12125

Bridge, G., Butler, T., & Lees, L. (Eds). (2012). *Mixed communities: Gentrification by stealth?* Policy Press.

Center for Transit Oriented Development. (2017, March). *The mixed-income housing TOD action guide*. https://www.nlc.org/wp-content/uploads/2017/03/Guide_Mixed-Income-TOD-Action-Guide.pdf

Chaskin, R. J., & Joseph, M. L. (2010). Building "community" in mixed-income developments: Assumptions, approaches, and early experiences. *Urban Affairs Review*, 45(3), 299–335. https://doi.org/10.1177/1078087409341544

Chaskin, R., Khare, A., & Joseph, M. (2012). Participation, deliberation, and decision making: The dynamics of inclusion and exclusion in mixed-income developments. *Urban Affairs Review*, 48(6), 863–906. https://doi.org/10.1177/1078087412450151

Chen, Y.-L. (2011). New prospects for social rental housing in Taiwan: The role of housing affordability crises and the housing movement. *International Journal of Housing Policy*, 11(3), 305–318. https://doi.org/10.1080/14616718.2011.599133

Cho, I. S., Trvic, Z., & Nasution, I. (2017). New high-density intensified housing developments in Asia: Qualities, potential and challenges. *Journal of Urban Design*, 22(5), 613–636. https://doi.org/10.1080/13574809.2017.1311770

Chu, C., Nomura, R., & Mori, S. (2019). Actual conditions of mixed public–private planning for housing complexes in Beijing. *Sustainability*, 11(8), 2409, 1–19. https://doi.org/10.3390/su11082409

Clark, W. A. V., Huang, Y., & Yi, D. (2019). Can millennials access homeownership in urban China? *Journal of Housing and the Built Environment*, 36(1), 69–87. https://doi.org/10.1007/s10901-019-09672-0

Coelho, K., Mahadevia, D., & Williams, G. (2020). Outsiders in the periphery: Studies of the peripheralisation of low income housing in Ahmedabad and Chennai, India. *International Journal of Housing Policy*. https://doi.org/10.1080/19491247.2020.1785660

Cole, I., & Goodchild, B. (2001). Social mix and the 'balanced community' in British housing policy – A tale of two epochs. *GeoJournal*, 51(4), 351–360. https://doi.org/10.1023/A:1012049526513

Curley, A. M. (2009). Draining or gaining? The social networks of public housing movers in Boston. *Journal of Social and Personal Relationships*, 26(2–3), 227–247. https://doi.org/10.1177/0265407509106716

Curley, A. M. (2010). Relocating the poor: Social capital and neighbourhood resources. *Journal of Urban Affairs*, 32(1), 237–294. https://doi.org/10.1111/j.1467-9906.2009.00475.x

Darcy, M. (2010). De-concentration of disadvantage and mixed income housing: A critical discourse approach. *Housing, Theory and Society*, 27(1), 1–22. https://doi.org/10.1080/14036090902767516

Davidson, M. (2010). Love thy neighbour? Social mixing in London's gentrification frontiers. *Environment and Planning A: Economy and Space*, 42(3), 524–544. https://doi.org/10.1068/a41379

Doney, R. H., McGuirk, P. M., & Mee, K. J. (2013). Social mix and the problematisation of social housing. *Australian Geographer*, 44(4), 401–418. https://doi.org/10.1080/00049182.2013.852500

Edmonds, L. (2018, April). *Financing the development in transit-oriented development: CDFI case study on the Denver Regional TOD Fund*. Urban Institute. https://www.urban.org/sites/default/files/publication/98056/financing_the_development_in_transit_oriented_development_0.pdf

Enterprise Community Partners. (2020, February 6). *Denver regional TOD fund term sheet*. https://www.enterprisecommunity.org/financing-and-development/community-loan-fund/denver-regionaltod-fund-term-sheet.pdf

Fraser, J. C., Oakley, D., & Levy, D. K. (2013). Guest editors' introduction: Policy assumptions and lived realities of mixed-income housing on both sides of the Atlantic. *Cityscape*, 15(2), 1–14. http://www.jstor.org/stable/41959106

Galster, G. C., & Friedrichs, J. (2015). The dialectic of neighborhood social mix: Editors' introduction to the special issue. *Housing Studies*, 30(2), 175–191. https://doi.org/10.1080/02673037.2015.1035926

Galster, G. (2007). Neighbourhood social mix as a goal of housing policy: A theoretical analysis. *European Journal of Housing Policy*, 7(1), 19–43. https://doi.org/10.1080/14616710601132526

Gans, H. J. (1962). *The urban villagers: Group and class in the life of Italian-Americans*. Free Press.

Goetz, E. G., & Chapple, K. (2010). You gotta move: Advancing the debate on the record of dispersal. *Housing Policy Debate*, 20(2), 209–233. https://doi.org/10.1080/10511481003779876

Goetz, E. G. (2012). Obsolescence and the transformation of public housing communities in the US. *International Journal of Housing Policy*, 12(3), 331–345. https://doi.org/10.1080/14616718.2012.709671

Goetz, E. G. (2013). Too good to be true? The variable and contingent benefits of displacement and relocation among low-income public housing residents. *Housing Studies*, 28(2), 235–252. https://doi.org/10.1080/02673037.2013.767884

Ho, K. C., & Chua, V. (2018). The neighbourhood roots of social cohesion: Notes on an exceptional case of Singapore. *Environment and Planning C: Politics and Space*, 36(2), 290–312. https://doi.org/10.1177/2399654417710659

Housing Authority of the City and County of Denver. (n.d.) *Transit oriented development*. http://www.denverhousing.org/aboutus/Documents/Transit%20Oriented%20Development.pdf

Hsiao, H. (2021). Transformation and issues of public housing policies facing aging society: Case review of Osaka City, Japan. *Japan Architectural Review*, 4(1), 5–13. https://doi.org/10.1002/2475-8876.12198

Jackson, L., Langille, L., Lyons, R., Hughes, J., Martin, D., & Winstanley, V. (2009). Does moving from a high-poverty to lower-poverty neighborhood improve mental health? A realist review of 'Moving to Opportunity.' *Health & Place*, 15(4), 961–970. https://doi.org/10.1016/j.healthplace.2009.03.003

Jacobs, J. (1961). *The death and life of great American cities*. Random House.

Joseph, M. L. (2008). Early resident experiences at a new mixed-income development in Chicago. *Journal of Urban Affairs*, 30(3), 229–257. https://doi.org/10.1111/j.1467-9906.2008.00394.x

Jourdan, D., Van Zandt, S., & Tarlton, E. (2013). Coming home: Resident satisfaction regarding return to a revitalized HOPE VI community. *Cities*, 35, 439–444. https://doi.org/10.1016/j.cities.2013.03.006

Kearns, A., McKee, M. J., Sautkina, E., Cox, J., & Bond, L. (2013). How to mix? Spatial configurations, modes of production and resident perceptions of mixed tenure neighbourhoods. *Cities*, 35, 397–408. https://doi.org/10.1016/j.cities.2013.03.005

King, R., Orloff, M., Virsilas, T., & Pande, T. (2017). Confronting the urban housing crisis in the Global South: Adequate, secure, and affordable (No. 40). *World Resources Institute*. https://files.wri.org/s3fs-public/towards-more-equal-city-confronting-urban-housing-crisis-global-south.pdf

Kleinhans, R., & Kearns, A. (2013). Neighbourhood restructuring and residential relocation: Towards a balanced perspective on relocation processes and outcomes. *Housing Studies*, 28(2), 163–176. https://doi.org/10.1080/02673037.2013.768001

Kleit, G. R., & Galvez, M. (2011). The relocation choices of public housing residents displaced by redevelopment: Market constraints, personal preferences or social information? *Journal of Urban Affairs*, 33(4), 375–407. https://doi.org/10.1111/j.1467-9906.2011.00557.x

Kumar, V. (2020). When heritage meets creativity: A tale of two urban development strategies in Kampong Glam, Singapore. *City & Community*, 19(2), 398. https://doi.org/10.1111/cico.12427

Lees, L. (2008). Gentrification and social mixing: Towards an inclusive urban renaissance? *Urban Studies*, 45(12), 2449–2470. https://doi.org/10.1177/0042098008097099

Lelévrier, C. (2013). Social mix neighbourhood policies and social interaction: The experience of newcomers in three new renewal developments in France. *Cities*, 35, 409–416. https://dx.doi.org/10.1016/j.cities.2013.03.003

Levin, I., Arthurson, K., & Ziersch, A. (2014). Social mix and the role of design: Competing interests in the Carlton Public Housing Estate Redevelopment, Melbourne. *Cities*, 40, 23–31. https://doi.org/10.1016/j.cities.2014.04.002

Levin, I., Arthurson, K., & Ziersch, A. (2018). Experiences of tenants' relocation in the Carlton Public Housing Estate Redevelopment, Melbourne. *Urban Policy and Research*, 36(3), 354–366. https://doi.org/10.1080/08111146.2018.1502661

McTarnaghan, S., Martin, C., & Srini, T. (2016, October). *Literature review of housing in Latin America and the Caribbean* (Research Report). Global Housing Research Initiative, Cities Alliance, Urban Institute. https://www.urban.org/research/publication/literature-review-housing-latin-america-and-caribbean-phase-i-global-housing-research-initiative

Mishra, A. K., & Mohanty, P. K. (2017). Urban policy in Asia Pacific countries: A case for inclusionary zoning and housing. *Asia-Pacific Journal of Regional Science*, 1(1), 191–215. https://doi.org/10.1007/s41685-017-0026-4

Mizuuchi, T., & Jeon, H. G. (2010). The new mode of urban renewal for the former outcaste minority people and areas in Japan. *Cities*, 27(Suppl. 1), S25–34. https://doi.org/10.1016/j.cities.2010.03.008

Mosselson, A. (2017). Caught between the market and transformation: Urban regeneration and the provision of low-income housing in inner-city Johannesburg. In P. Watt & P. Smets (Eds.), *Social housing and urban renewal: A cross-national perspective* (pp. 351–390). Emerald Publishing Limited.

Mueller, E. J., Hilde, T. W., & Torrado, M. J. (2018). Methods for countering spatial inequality: Incorporating strategic opportunities for housing preservation into transit-oriented development planning. *Landscape and Urban Planning*, 177(September), 317–327. https://doi.org/10.1016/j.landurbplan.2018.01.003

Oakley, D., & Burchfield, K. (2009). Out of the projects, still in the hood: The partial constraints on public-housing residents' relocation in Chicago. *Journal of Urban Affairs*, 31(5), 598–614. https://doi.org/10.1111/j.1467-9906.2009.00454.x

Padeiro, M., Louro, A., & Marques Da Costa, N. (2019). Transit-oriented development and gentrification: A systematic review. *Transport Reviews*, 39(6), 733–754. https://doi.org/10.1080/01441647.2019.1649316

Phang, S. Y. (2018). *Policy innovations for affordable housing in Singapore: From colony to global city*. Palgrave Advances in Regional and Urban Economics.

Pollack, S., Bluestone, B., & Billingham, C. (2010, October). *Maintaining diversity in America's transit-rich neighborhoods: Tools for equitable neighborhood change*. Northeastern University, Dukakis Center for Urban and Regional Policy. https://housingtrustfundproject.org/wp-content/uploads/2011/10/TRNEquityFull.pdf

Popkin, S. J., Levy, D. K., & Buron, L. (2009). Has HOPE VI transformed residents' lives? New evidence from the HOPE VI Panel Study. *Housing Studies*, 24(4), 477–502. https://doi.org/10.1080/02673030902938371

Ramanathan, S., & Gandhi, V. (2018, July 15–18). Balancing environment, economy and equity: Planning initiatives in Brazil, Mongolia and India. *Proceedings of the 18th International Conference of the International Planning History Society* (Yokohama, Japan: International Planning History Society). https://journals.open.tudelft.nl/index.php/iphs/issue/view/620

Ronald, R., & Hirayama, Y. (2007). Situating the Japanese housing system. In Y. Hirayama & R. Ronald (Eds.), *Housing and social transition in Japan* (pp. 193–209). Routledge.

Ronald, R., & Lee, H. (2012). Housing policy socialization and de-commodification in South Korea. *Journal of Housing and the Built Environment*, 27(2), 111–131. https://doi.org/10.1007/s10901-011-9257-2

Ruiz-Tagle, J. (2017). Territorial stigmatization in socially-mixed neighborhoods in Chicago and Santiago: A comparison of Global-North and Global-South urban renewal problems. In P. Watt & P. Smets (Eds.), *Social housing and urban renewal: A cross-national perspective* (pp. 311–350). Emerald Publishing Limited.

Sarkissian, W. (1976). The idea of social mix in town planning: A historical review. *Urban Studies*, 13(4), 231–246. https://journals.sagepub.com/doi/pdf/10.1080/00420987620080521

Satterthwaite, D., & Mitlin, D. (2014). *Reducing urban poverty in the Global South*. Routledge.

Sautkina, E., Bond, L., & Kearns, A. (2012). Mixed evidence on mixed tenure effects: Findings from a systematic review of UK studies, 1995–2009. *Housing Studies*, 27(6), 748–782. https://doi.org/10.1080/02673037.2012.714461

Shin, H. B., Lees, L., & López-Morales, E. (2016). Introduction: Locating gentrification in the Global East. *Urban Studies*, 53(3), 455–470. https://doi.org/10.1177/0042098015620337

Sinxadi, L., Awuzie, B. O., & Haupt, T. (2019, December 16–17). Tackling spatial inequalities through mixed income housing: A qualitative analysis of stakeholder perceptions. *14th International Postgraduate Research Conference 2019: Contemporary and Future Directions in the Built Environment. Conference Proceedings* (pp. 314–325). University of Salford, Manchester UK, School of Science, Engineering & Environment. http://usir.salford.ac.uk/id/eprint/56438/

Slater, T. (2008). 'A literal necessity to be re-placed': A rejoinder to the gentrification debate. *International Journal of Urban and Regional Research*, 32(1), 212–223. https://doi.org/10.1111/j.1468-2427.2008.00781.x

South-East Ottawa Community Health Centre. (n.d.) *No community left behind: Building safer and vibrant neighborhoods.* http://nocommunityleftbehind.ca/

Steel, G., van Noorloos, F., & Klaufus, C. (2017). The urban land debate in the Global South: New avenues for research. *Geoforum*, 83(July), 133–141. https://doi.org/10.1016/j.geoforum.2017.03.006

Tian, Y., Bi, X., & Li, D. (2007). Feasibility analysis of mixed-income housing in China. *Frontiers in Architecture and Civil Engineering in China*, 1(3), 371–377. https://doi.org/10.1007/s11709-007-0050-y

United Nations. (2019). *World urbanization prospects: The 2018 revision.* https://population.un.org/wup/Publications/Files/WUP2018-Report.pdf

Van Ham, M., & Manley, D. (2010). The effect of neighbourhood housing tenure mix on labour market outcomes: A longitudinal investigation of neighbourhood effects. *Journal of Economic Geography*, 10(2), 257–282. https://doi.org/10.1093/jeg/lbp017

Varady, D. P., Raffel, J. A., Sweeney, S., & Denson, L. (2005). Attracting middle-income families in the HOPE VI public housing revitalization program. *Journal of Urban Affairs*, 27(2), 149–164. https://doi.org/10.1111/j.0735-2166.2005.00229.x

Varady, D. (Ed.). (2005). *Desegregating the city ghettos, enclaves, and inequality.* State University of New York Press.

Wang, Y. P., & Murie, A. (2000). Social and spatial implications of housing reform in China. *International Journal of Urban and Regional Research*, 24(2), 397–417. https://doi.org/10.1111/1468-2427.00254

Watt, P., & Smets, P. (Eds.). (2017). *Social housing and urban renewal: A cross-national perspective.* Emerald Publishing Limited.

Weder di Mauro, B. (2018, April). *Building a cohesive society: The case of Singapore's housing policies* (Policy Brief no. 128). Centre for International Governance Innovation. https://www.cigionline.org/publications/building-cohesive-society-case-singapores-housing-policies

Yang, S., Kim, H., Kim, S.-N., & Ahn, K. (2018). What is achieved and lost in living in a mixed-income neighborhood? Findings from South Korea. *Journal of Housing and the Built Environment*, 33(4), 807–828. https://doi.org/10.1007/s10901-017-9586-x

Yap, K. S. (2016). The enabling strategy and its discontent: Low-income housing policies and practices in Asia. *Habitat International*, 54(3), 166–172. https://doi.org/10.1016/j.habitatint.2015.11.026

Promoting a geography of opportunity in Accra, Ghana: Applying lessons from mixed-income development successes and shortcomings

Mark L. Joseph, Isaac K. Arthur, and Edmund Kwame Botchway

ABSTRACT
Urban poverty in both the developed and developing world is often spatially organized with deprivation highly concentrated in segregated areas of cities. With the rapid urbanization and lack of effective urban planning in several countries in sub-Saharan Africa, segregation, economic deprivation and social exclusion are particularly severe challenges. In the United States, almost 30 years of poverty deconcentration policy has had mixed results and offers cautions to other countries looking to confront urban segregation. Accra, the capital city of Ghana, offers an intriguing example of a city with substantial clusters of poverty and slum areas, but also some neighborhoods with high existing levels of economic integration. Drawing on the theoretical and empirical context of poverty deconcentration efforts in the United States, this paper presents a conceptual framework with two alternative pathways for urban development: an inclusionary pathway and an exclusionary pathway. We use this framework to review and critique Ghana's existing urban policy and offer implications for inclusionary urban policy in Accra and other similar cities in developing countries.

Introduction

Social inequality is a rising policy challenge across the world and is particularly evident in metropolitan areas of both developed and developing nations as poverty and deprivation are often highly concentrated in segregated areas of cities. This residential segregation leads to social and economic marginalization, persistent poverty and a host of other social challenges such as disease, crime, and delinquency. Galster and Killen (1995) coined the term *the geography of opportunity* to describe the ways in which place matters for social and economic mobility and to highlight the importance of urban policies that connect the urban poor to broader society (see also, Briggs, 2003, 2005; Pastor, 2001; Rosenbaum, 1995).

In the United States, over 30 years of poverty deconcentration policy has had mixed results and offers cautions to other countries looking to confront urban segregation (J. Fraser et al., 2013; M. L. Joseph, 2013). One major policy approach to integrating the poor into more economically-diverse communities has been the building of mixed-income developments with housing for both the poor and affluent (M.L. Joseph & Yoon, 2019). A large literature documents the positive outcomes of these policies in terms of improving quality and safety of the physical environment but also indicates a general failure of these policies thus far to promote social and economic mobility among the poor (Chaskin & Joseph, 2015; Levy et al., 2013; M.L. Joseph, 2019). Further, research has documented significant social challenges in these mixed-income communities including tensions over norms of behavior and stigmatization and isolation of the poor (Chaskin & Joseph, 2012; Graves, 2010; J.C.

Fraser et al., 2013; Chaskin, Khare et al., 2012; Kleit, 2005; McCormick et al., 2012; Tach, 2009). Similar poverty deconcentration policies have been implemented across Europe as well as in Canada and Australia with similarly mixed results (Arthurson, 2002; August, 2008, 2015; Kleinhans & Van Hamm, 2013).

With the rapid urbanization, rising inequality and lack of effective urban planning in several countries in sub-Saharan Africa, segregation, economic deprivation and social exclusion are increasingly severe challenges in this region of the developing world (Amoako, 2016; Otiso & Owusu, 2008; Owusu & Agyei-Mensah, 2011; Songsore & McGranaham, 1993). As Otiso and Owusu (2008) pointed out in their comparative study of urbanization in Ghana and Kenya, although the racial segregation that had been established in the colonial era was abolished at independence, subsequent development has often maintained segregation on the basis of income and in some cases ethnicity and religion. Africa's increasing integration into the global economy, the rise of an African middle class and the increasing withdrawal of the state from urban housing and service provision is generating the conditions for ever-increasing geographic separation between the affluent and poor. Otiso and Owusu (2008) have referred to this trend as a "spatial logic of exclusion, intolerance and insularity" (p. 152).

The Greater Accra Metropolitan Area, the capital city region of Ghana in West Africa, with a residential population of 4.7 million people, is a prime example of the challenges of rapid urbanization, residential segregation, and concentration of poverty (Ghana Statistical Service, 2019; World Bank Group, 2017). There has been a boom of real estate investment in Accra over the last 2 decades by commercial developers and direct foreign investment. This has generated a house price-to income ratio of 14:1, making Accra one of the most inequitable housing environments in Africa (Gillespie, 2018). While Accra has substantial clusters of poverty and slum areas, there are also several neighborhoods with high levels of existing economic integration where upscale homes for the Ghanaian elite and international expatriates have been built among dilapidated dwellings for the poor. However, the current income mix in these neighborhoods is tenuous because ongoing development processes and legal efforts by the affluent are leading to the displacement of the poor. Existing mixed-income areas are increasingly becoming enclaves for the rich (Tetteh, 2016).

The Accra context presents an intriguing opportunity to consider the possibilities for urban policy and practice that would leverage the existing residential diversity to promote more intentional opportunities for social and economic inclusion and mobility for the poor. Tetteh (2016, p. 275) makes a recommendation for the government in Accra "to utilize and expand the repertoire of planning tools available to the City to encourage the mixing of diverse economic groups in the emergent new urban spaces, particularly in planned or proposed new residential projects." In his assessment of Ghanaian housing policy, Boamah (2014) agrees: "Planning regulations should be employed to ensure that developers pursue mix development and accommodate affordable housing in their development schemes. This is necessary in minimizing income driven social segregation in the country's residential neighborhoods." The Government of Ghana's National Housing Policy (Government of Ghana, 2015, pp. 13–14, emphasis added) also made the case for greater integration: "Economic growth and prosperity enhances the creation of *integrated communities* and fosters a sense of pride, which could encourage family self-sufficiency" and commits to "ensure adequate and sustainable funding for the supply of *a diverse mix of housing* in all localities."

Unfortunately, the Government of Ghana does not have a strong track record for following through on comprehensive urban planning. The National Urban Policy Framework released by the government in 2012 (Government of Ghana, 2012, p. 3) noted that "This is the first time in the history of Ghana that a comprehensive urban policy has been formulated to promote a sustainable, spatially integrated and orderly development of urban settlements with adequate housing and services." The report went on to acknowledge that "with little experience in urban management, local governments have often been unable to develop strategies and plans to mobilize the resources they need to deal with urban growth" and that "successive government interventions and response to urbanization and urban growth have been piece-meal and fragmented in character" (Government of Ghana, 2012, p. 3).

This paper draws relevant lessons from the American poverty deconcentration experience to inform more proactive and effective approaches to urban development in Accra and similar cities in the developing world. Our major contribution to the urban studies literature is a conceptual framework of inclusionary and exclusionary urban development pathways that can inform future policy development and analysis in all global settings experiencing urban growth and displacement. We first set the context for a comparison of urban development in Ghana and the U.S. by describing key differences in socioeconomic development as well as identifying commonalities in the way that urban development can exacerbate social exclusion of the poor. We then review in more detail the historical segregation patterns and modern-day context of state-sanctioned urban segregation, gentrification and displacement in Accra. Next, we review the theory and outcomes of mixed-income development efforts in the U.S. We establish the role of gentrification in urban development and the case for the mixed-income development approach and summarize the empirical evidence about mixed-income implementation in the U.S. We then present a conceptual framework with two alternative pathways for urban development in Accra and other developing countries: an inclusionary pathway and an exclusionary pathway. We conclude with recommendations for inclusionary urban policy and offer implications for urban development in Accra. We closely review the policy prescriptions in the 2015 Housing Plan released by the Government of Ghana and indicate where there is alignment with our proposed inclusionary policy framework. However, we conclude that while unique conditions are in place in Accra that make greater social inclusion into a geography of opportunity possible, the more likely path based on current trends and government inaction is one of displacement of the poor, privatized development for the elite, weakening community cohesion, and increased poverty and marginalization.

Establishing the basis for comparing urban policy in the U.S. and Ghana

This paper draws lessons from the mixed-income development experience in the U.S. to make recommendations for urban policy in Ghana. In this way, we follow other comparative studies that have leveraged research and practice from the developed world to inform policy in Ghana (see, for example, Acquah, 2021; Alhassan & Castelli, 2020; Boateng & Anngela-Cole, 2016; Siekpe & Greene, 2006). While there are fundamental differences in the urban development contexts between the U.S. and Ghana, there are also significant similarities that make this comparison instructive for policymakers in Ghana and other developing countries facing exclusionary housing pressures.

Fundamental differences in urban housing contexts
In addition to the major differences in the demographic, political, economic and cultural contexts of the U.S. and Ghana (see Alhassan & Castelli, 2020, for a summary comparison of Ghana in a global North-South context and Acquah, 2021 for a U.S.-Ghana comparison), there are some important specific differences in the contexts for urban housing development that should be noted. The challenges common to many state functions in Ghana, such as weak infrastructure and systems, poor coordination, and rampant corruption, are also inherent in the urban housing sector and political influence and manipulation can often undermine professional urban planning practice (Cobbinah & Darkwah, 2017). In Ghana, urban planning is particularly complicated by the pluralistic land tenure system whereby both traditional and formal political systems manage customary and statutory land respectively (Cobbinah & Darkwah, 2017; Frimpong Boamah & Walker, 2017). This often leads to situations where state officials and traditional leaders have competing claims to land ownership, complicating development activities (Boamah & Amoako, 2020; Otiso & Owusu, 2008). In Ghana, mayors are nominated by the president and elected by the members of the metropolitan assembly, not democratically elected by the city's constituents. This structure of governance situates the president and his executives as the indirect yet powerful custodians of urban policy where presidents set the agenda and mayors are primarily accountable to the president instead of residents of their cities (Ahwoi, 2010; Antwi-Boasiako, 2010; Nanja, 2019).

Similarities in urban policy challenges

Despite these fundamental contextual differences, the U.S. and Ghana, like other countries in the developed and developing worlds, face some very similar challenges of exclusion and displacement in the face of urban revitalization. The spatial organization of poverty is a global phenomenon. In major cities across the world, poverty tends to be clustered geographically and a rise in social inequality tends to be associated with increased income segregation (Amnesty International, 2011; Huxley, 2006, 2007; Mackie et al., 2014; Nijman & Wei, 2020). U.S. cities have been particularly renowned for their stark segregation by race and income. Likewise, the rapid urbanization of African countries has been coupled with increasing income inequality (Novignon, 2017) and there are clearly observable patterns of economic segregation within most Ghanaian cities (Grant, 2015; Satterthwaite & Mitlin, 2014). In Accra, an increasing number of the affluent live in gated communities. And many of the Ghanaian poor are isolated in slum areas known as *zongos*, which are physically separated from the core of cities. Songsore and McGranaham (1993) have documented that residential segregation in Accra is perpetuated by the provision of estate houses for a small elite whereas the lower income residents in the city are left to find housing in more crowded, poorly planned neighborhoods with little access to improved sanitation and other social amenities. These segregated neighborhoods have become clusters of poverty, deprivation, poor health and disease (Agyei-Mensah & Owusu, 2009).

However, in both the U.S. and Ghana, while exclusion and residential segregation has endured in much of the urban core, there has been an emergence of pockets of neighborhood revitalization and affluence leading to an increasing number of mixed-income communities. In the U.S., this phenomenon is associated with the renewed taste for urban living, resulting in the gentrification of inner-city neighborhoods with in-migration of higher-income residents and the displacement of the urban poor

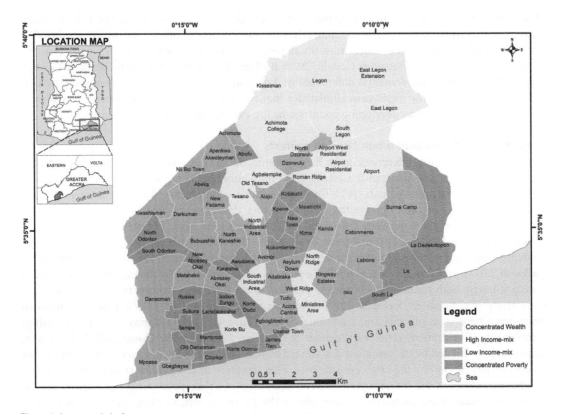

Figure 1. Income mix in Accra.

Figure 2. Juxtaposition of affluent housing and shacks in East Legon, Accra.
Photo credit: Mark Joseph.

(Freeman, 2006; Hyra, 2008; Lees, 2008). Likewise in Accra, as can be seen in Figure 1, while there are numerous slum areas with highly concentrated poverty, there is also an array of neighborhoods with varying levels of income mix.

The rapid urban sprawl, informalization of the urban space, and market-driven housing development in Accra has led to a considerable degree of integration and what could be considered "naturally-occurring" mixed-income neighborhoods. It is not uncommon to see people living in shacks fortified with corrugated metal, uncompleted buildings and other makeshift structures directly adjacent to mansions (see, Figure 2).

This existing income mix in communities throughout Accra presents a tremendous opportunity for upgrading and sustaining the socioeconomic integration that is already present in many parts of the metropolitan area. However, current real estate trends in Accra are to displace and supplant low-income housing with high-end development. Sassen (2014, p. 15) characterizes these developed and developing world trends of urbanization, widening inequality, gentrification and displacement as "expulsions."

Further examination of the challenges of the housing policy context in Accra

Accra has historically been characterized by inequality, segregation, and violent class struggles over urban spaces (Gillespie, 2015). The earliest housing policies by the British colonial government were focused not on the provision of housing for the masses but for expatriate workers and senior indigenous staff of the colonial government. This led to the development of exclusive neighborhoods such as Cantonments, which still remains an enclave for expatriates (Abiodun, 1976; Konadu-Agyemang, 2001). A relatively short-lived shift toward public sector housing provision for the general public ensued post-independence (Boamah, 2014). Between 1957 and 1966, the State embarked on mass public housing programs. In that period, the Tema Development Corporation and the State Housing Corporation together delivered over 11,000 low-cost housing units (Boamah, 2014). After the overthrow of the Kwame Nkrumah-led government in 1966, the new administration ended all rental subsidies and increased the rent on all state housing units. The state maintained that housing policy stance until liberalization policies were implemented in the 1990s. The International Monetary Fund and World Bank pushed for structural adjustment programs which emphasized economic liberalization and an aggressive decrease of state involvement in different sectors of the Ghanaian economy.

This continued through the 1990s until the severe deepening of inequality prompted policy changes. In 2001, the Social Security and National Insurance Trust acquired about 3,000 acres of land in different locations across the country, including Accra, for the provision of public housing. Most of these projects have, however, been abandoned by subsequent governments (Boamah, 2014). Today, the state has assumed a neoliberal position toward urban development and housing provision, relinquishing its direct role and instead acting as an intermediary to promote and facilitate the investment of private capital (Boamah & Amoako, 2020; Fält, 2016; Gillespie, 2015).

The majority of the city of Accra's new inhabitants live in informal settlements (Stow et al., 2010). Most Ghanaian households, 79%, do not have adequate sleeping rooms; more than 50% of households with an average of four members occupy only one sleeping room (See, Boamah, 2014; Ghana Statistical Service, 2013). The long absence of an urban policy context to guide the development and planning of the city has allowed the informal sector to self-organize within a largely unstructured and minimally regulated housing regime (Boamah, 2014). To the extent that there is any public sector policy, it is driven largely by market incentives and land speculation resulting in urban development that has further segregated urban spaces (Asiedu & Arku, 2009; Boamah, 2014; Fält, 2016; Tetteh, 2016). The National Urban Policy Framework released by the Government of Ghana in 2012 concluded that:

> "[There are] fundamental problems associated with urban development and management in the country. These include a weak urban economy, land-use disorder and uncontrolled urban sprawl, increasing environmental deterioration, inadequate urban services, urban poverty, slums and squatter settlements, weak urban governance and institutional coordination, delimitation of urban areas of jurisdiction and lack of integrated planning across jurisdictional boundaries, weak rural-urban linkages, limited data and information on urban areas, inadequate urban investment and financing, weak information, education and communication strategy, and weak urban transportation planning and traffic management and a host of other challenges associated with our decentralization programme." (Government of Ghana, 2012, p. 4)

The resulting concentration of the urban poor in spaces without access to amenities and other opportunities has health and other economic implications. As Agyei-Mensah and Owusu (2009, p. 511) described: "spatial segregation of relatively disadvantaged groups ... is likely to accentuate patterns of social polarization and to inhibit efforts by the disadvantaged to improve their individual and collective conditions." According to Owusu and Agyei-Mensah (2011, p. 348) "the problem lies in the spatial coexistence of poor people and poor environments, unemployment, high crime rates, lack of economic dynamics and neighborhood cohesion, social tension and negative local images."

In the absence of leases and other contractual ties, these forms of informal housing and squatting are highly unstable. This can be seen in both highly affluent neighborhoods, such as East Legon, Cantonments, and part of Spintex as well as middle-income neighborhoods, such as parts of North Kaneshie, Adenta, and Madina, and low-income neighborhoods such as Nima, Mamobi and other areas. As observed by Agyei-Mensah & Owusu (2009, 503), "pockets of old and dilapidated houses (what one may even describe as slums) exist within [East Legon]." As the state takes more land to redistribute for luxury and market-rate real estate development, the urban poor (see, Gillespie, 2015) push back through the appropriation and redistribution of urban space from the rich through acts of quiet encroachment (see, Bayat, 1997). This accounts for the juxtaposition of makeshift structures and large gated houses in many Accra neighborhoods. As noted by Grant and Yankson (2003, p. 65), "Accra is characterized by fragmented economic and residential geographies that if left unchecked will undermine sustainable urban development."

More on gentrification and displacement pressures in Accra

As noted earlier, urban governance in Accra has adopted an entrepreneurial approach where the state interprets its primary role as facilitator of private-sector growth (see, Gillespie, 2015; Grant, 2009; Obeng-Odoom, 2013). In fulfilling this role as an intermediary between the private sector and customary land systems, the state has adopted the following mechanisms: privatization of communal land; cleansing of street hawkers and eviction; and expulsion of squatters (Gillespie, 2015). For example, it is estimated that some of the indigenous Ga communities [for instance, the La ethnic group] in Accra have lost more than 80% of their customary land (Gillespie, 2015). Much of the appropriated land is redistributed to private developers to undertake luxury developments targeted at expatriates, and higher income individuals and households. As a result, the original owners of the land in places like Osu, La, and Jamestown among others are crammed into impoverished and overcrowded settlements without any benefit of the development of their lands (Gillespie, 2015). A stark demonstration of the expulsion of these residents can be seen in the sharp contrast between places like La and its immediate surroundings, and the "spacious, leafy Cantonments and Ridge estates, the American-style luxury mansions in AU Village, and the high-rise commercial center of Airport City, all built on land originally expropriated from these communities for public use" (Gillespie, 2015, p. 71; see also, Fält, 2016). These instances of state-led gentrification of Accra are widespread. Even though this decongestion by expulsion and criminalization of informal settlements started long ago, the former mayor of Accra, Alfred Oko Vandepuije, reenergized the slum clearance mechanisms when he pledged to transform Accra into a "Millennium City" (Crentsil & Owusu, 2018; Fält, 2016; Gillespie, 2015; Obeng-Odoom, 2013). The current mayor of Accra, Mohammed Adjei Sowah has continued this policy, evident in the announcement by the City of Accra in March 2017, that it was commencing mass demolitions (Adogla-Bessa, 2017). As cities around the world, including Accra, went into lockdown in the spring of 2020 to mitigate the spread of COVID-19, the Accra Metropolitan Assembly moved to demolish several makeshift-wooden structures in the Old Fadama district, rendering over a thousand slum-dwellers homeless (Cromwell, 2020; GhanaWeb, 2020).

Poverty deconcentration theory, policy and results in the United States

We now turn to a discussion of how the challenges of urban exclusion and poverty concentration have been addressed in the United States. As stated earlier, despite the major differences in economic, social, political and cultural contexts between Ghana and the U.S., both countries face the rising challenge of gentrification and the economic marginalization of the urban poor. In both contexts, mixed-income communities present a win-win option in which public-private ventures aim to yield benefits for both the affluent and the poor. In the U.S., there has been almost 30 years of national and local policy aimed at deconcentrating poverty by promoting mixed-income housing and neighborhoods (J. Fraser et al., 2013; M.L. Joseph, 2019). Mixed-income development involves the construction of housing for higher-income households in high poverty, segregated areas of a city in order to promote a socioeconomic population mix. The general theory behind mixed-income development in the U.S. and around the world is that through intentional social mixing the resources and opportunities usually available only to affluent members of society can be made more accessible to low-income households (M.L. Joseph & Yoon, 2019). Joseph et al. (2007) identify four specific theoretized benefits of mixed-income development: (1) broadening the social capital and social networks of low-income households; (2) facilitating greater cross-class social learning and role modeling; (3) reducing community instability and promoting greater social control; and (4) generating more political and economic influence from higher-income residents to secure and sustain community improvements.

The first major federal mixed-income policy in the United States was the HOPE VI program (see, Popkin et al., 2004). From 1992 to 2008, with a total $6 billion investment from the U.S. Department of Housing and Urban Development, 259 grants were made to local housing authorities for the demolition and redevelopment of high-poverty public housing developments into new complexes with public housing, other subsidized housing and market-rate housing (Gress et al., 2019). In 2010, the Obama administration replaced HOPE VI with the Choice Neighborhoods Program which established stricter requirements for ensuring that a higher percentage of original residents move into the new developments, elevated the focus on education and workforce development programming, and broadened the purview of the redevelopment efforts beyond the housing site itself to include the neighborhood surrounding the site (Urban Institute & MDRC, 2015). At the writing of this article, the Choice

Neighborhoods program had funded almost 100 planning grants at around $500,000 each and almost 40 implementation grants at $30-$35 million each (U.S. Department of Housing and Urban Development, 2021).

The implementation of mixed-income policy in the U.S. has yielded mixed results and provides a cautionary tale to urban planners and policymakers in Ghana and other developing countries that may seek to replicate this strategy (M.L. Joseph, 2019). While the goals of catalyzing housing and neighborhood redevelopment through public and private sector investment have largely been met, the social goals of promoting social inclusion and economic mobility among the poor have failed to materialize (M.L. Joseph & Yoon, 2019). Mixed-income development in the U.S. has yielded far greater benefits to city tax coffers, developer and investor profits and higher-income gentrifiers than to low-income households trapped for decades in marginalized neighborhoods and now tenuously attached to a rapidly changing urban landscape (Khare, 2021).

There has been tremendous success from mixed-income housing development in terms of the physical transformation of formerly deteriorated housing and neighborhoods characterized by high crime and instability into beautifully-designed housing developments (Levy et al., 2013). Federal government funding, incentives and requirements have successfully encouraged the creation of thousands of units of mixed-income housing in cities across the U.S. In these housing complexes, there are often units for very low-income families living below the poverty level, moderate-income households that benefit from a modest housing subsidy, and higher-income households able to pay full market rates. The level of actual physical integration varies. Some housing complexes integrate some buildings with subsidized units with other buildings with market-rate units. Other housing complexes have an economic mix within buildings. Most of these mixed-income developments in the HOPE VI and Choice Neighborhoods programs adhere to a common external design and quality for both the market-rate and subsidized units so that it is not possible to distinguish one from the other. Investments in the mixed-income housing have spurred other residential and commercial investments in the surrounding neighborhood. Rates of local crime and delinquency have decreased (Levy et al., 2013).

Another important element of success is that the physical and environmental improvements have yielded an improved quality of life among the urban poor living in the new mixed-income housing. Low-income residents that have been able to return to live in the new developments report high satisfaction with their new homes, reduced stress and anxiety about safety and instability, and reduced stigma in terms of where they live (Chaskin & Joseph, 2015). Low-income residents are largely pleased with the design and quality of their new units and grateful to be able to live affordably in such a stable, attractive housing setting.

A major shortcoming of the U.S. experience with mixed-income development has been the relatively low proportion of the targeted urban populations that have benefited from the housing investments. Very few of the residents who originally lived in the high-poverty public housing developments have returned to the new mixed-income housing (Joseph & Chaskin, 2012). Across the 259 HOPE VI developments, the median return rate was just 17% of original residents (Gress et al., 2019). These low return rates are explained by a variety of factors including extensive delays in completing the new units, screening protocols and selection criteria such as drug testing and financial credit checks, and fear on the part of low-income residents that they will be overly monitored and unwelcome in the new mixed environment (Joseph & Chaskin, 2012). Relocation data suggests that displaced residents have generally moved to other high-poverty neighborhoods rather than to communities with greater opportunity (see, for example, Chaskin, Joseph et al., 2012).

Another major negative outcome of mixed-income housing in the U.S. is that while those residents who have been able to return to the new housing have enjoyed better quality housing and more stable neighborhoods, they have had to confront social stigma and marginalization from their higher-income neighbors and have generally not experienced changes in their economic trajectory and financial security (Chaskin & Joseph, 2015; Levy et al., 2013; McCormick et al., 2012). Low-income households have experienced a sense of lack of welcome and belonging, increased monitoring by property staff and local security, and a lack of voice and influence in community affairs. Improved amenities in the communities such as retail and commercial enterprises are often geared toward the needs and economic status of more affluent residents. There have been limited connections to new economic opportunities and low-income households have generally not experienced substantive improvements in their income or financial stability (Levy et al., 2013; M.L. Joseph & Yoon, 2019).

In summary, returning to Joseph et al.'s (2007) theoretical propositions about the possible positive benefits of mixed-income development for the urban poor, research suggests that the realities in the U.S. have been extremely mixed and largely disappointing. There have been improved housing and neighborhood conditions for those few low-income households that have avoided displacement and remained in mixed-income communities. But there has been limited social interaction and network-building, limited exchange of resources from the affluent to the poor, and increased stigmatization of the poor by their higher-income neighbors. Chaskin and Joseph (2015) term this outcome "incorporated inclusion," whereby the urban poor are physically integrated into urban neighborhoods, but remain social and economically marginalized.

These mixed results with mixed-income development policy in the U.S. provide a warning to policymakers in Accra and other rapidly urbanizing cities that have an opportunity to design and implement an urban strategy to counter gentrification and displacement with efforts to promote and sustain socioeconomic integration. Urban planners face a choice of repeating the exclusionary results experienced in the U.S. or making design and governance choices that promote mixed-income communities with more inclusionary outcomes. We turn now to elucidating a conceptual framework that contrasts an inclusionary pathway with an exclusionary pathway.

Conceptual framework

Leveraging existing income mix to promote upward mobility for the poor

Existing theory and practice enables us to chart two possible pathways ahead for Accra: an inclusionary pathway in which the existing economic integration and social mix in middle and higher-income neighborhoods is leveraged for positive outcomes for the low-income population and an exclusionary pathway where the benefits and amenities of middle and higher-income neighborhoods are hoarded and enjoyed only by affluent Ghanaian elites and expatriates. Our conceptual model (see, Figure 3) has four elements: (1) the

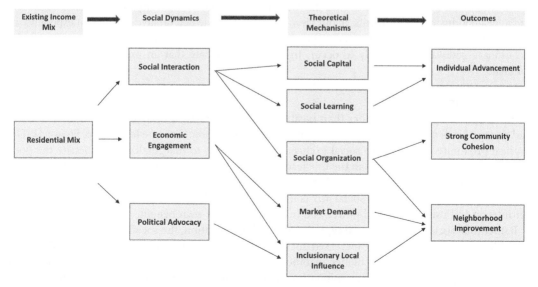

Figure 3. An inclusionary pathway to leverage income mix for positive benefits for the urban poor.

existing income mix, which could lead to (2) inclusionary or exclusionary social dynamics among community residents and other stakeholders, which then operate through (3) possible theoretical mechanisms to generate (4) inclusionary or exclusionary outcomes for the urban poor.

Inclusionary pathway

In the inclusionary pathway, the residential mix could lead to several positive social dynamics. The physical proximity of poor and affluent residents could lead to social interaction among population groups that typically do not come into such regular, informal daily contact and facilitate the establishment of some familiarity and personal relationships. The proximity could also lead to opportunities for economic engagement, with the affluent hiring the lower-income residents for ad-hoc and more extended employment and patronizing their informal businesses. Sharing the same geographic space also could mean that when affluent residents use their power and influence to advocate with local political representatives for resources and services for the neighborhood, those benefits could accrue to the broader neighborhood population.

The social interaction among affluent and impoverished could generate positive outcomes through three mechanisms. First, the interaction could lead to increased social capital whereby the lower-income residents gain networks and connections to new resources and information and develop shared norms and expectations with their higher income neighbors (Coleman, 1988). Second, the interaction could lead to increased social learning, whereby the lower-income residents gain new knowledge and skills through observing and engaging with affluent residents (Bandura, 1977). Third, the interactions could lead to stronger social organization as the impoverished and affluent residents work together and collaborate to establish and achieve a shared set of aims for life in their neighborhood (Sampson & Groves, 1989).

The economic engagement among affluent and poor residents could lead to increased market demand for the goods and services produced by the lower-income residents. This engagement could also lead to affluent residents using their local power and influence in an inclusionary way to advocate for state support of the ability of those lower-income residents to provide those goods and services and to counteract efforts by the state to displace those residents (Logan & Molotch, 1987). Likewise, the political advocacy for neighborhood amenities and services by the higher-income residents could also result in inclusionary local influence deployed for the benefit of the lower-income residents as well as the affluent.

In terms of positive outcomes, then, the social capital and social learning could lead to individual advancement for low-income residents. The social organization could lead to greater community cohesion and to neighborhood improvements. And the market demand and inclusionary local influence could also lead to neighborhood improvements. In our view, given the documented urban development experience in the U.S. and the current developmental trajectory in Accra and other cities in the developing world, the inclusionary pathway is not likely to occur. Instead, we anticipate that an exclusionary pathway will dominate.

Exclusionary pathway

In the exclusionary pathway, rather than positive social dynamics, the residential income mix could lead to negative dynamics and tensions among residents of different income levels (See, Figure 4). The physical proximity could lead to social exclusion and attempts to marginalize and alienate the poor from the more affluent. Rather than the mix leading to productive economic engagement, it could lead to more exploitative economic activity, whereby the affluent take advantage of the weaker economic positioning of the poor. And the social mix could lead to the affluent acting exclusively out of political self-interest and using their local power and influence for their own benefit.

Rather than social learning, social capital and social organization, the social exclusion could lead to social distance, class stigma and increased social control. Rather than a vibrant local neighborhood economy where the affluence of higher-income neighborhood generates productive opportunity and activity by the poor, the economic exploitation could lead to economic stagnation where the affluent seek goods and services outside the neighborhood or only from elite-serving establishments and the

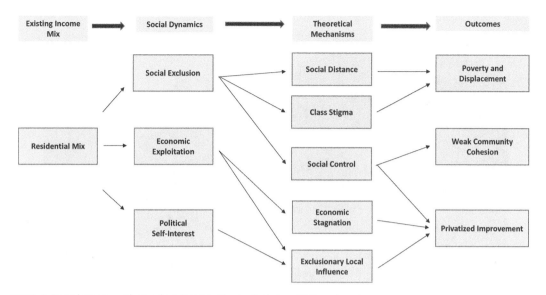

Figure 4. An exclusionary pathway where income mix negatively impacts the urban poor.

economic activity by the poor is deprived of investment. And rather than inclusionary local influence emerging that benefits all residents, the economic exploitation and political self-interest result in exclusionary local influence that hoards the benefits of the neighborhood for the affluent. Rather than promoting physical and economic integration, the higher income residents could literally and figuratively wall themselves off from the poor living around them.

The exclusionary pathway, rather than promoting individual advancement, community cohesion and neighborhood improvements for all, would generate poverty and displacement, weak community cohesion and privatized improvements like paved roads that only lead to affluent homes, electric generators that deliver electricity just to the wealthy, and large household water tanks to deliver running water only to the well-off. And the affluent would live behind gates, barbed wire and electrified barriers (see, Figure 5).

This is the future that Otiso and Owusu (2008) anticipate: "the exponential expansion of such fortified enclaves ... a globally tested mechanism for the propertied middle [and upper] classes to insulate themselves from the threats—real or imagined—to their physical security and sense of well-being." A report by Institute of Statistical, Social and Economic Research (ISSER; 2012) warns that while self-contained housing and gated communities promote security and privacy the separation created by these forms of housing can diminish ethnic and social cohesion.

A bright spot is offered by Asiedu and Arku's (2009) research on gated communities in Accra. Their research with residents who live in proximity to gated residents did not reveal any resentment toward those who live behind the gates and in fact there appeared to be positive and extensive levels of interaction between the two communities, though the interactions were mainly focused on economic transactions and job opportunities such as gardening, housecleaning and landscaping rather than social interaction. This research finding suggests the possibility of making the inclusionary pathway real, at least in some urban neighborhoods, with the appropriate policy action and intentionality.

Proposed framework for an inclusionary policy

There are many steps that can be taken by state actors, private developers, nongovernmental organizations, and community leaders to counter the exclusionary pathway and promote the inclusionary pathway. Indeed, the National Housing Policy released by the Government of Ghana in 2015 establishes a commitment to a more inclusive, democratic and integrated society.

Figure 5. Accra resident with security gate.
Photo credit: Mark Joseph.

We now present a framework for inclusionary policy (see, Figure 6). Our proposed inclusionary policy prioritizes seven inclusionary practices that would help leverage the residential income mix to generate the social dynamics, theoretical mechanisms and outcomes associated with the inclusionary pathway. We see the seven inclusionary practices related to each other as follows. A foundational practice is *proactive leadership* in the public and non-governmental sector with the vision and will to advance a more inclusive form of urban development. That leadership would generate the *incentives and influence* to promote more inclusive development by private sector developers. This would generate more *affordable housing* as a component of development projects. The resultant mixed-income communities would provide a platform for greater *economic leverage*, to harness the resources of the affluent for community revitalization. *Inclusive governance* would be needed to ensure that the urban poor retained representation and a voice in the decisions and affairs of their

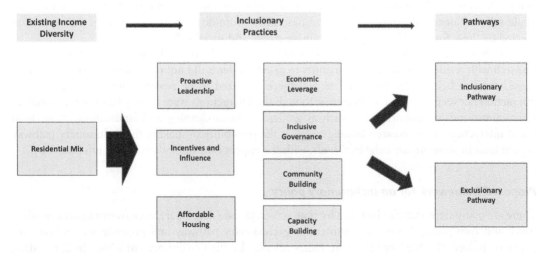

Figure 6. Inclusionary policy.

communities. *Community building* would promote connections and social cohesion across lines of income. And finally *capacity building* would equip local housing and community development officials and residents with the knowledge and skills to promote and sustain a more inclusive approach.

The National Housing Policy released in 2015 by the Government of Ghana made a number of promising statements and propositions that align very well with our proposed inclusionary practices (Government of Ghana, 2015). While previous national government plans for development and inclusion have ultimately not been implemented, we believe the 2015 plan could provide a strong policy framework for future urban development in Ghana. We now explore each of the inclusionary practices in more detail.

Proactive leadership

Leadership is needed at multiple levels to set a clear vision for a more inclusive approach to urban development, to develop and implement the strategies would advance that approach, and to hold all relevant actors accountable to it. This includes national, regional and municipal government leaders, customary, traditional leaders, and leaders of nongovernmental organizations. Above all, it will be critical for the city government to replace its current policies of decongestion through slum clearance and displacement with a more balanced approach to revitalization that promotes mixed-income communities with retention of the poor as neighborhoods develop. The 2015 National Housing Policy is a strong and comprehensive starting point for leadership at the national level on this issue. The policy states a commitment to deploy public resources to support different income levels of households while prioritizing the needs of vulnerable groups (Government of Ghana, 2015). There remains a critical question of where the ongoing leadership will, strategy and accountability will come from to ensure that issues of inclusion are kept at the forefront as Accra and its neighborhoods continue their rapid development and growth. What mechanisms will ensure that the directives in the Policy are carried out by local political representatives, civil servants, customary leaders, private corporations and non-governmental leaders?

Incentives and influence

In a neoliberal, market-driven development environment, where the government's priority has been to create an attractive environment for private investment, inclusionary policy will require establishing incentives for housing developers and other corporate and civic actors to promote the more balanced approach. The National Housing Policy calls for encouraging the "inclusion of rental housing in new residential developments by developers" (Government of Ghana, 2015, p. 18). Inclusionary housing programs, where private housing developers are incentivized (sometimes mandated) to incorporate affordable housing units in their market-rate developments, have been successful at generating affordable housing units in the United States. The government could use its power of land transfer to incorporate requirements for the inclusion of affordable housing on any housing development on that land. The 2015 National Housing Policy proposes to create a National Housing Fund to attract and direct private capital into housing and infrastructure development. Proposed sources for the Fund include government funds, national housing bonds, and other grant funding. The Fund would be designed as an investment that will yield tax-deductible competitive returns (Government of Ghana, 2015).

Another form of incentive that could work especially well in communities with a strong proportion of higher-income residents would be for the government to offer matching grants to be combined with local private investment to address key needs in mixed-income communities, such as roads, security, water, electricity and other infrastructure.

Affordable housing

The creation of quality, durable affordable housing in mixed-income neighborhoods with strong infrastructure and amenities is key to an inclusionary approach. As stated by the president of Ghana, Nana Akufo-Addo, in his State of the Nation Address in 2019: "There is an acute shortage of user-friendly, decent housing for people in middle and low-income brackets in our country. This is a long-standing problem that gets worse with each passing day. It is time to tackle the issue and find a resolution" (Akufo-Addo, 2021, p. 9). To date, efforts by the national and local governments to build affordable housing at scale have fallen far short of the need and not been sustained. The 2015 National Housing Policy acknowledged that the investments made in developers "did not adequately promote affordable or low-income housing" and the tax incentives resulted in more housing for higher-income residents than for vulnerable populations. The policy commits to prioritize affordable and social housing. (Government of Ghana, 2015, p. 36). Wherever possible, the state should look to leverage private investment and market demand for upscale housing to generate opportunities to create affordable housing. Given the scale of need, it will be important to broaden the range of actors working to produce affordable housing. The 2015 National Housing Policy aims to engage "non-conventional partners such as faith-based organizations, civil society organizations, policy think-tanks and research and academic institutions as intermediaries in low-income housing interventions" (Government of Ghana, 2015, p. 23).

Economic leverage
In Accra as in metropolitan areas across the developing world, there is a vibrant, bustling informal sector of goods and services. However, given the lack of formal state approval, support and regulation, this informal sector is rife with instability, risk and exploitation. An inclusionary policy would leverage the entrepreneurialism and vitality of the informal sector along with the proximity of low-income individuals to centers of affluence in mixed-income communities. The 2015 National Housing Policy proposes to support more economic viability among low-income slum dwellers along with elevating their voice in decision-making (Government of Ghana, 2015). Providing a promising example of grass-roots engagement, Gillespie (2018) described a pioneering cooperative housing project in the Ashaiman neighborhood of Greater Accra led by a transnational civil society organization working in partnership with the United Nations Human Settlement Program which incorporates the urban poor into financial markets on a collective basis by extending loans to organized groups. The People's Dialogue on Human Settlements is the local non-governmental organization which completed the Amui Dzor Housing Project in partnership with United Nations Human Settlement Program (People's Dialogue on Human Settlements Ghana, 2020).

Other strategies to leverage local entrepreneurial vitality could include support for microenterprises through business development loans with a particular focus on helping low-income residents of mixed-income communities build strong customer base among the higher-income residents of those communities. Residents with successful careers in business could be recruited to serve as mentors and connectors for low-income residents, particularly youth.

Inclusive governance
Along with greater state intentionality around economic investment and programs, an inclusionary policy would also include attention to decision-making, agency, participation and voice. Who has a say in shaping urban policy at the municipal level and at the neighborhood level? An inclusionary approach would strengthen mechanisms for influence from a broader constituency that includes the poor and would aim to counterbalance the current dominance of elites. The 2015 National Housing Policy commits to inclusivity in principle and makes a pledge to take into account the interests of a wide variety of stakeholders in the development of policy, including housing associations, cooperatives and management boards at the community level (Government of Ghana, 2015). A key element of this strategy will be community organizing and mobilizing among low-income residents of mixed-income communities for more effective collective advocacy with higher-income residents to influence local politicians and customary leaders to promote inclusionary strategies.

Community building

Our inclusionary conceptual framework calls for positive social interaction across lines of income and class that would promote increased social capital, social learning and social organization. Research in mixed-income communities in the United States has established that these positive social dynamics do not emerge naturally in socioeconomically integrated environments. An inclusionary policy would include strategies for building community, including strengthening and broaden existing social networks and neighborhood activities and designing and generating new opportunities for relationship and norm and trust-building among residents of mixed-income communities. This would entail a broadening from a community organizing approach, which is focused on power-building to influence external actors, to also include a community building approach which focused on building strong social networks and support within a community. Churches and other faith organizations would be an important asset in this community building work. Neighborhood civic associations tend to emerge in slums areas to address the high levels of deprivation but not necessarily in areas without extreme levels of poverty. A key component of this strategy could be to support the formation of neighborhood civic associations in mixed-income communities as well.

Capacity building

Finally, the work of inclusionary policy requires not only vision and will but also skill to navigate the complexities of politics and power dynamics in rapidly changing communities with numerous interests with competing agendas. All actors, governmental, for-profit, and nongovernmental, would benefit from technical assistance and training to strengthen their ability to plan, execute and sustain more inclusionary practices. There is a need to build the acumen of those local political and customary representatives to be more effective in promoting and insisting upon an inclusionary approach with government entities and private developers. Given the dominance of private, for-profit developers in housing development and their focus on meeting market demand for high-end housing, the capacity-building could also include efforts to grow and strengthen the capacity of nongovernmental organizations in the housing and community development sector. The previously cited organization the Peoples Dialogue on Human Settlement is an example of an initiative that could be the target for investment and replication (People's Dialogue on Human Settlements Ghana, 2020).

Conclusion

Our conceptual framework and assessment of the current development trajectory in Accra makes clear that there is likely a severely challenging path ahead for inclusive urban development without comprehensive and disciplined planning and accountability by the government. The National Housing Policy released in 2015 was impressive in its scope, principles and comprehensiveness. However, the national elections in 2016 returned power from the National Democratic Congress, under which the Policy was finalized and released, to the opposition party the New Patriotic Party, placing the commitment to the Policy in jeopardy. The New Patriotic Party was returned to power by the electorate in December 2020, giving it four more years to advance its policies for social development in Ghana. Under President Nana Akufo Addo, the Ghanaian Ministry of Work and Housing continues to assert its commitment to bridge the affordable housing deficit in the country (Ministry of Works and Housing, 2021). The Government of Ghana over the last decade has initiated several large-scale housing projects including the Saglemi and Kpone Affordable Housing projects, National Housing Mortgage Fund project, and Tema Kaizer flat projects. However, most of these housing projects have remained stalled for years (Amoatey, 2015). In the President's 2021 State of the Nation 2021 Address, he acknowledged that less than 2,000 units had been produced (2021 State of the Nation Address). Furthermore, the units that have been produced remain largely unaffordable to a large section of the Ghanaian population (Ministry of Works and Housing, 2021).

It seems clear that current urban planning infrastructure remains exceedingly under capacity and poorly positioned to provide the necessary intentionality, strategy and accountability to promote the inclusionary policy we have recommended here. The creation and ratification of a comprehensive housing policy with many elements aligned with inclusive, mixed-income development was an important foundational step for Ghana and Accra. The displacement and exclusion experienced in mixed-income communities in the United States should serve as a cautionary example to motivate bold action by current government and civic leaders to accelerate implementation of the policy directives.

Acknowledgments

We thank Prof. George Owusu for his input on an earlier version of this paper. We thank Jonathan Duffie and Bashara Abubakari for their research assistance. We gratefully acknowledge the support of colleagues in the Department of Geography and Resource Development at the University of Ghana, Legon, where the authors first developed and presented the ideas in this paper.

Disclosure statement

No potential conflict of interest was reported by the author(s).

References

Abiodun, J. (1976). Housing problems in Nigerian cities. *Town Planning Review*, 47(4), 339–347. https://doi.org/10.3828/tpr.47.4.r7g4372515673600

Acquah, A. (2021). Higher education finance between Ghana and the United States. *Current Issues in Comparative Education*, 23(1), 90–108. https://doi.org/10.52214/cice.v23i1.8143

Adogla-Bessa, D. (2017). AMA to commence mass demolition exercise tomorrow. *CitiFMOnline*. Retrieved June 10, 2020, from: http://citifmonline.com/2017/03/21/ama-to-commence-mass-demolition-exercise-tomorrow/

Agyei-Mensah, S., & Owusu, G. (2009). Segregated by neighbourhoods? A portrait of ethnic diversity in the neighbourhoods of the Accra Metropolitan Area. *Ghana Population, Space and Place*, 16(6), 499–516. https://doi.org/10.1002/psp.551

Ahwoi, K. (2010). *Local government & decentralisation in Ghana*. Unimax Macmillan.

Akufo-Addo, N. (2021). *2021 State of the Nation Address*. Myjoyonline. Retrieved June 27, 2021 from https://www.myjoyonline.com/full-text-akufo-addos-2021-state-of-the-nation-address/

Alhassan, J., & Castelli, M. (2020). Politics as an explanation to the health divide in different settings: A comparative study of England and Ghana. *International Journal of Health Services*, 50(1), 110–122. https://doi.org/10.1177/0020731419876786

Amnesty International. (2011). *Stop forced evictions: Protect people living in slums*. Retrieved July 10, 2020 from https://www.amnesty.org/en/documents/ACT35/026/2011/en/

Amoako, C. (2016). Brutal presence or convenient absence: The role of the state in the politics of flooding in informal Accra, Ghana. *Geoforum*, 77, 5–16. https://doi.org/10.1016/j.geoforum.2016.10.003

Amoatey, C. (2015). Analysing delay causes and effects in Ghanaian state housing construction projects. *International Journal of Managing Projects in Business*, 8(1), 198–214. https://doi.org/10.1108/IJMPB-04-2014-0035

Antwi-Boasiako, K. B. (2010). Public administration: Local government and decentralization in Ghana. *Journal of African Studies and Development*, 2(7), 166–175. https://academicjournals.org/article/article1380006757_Antwi-Boasiako.pdf

Arthurson, K. (2002). Creating inclusive communities through balancing social mix: A critical relationship or tenuous link? *Urban Policy and Research*, 20(3), 245–261. https://doi.org/10.1080/0811114022000005898

Asiedu, A. B., & Arku, G. (2009). The rise of gated housing estates in Ghana: Empirical insights from three communities in metropolitan Accra. *Journal of Housing and the Built Environment*, 24(3), 227–247. https://doi.org/10.1007/s10901-009-9146-0

August, M. (2008). Social mix and Canadian public housing redevelopment: Experiences in Toronto. *Canadian Journal of Urban Research*, 17(1), 82–100. https://www.jstor.org/stable/26193206

August, M. (2015). Revitalization gone wrong: Mixed-income public housing redevelopment in Toronto's Don Mount Court. *Urban Studies*, 53(16), 3405–3422. https://doi.org/10.1177/0042098015613207

Bandura, A. (1977). *Social learning theory*. Prentice Hall.

Bayat, A. (1997). Un-civil society: The politics of the 'informal people.' *Third World Quarterly*, 18(1), 53–72. https://doi.org/10.1080/01436599715055

Boamah, E. F., & Amoako, C. (2020). Planning by (mis)rule of laws: The idiom and dilemma of planning within Ghana's dual legal land systems. *Politics and Space*, 38(1), 97–115. https://doi.org/10.1177/2399654419855400

Boamah, N. A. (2014). Housing policy in Ghana: The feasible paths. *Ghana Journal of Development Studies*, 11(1), 1–18. https://doi.org/10.4314/gjds.v11i1.1

Boateng, A., & Anngela-Cole, L. (2016). Funeral practices in Ghana and the United States: A cultural comparison. *International Journal of Social Science Studies*, 4(1). https://doi.org/10.11114/ijsss.v4i1.1221

Briggs, X. (2003). Re-shaping the geography of opportunity: Place effects in global perspective. *Housing Studies*, 18(6), 915–936. https://doi.org/10.1080/0267303032000135500

Briggs, X. (2005). *The geography of opportunity: Race and housing choice in metropolitan America*. Brookings Institution Press. https://www.brookings.edu/wp-content/uploads/2016/07/geographyofopportunity_chapter-1.pdf

Chaskin, R. J., & Joseph, M. L. (2012). "Positive" gentrification, social inclusion, and the "right to the city" in mixed-income communities: Uses and expectations of space and place. *International Journal of Urban and Regional Research*, 37(2), 280–302. https://doi.org/10.1111/j.1468-2427.2012.01158.x

Chaskin, R. J., & Joseph, M. L. (2015). *Integrating the inner city: The promise and perils of mixed-income public housing transformation*. University of Chicago Press.

Chaskin, R. J., Joseph, M. L., Voelker, S., & Dworsky, A. (2012). Public housing transformation and resident relocation: Comparing destinations and household characteristics in Chicago. *Cityscape*, 14(1), 183–214.

Chaskin, R. J., Khare, A. T., & Joseph, M. L. (2012). Participation, deliberation, and decision-making: The dynamics of inclusion and exclusion in mixed-income developments. *Urban Affairs Review*, 48(6), 863–906. https://doi.org/10.1177/1078087412450151

Cobbinah, P. B., & Darkwah, R. M. (2017). Urban planning and politics in Ghana. *GeoJournal*, 82(6), 1229–1245. https://doi.org/10.1007/s10708-016-9750-y

Coleman, J. S. (1988). Social capital in the creation of human capital. *American Journal of Sociology*, 94, 95–120. https://doi.org/10.1086/228943

Crentsil, A., & Owusu, G. (2018). Accra's decongestion policy: Another face of urban clearance or bulldozing approach? *Revue internationale de politique de développement*. 10(3), 213–228. https://doi.org/10.4000/poldev.2719

Cromwell, A. (2020). Over 100 slum dwellers homeless after demolishing exercise at Old Fadama. Myjoyonline. Retrieved September 6, 2020, from https://www.myjoyonline.com/news/national/over-1000-slum-dwellers-homeless-after-demolishing-exercise-at-old-fadama/.

Dasgupta, B., Lall, S., & Lozano-Gracia, N. (2014). *Urbanization and housing investment*. (Policy Research Working Paper 7110). World Bank Group. https://doi.org/10.13140/2.1.2284.5123.

Fält, L. (2016). From shacks to skyscrapers: Multiple spatial rationalities and urban transformation in Accra, Ghana. *Urban Forum, 27*(4), 465–486. https://doi.org/10.1007/s12132-016-9294-8

Fraser, J., Oakley, D., & Levy, D. (2013). Guest editors' introduction: Policy assumptions and lived realities of mixed-income housing on both sides of the Atlantic. *Cityscape, 15*(2), 1–14. https://www.huduser.gov/portal/publications/Cityscape_Jul2013.pdf

Fraser, J. C., Chaskin, R. J., & Bazuin, J. T. (2013). Making mixed-income neighborhoods work for low-income households. *Cityscape, 15*(12), 83–100. https://www.huduser.gov/portal/periodicals/cityscpe/vol15num2/ch6.pdf

Freeman, L. (2006). *There goes the 'hood: Views of gentrification from the ground up*. Temple University Press.

Frimpong Boamah, E., & Walker, M. (2017). Legal pluralism, land tenure and the production of "nomotropic urban spaces" in post-colonial Accra, Ghana. *Geography Research Forum, 36*, 24. https://grf.bgu.ac.il/index.php/GRF/article/view/492/452

Galster, G., & Killen, S. (1995). The geography of metropolitan opportunity: A reconnaissance and conceptual framework. *Housing Policy Debate, 6*(1), 7–43. https://doi.org/10.1080/10511482.1995.9521180

Ghana Statistical Service. (2013). *2010 population and housing census of Ghana, National analytical report*. Retrieved July 10, 2020 from https://statsghana.gov.gh/gssmain/fileUpload/pressrelease/2010_PHC_National_Analytical_Report.pdf

Ghana Statistical Service. (2019). Population by regions: Greater Accra. *Journal of Architectural & Planning Research, 8*, 96–115. https://statsghana.gov.gh/regionalpopulation.php?population=MTM0NTk2MjQzOS4yMDE1&&Greater%20Accra°id=3researchandtheoreticaldevelopment

GhanaWeb. (2020). *Old Fadama demolition: Evacuate affected persons to Trade Fair- Amnesty International*. Retrieved July 10, 2020 from https://www.ghanaweb.com/GhanaHomePage/NewsArchive/Old-Fadama-demolition-Evacuate-affected-persons-to-Trade-Fair-Amnesty-International-926830

Gillespie, T. (2015). Accumulation by urban dispossession: Struggles over urban space in Accra, Ghana. *Transactions of the Institute of British Geographers, 41*(1), 66–77. https://doi.org/10.1111/tran.12105

Gillespie, T. (2018). Collective self-help, financial inclusion, and the commons: Searching for solutions to Accra's housing crisis. *Housing Policy Debate, 28*(1), 64–78. Retrieved July 14, 2020, from https://www.pdghana.org/housing-and-community-infrastructure-upgrading/

Government of Ghana. (2012). *National urban policy framework*. Ministry of Local Government and Rural Development. Retrieved July 10, 2020, from http://www.mlgrd.gov.gh/files/file/download/332/?next=/library/documents/

Government of Ghana. (2015). *National housing policy*. Ministry of Water Resources, Works and Housing. Retrieved July 10, 2020, from http://www.mlgrd.gov.gh/files/file/download/331/?next=/library/documents/

Grant, R. (2009). *Globalizing city: The urban and economic transformation of Accra, Ghana*. Syracuse University Press.

Grant, R. (2015). *Africa: Geographies of change*. Oxford University Press.

Grant, R., & Yankson, P. (2003). Accra profile. *Cities, 20*(1), 65–74. https://doi.org/10.1016/S0264-2751(02)00090-2

Graves, E. M. (2010). The structuring of urban life in a mixed-income housing community. *City and Community, 9*(1), 109–131. https://doi.org/10.1111/j.1540-6040.2009.01305.x

Gress, T. H., Joseph, M. L., & Cho, S. (2019). Confirmations, new insights, and future implications for HOPE VI mixed-income redevelopment. *Cityscape, 21*(2), 185–212. https://www.huduser.gov/portal/periodicals/cityscpe/vol21num2/article11.html

Huxley, M. (2006). Spatial rationalities: Order, environment, evolution and government. *Social & Cultural Geography, 7*(5), 771–787. https://doi.org/10.1080/14649360600974758

Huxley, M. (2007). Geographies of governmentality. In J. W. Crampton & S. Elden (Eds.), *Space, knowledge and power: Foucault and geography* (pp. 185–204). Ashgate.

Hyra, D. S. (2008). *The new urban renewal: The economic transformation of Harlem and Bronzeville*. University of Chicago Press.

Institute of Statistical, Social and Economic Research (ISSER). (2012). *Ghana social development outlook, 2012*. University of Ghana.

Joseph, M. L. (2013). Mixed-income symposium summary and response: Implications for antipoverty policy. *Cityscape, 15*(2), 215–221. https://www.huduser.gov/portal/periodicals/cityscpe/vol15num2/ch16.pdf

Joseph, M. L. (2019). Promoting poverty deconcentration and racial desegregation through mixed-income development. In M. W. Metzler & H. S. Webber (Eds.), *Facing segregation: Housing policy solutions for a stronger society* (pp. 146–168). Oxford University Press.

Joseph, M. L., & Chaskin, R. J. (2012). Mixed-income developments and low rates of return: Insights from relocated public housing residents in Chicago. *Housing Policy Debate, 22*(3), 377–406. https://doi.org/10.1080/10511482.2012.680479

Joseph, M. L., Chaskin, R. J., & Webber, H. S. (2007). A theoretical basis for addressing poverty through mixed-income development. *Urban Affairs Review, 42*(3), 369–409. https://doi.org/10.1177/1078087406294043

Joseph, M. L., & Yoon, M. (2019). Mixed-income development. In A. Orum (Ed.), *Wiley-Blackwell encyclopedia of urban and regional studies* (pp. 11). John Wiley & Sons Press. https://doi.org/10.1002/9781118568446.eurs0205

Khare, A. T. (2021). *Poverty, power and profit: Structural racism in Chicago's public housing reforms* [Unpublished manuscript].

Kleinhans, R., & Van Hamm, M. (2013). Lessons learned from the largest tenure-mix operation in the world: Right to buy in the United Kingdom. *Cityscape: A Journal of Policy Development and Research, 15*(2), 101–117. https://www.huduser.gov/portal/periodicals/cityscpe/vol15num2/ch7.pdf

Kleit, R. G. (2005). HOPE VI new communities: Neighborhood relationships in mixed-income housing. *Environment and Planning A: Economy and Space, 37*(8), 1413–1441. https://doi.org/10.1068/a3796

Konadu-Agyemang, K. (2001). *The political economy of housing and urbanization in Africa: Ghana's experience from colonial times to 1998*. Praeger.

Lees, L. (2008). Gentrification and social mixing: Towards an inclusive urban renaissance? *Urban Studies, 45*(12), 2449–2470. https://doi.org/10.1177/0042098008097099

Levy, D. K., McDade, Z., & Bertumen, K. (2013). Mixed-income living: Anticipated and realized benefits for low-income households. *Cityscape, 15*(2), 15–28. https://www.huduser.gov/periodicals/cityscpe/vol15num2/ch1.pdf

Logan, J. R., & Molotch, H. L. (1987). *Urban fortunes: The political economy of place*. University of California Press.

Mackie, P. K., Bromley, R. D., & Brown, A. (2014). Informal traders and the battlegrounds of revanchism in Cusco, Peru. *International Journal of Urban and Regional Research, 38*(5), 1884–1903. https://doi.org/10.1111/1468-2427.12161

McCormick, N., Joseph, M. L., & Chaskin, R. J. (2012). The new stigma of relocated public housing residents: Challenges to social identity in mixed-income developments. *City and Community, 11*(3), 285–308. https://doi.org/10.1111/j.1540-6040.2012.01411.x

Ministry of Works and Housing. (2021). *Affordable housing: Government intends to build more*. Retrieved May 27, 2021, from https://www.mwh.gov.gh/affordable-housing/

Nanja, S. (2019). Appointment of Ghana's local government chief executives: A setback on accountability? *Journal of Public Administration, 1*(1), 5–16. https://www.sryahwapublications.com/journal-of-public-administration/pdf/v1-i1/2.pdf

Nijman, J., & Wei, Y. D. (2020). Urban inequalities in the 21st century economy. *Applied Geography, 117*, 102188. https://doi.org/10.1016/j.apgeog.2020.102188

Novignon, J. (2017). Household income inequality in Ghana: A decomposition analysis. *African Journal of Economic and Management Studies, 8*(4), 515–526. https://doi.org/10.1108/AJEMS-03-2017-0045

Obeng-Odoom, F. (2013). *Governance for pro-poor urban development: Lessons from Ghana*. Routledge.

Otiso, K., & Owusu, G. (2008). Comparative urbanization in Ghana and Kenya in time and space. *GeoJournal, 71*(2–3), 143–157. https://doi.org/10.1007/s10708-008-9152-x

Owusu, G. (2008). Indigenes' and migrants' access to land in periurban areas of Accra, Ghana. *International Development Planning Review, 30*(2), 177–198. https://doi.org/10.3828/idpr.30.2.5

Owusu, G., & Agyei-Mensah. (2011). A comparative study of ethnic residential segregation in Ghana's two largest cities, Accra and Kumasi. *Population and Environment, 32*(4), 332–352. https://doi.org/10.1007/s11111-010-0131-z

Pastor, M. (2001). Geography and opportunity. In N. J. Smelser, J. Wilson, & F. Mitchell (Eds.), *America becoming: Racial trends and their consequences* (pp. 435–468). The National Academies Press.

People's Dialogue on Human Settlements Ghana. (2020). *Housing & community infrastructure upgrading: Amui Dzor Cooperative Multi-Compound Housing*. Retrieved July 10, 2020 from https://www.pdghana.org/housing-and-community-infrastructure-upgrading/

Popkin, S. J., Katz, B., Cunningham, M. K., Brown, K. D., Gustafson, J., & Turner, M. A. (2004). *A decade of HOPE VI: Research findings and policy challenges*. Urban Institute.

Rosenbaum, J. E. (1995). Changing the geography of opportunity by expanding residential choice: Lessons from the Gautreaux Program. *Housing Policy Debate, 6*(1), 231–269. https://doi.org/10.1080/10511482.1995.9521186

Sampson, R. J., & Groves, W. B. (1989). Community structure and crime: Testing social-disorganization theory. *American Journal of Sociology, 94*(4), 774–802. https://doi.org/10.1086/229068

Sassen, S. (2014). *Expulsions: Brutality and complexity in the global economy*. Harvard University Press.

Satterthwaite, D., & Mitlin, D. (2014). *Reducing urban poverty in the global south*. Routledge.

Siekpe, J. S., & Greene, W. E. (2006). Employment and labor laws: Comparing Ghana, South Africa, and the U.S. *Journal of African Business, 7*(1–2), 229–249. https://doi.org/10.1300/J156v07n01_11

Songsore, J., & McGranaham, G. (1993). Environment, wealth and health: Towards an analysis of intra-urban differentials within Accra, Ghana. *Environment and Urbanization, 5*(2), 10–34. https://doi.org/10.1177/095624789300500203

Space and Place 16 499–516

Stow, D. A., Lippitt, C. D., & Weeks, J. R. (2010). Geographic object-based delineation of neighborhoods of Accra, Ghana using QuickBird satellite imagery. *Photogrammetric Engineering and Remote Sensing, 76*(8), 907–914. https://doi.org/10.14358/pers.76.8.907

Tach, L. M. (2009). More than bricks and mortar: Neighborhood frames, social processes, and the mixed-income redevelopment of a public housing project. *City and Community, 8*(3), 269–299. https://doi.org/10.1111/j.1540-6040.2009.01289.x

Tetteh, K. (2016). *The new middle class and urban transformation in Africa: A case study of Accra, Ghana* [Master's thesis]. Kwame Nkrumah University of Science and Technology, The University of British Columbia Open Collections. https://open.library.ubc.ca/cIRcle/collections/ubctheses/24/items/1.0300342

Urban Institute & MDRC. (2015). *Choice Neighborhoods: Baseline conditions and early progress. Prepared for the U.S. Department of Housing and Urban Development.* https://www.huduser.gov/portal/sites/default/files/pdf/Baseline-Conditions-Early-Progress.pdf

U.S. Department of Housing and Urban Development (2021). *Choice Neighborhoods.* Retrieved July 1, 2021 from https://www.hud.gov/cn

World Bank Group. (2017). *Enhancing urban resilience in the greater Accra metropolitan area. Global practice on social, urban, rural and resilience.* Retrieved June 24, 2020, from http://documents.worldbank.org/curated/en/949241495793834492/pdf/115296-REPLACEMENT-PUBLIC-Accra-v5-highres-nocutmarks.pdf

Low-income housing development in India: Strategies for income mixing and inclusive urban planning

Naganika Sanga

ABSTRACT

Federal housing programs in rapidly urbanizing countries like India are targeting the expansion of low-income housing stocks. However, most of these large-scale low-income housing developments occur in the urban peripheries, and they are cut off from opportunities and essential urban infrastructure. They not only indicate policy failure but also exacerbate urban segregation in growing cities. Federal policies to tackle these problems in India are geared toward relatively small-scale mixed-income initiatives like inclusionary housing and public-private partnerships. Evaluating these efforts based on four cases in the city of Vijayawada in Andhra Pradesh, this paper expands the literature on social-mix and mixed-income housing initiatives that is dominated by studies from the Global North. It identifies multi-pronged approaches to address (1) the failure of the current Indian federal policy involving small-scale mixed-income initiatives, and (2) the need to integrate housing initiatives with urban development at multiple levels, especially in the urban peripheries.

Introduction

Rising income inequalities and residential segregation are global phenomena (van Ham et al., 2021). These issues are more severe in the developing economies of the Global South (Comandon & Veneri, 2021). In these countries, rapid urbanization has exacerbated affordable housing shortages, resulting in the proliferation of informal settlements (Satterthwaite & Mitlin, 2014). Meanwhile, rising income disparities due to globalization forces have created enclaves of prosperity and affluence adjacent to spaces of abject poverty that do not have access to basic services (Smets & Salman, 2008). Spurred by international development goals, national governments in many Global South countries like India are pursuing expansive low-income housing policies aimed at providing improved structural housing conditions to low-income families (Buckley et al., 2016b; Tiwari et al., 2016). Most of these projects are located in urban peripheries due to high land costs in urban centers. Scholars and observers have pointed out that these efforts have often emphasized the expansion of low-income housing production without due consideration for overall urban development patterns and access to opportunities (Turok, 2016). In India, more than 200,000 units constructed under two national housing programs, *Jawaharlal Nehru National Urban Renewal Mission* and *Rajiv Awas Yojana*, during the period between 2005 and 2013 were vacant in 2016 due to their distance from economic centers and other social infrastructure (The Economic Times, 2016). Others have noted how patterns of spatial segregation are also being reproduced in the urban peripheries due in part to the development of enclaves of low-income housing without proper connectivity to jobs and infrastructure (Caldeira, 2017; Coelho et al., 2020). These patterns of *state-sponsored segregation* need careful study to encourage the integrated development of low-income housing projects to avoid the problems witnessed in some public housing projects in the Global North. It poses two key challenges to low-income housing provision in these rapidly urbanizing contexts. First, how can a balance be struck between producing high numbers of affordable housing units while ensuring that these units are connected to economic and social opportunities? Second, how can the integration of different socioeconomic groups be encouraged while preserving their community ties and preventing displacement?

This paper argues that social integration and affordable production are not mutually exclusive objectives and that they may be achieved together when governments integrate low-income housing policies with broader urban development strategies. This integration needs to be pursued at multiple levels and scales to provide improved opportunities for low-income families and facilitate socioeconomic integration in growing cities. Current literature on housing policies for socioeconomic integration in the Global North predominantly focuses on mixed-income housing policies—"a deliberate effort to construct and/or own a multifamily development that has the mixing of income groups as a fundamental part of its financial and operating plans" (Brophy & Smith, 1997)—at the neighborhood level (Andersson & Musterd, 2010; Chapple, 2015). However, as Tach et al. (2014) have argued, income mixing initiatives at broader spatial scales, such as comprehensive planning and inclusive development policies, can help deliver equitable housing and employment opportunities for all income groups. As this paper will demonstrate based on the experience from India, there is a need to deploy place-based housing strategies for socioeconomic integration and income mixing at both the city level and in urban expansion areas.[1] These interventions should be paired with small-scale mixed-income housing initiatives like inclusionary housing policies to foster integrated and inclusive urban development.

Evidence gathered from four case studies of local implementation of federal mixed-income housing policies in Vijayawada, a city in Andhra Pradesh, India, shows that federal housing policies that encourage small-scale mixed-income housing strategies are not being implemented at the local level. Instead, given the acute shortages of low-income housing, local authorities are pursuing other strategies to find land and capital for producing large-scale low-income housing. When adopted through comprehensive planning and other land-use regulatory frameworks, these other strategies can provide sustained mechanisms for creating integrated communities and facilitate the development of mixed-income housing at small scales. This paper proposes incremental policy changes based on stakeholder perceptions and reception to existing policy ideas and suggests immediate intervention in the urban expansion areas where much of the future development is set to happen.

Socioeconomic segregation in Indian cities

India's urbanization processes and its land use regulations are exclusionary toward the poor (Bhan, 2013; Kundu, 2014). Land use planning standards through building and zoning regulations often deem small building lots, low-quality construction materials, and built-up areas without large setbacks illegal. These regulations often serve to hinder poor people's access to decent living conditions (Mishra, 2017). The rising costs of urban land further disenfranchise the poor from accessing formal housing opportunities in cities (Steel et al., 2017; Turok, 2016). Consequently, squatting and densification of existing informal settlements within the urban core, particularly in those that offer employment opportunities, are a regular feature in Indian cities. These processes have resulted in the "ghettoization" of the poor into informal settlements, otherwise labeled as *slums*[2] in government policy documents and regular parlance. These informal settlements are deprived of basic infrastructure services, face environmental precarity, and battle constant threats of eviction. At the turn of the 21st century, informal settlements were slowly becoming accepted as poor people's response to the market's failure and rigid government land use and development control (Buckley & Kalarickal, 2005; Roy, 2005; Satterthwaite & Mitlin, 2014). These pockets of poverty are growing together with the emergence of enclaves of affluence in fast-growing cities due to rising inequalities in the era of globalization (van Ham et al., 2021).

Recent studies have found that segregation is also clearly prevalent at the street and neighborhood levels in Indian cities along caste lines (Bharathi et al., 2021). These authors point out that such deeply embedded patterns of segregation are comparable to race-based socioeconomic segregation in the United States (Bharathi et al., 2021). Thus, reviewing the U.S. experience in addressing residential segregation may offer lessons in understanding India's efforts.

Integrated urban and housing development: Income mixing strategies beyond public housing redevelopment

As the literature has widely documented, the U.S. government has launched mixed-income housing projects during the past 20 years, largely in response to the concentration of poverty in inner-city neighborhoods in general and public housing projects in particular (Goetz, 2000; Schwartz & Tajbakhsh, 1997; Vale & Shamsuddin, 2017). The objective of mixed-income housing development, a type of social mix housing, is to promote socioeconomic integration and advancement of marginalized communities through exposure to the social and economic advantages accessible to their high-income neighbors (Arthurson, 2010b; Chaskin & Joseph, 2015; Imbroscio, 2016). Social scientists have argued that inner-city crime and socioeconomic distress resulted primarily from the concentration of poverty in public housing projects that adversely impacted low-income residents (Bloom et al., 2015; Chaskin & Joseph, 2015). These adverse effects ranged from poor behavioral effects on children due to the lack of appropriate role models to reduced socioeconomic opportunities for adults and low collective bargaining power in city politics for improved infrastructure and the built environment (Chaskin & Joseph, 2011; Curley, 2010). However, empirical results from mixed-income housing initiatives that aimed at mitigating these adverse effects show conflicting results (Thurber et al., 2018).

It appears that the direction of income mixing and whether it is by residents' own choice are important in determining the success and desirability of those mixed-income housing initiatives. Mixed-income housing initiatives that relocated some low-income families to high-income neighborhoods were found to have improved development outcomes in health, education, employment, and safety in young children (Chetty et al., 2016). In contrast, those that redeveloped existing public housing projects by displacing low-income families were found to be harmful (Bloom et al., 2015; Musterd & Andersson, 2005). Overall, scholars argue that low-income families mainly benefit from access to the improved living environment, including schools, transportation, and neighborhood services that mixed-income developments offer (Berube, 2006; Curley, 2010; Fraser et al., 2013), rather than close social interaction through proximity to higher-income groups themselves (Arthurson et al., 2015; Bloom et al., 2015). Given these findings, it seems that cities could pursue two types of strategies to improve low-income residents' access to social and economic opportunities. The first is to enhance connectivity to opportunities and infrastructure in the existing low-income neighborhoods while protecting them against gentrification; the second is to create new developments that are socioeconomically integrated. Given this study's focus on new developments, the rest of the paper will focus on the second type of strategy.

Strategies for new mixed-income housing developments could occur at smaller scales through project-based financial subsidies or land-use planning instruments like inclusionary housing. *Inclusionary housing policies* require developers to provide a specific portion of income-restricted units in new development as determined by the local authority (Kontokosta, 2014). Cities widely use inclusionary housing policies to mandate or incentivize the production of affordable housing by private developers (Thaden & Wang, 2017). The underlying objective is that being tied to market demand would result in the location of inclusionary housing units in high opportunity areas with high-quality infrastructure (Calavita & Mallach, 2010). However, the need for the equitable spatial distribution of opportunities is not limited to infrastructure within neighborhoods. Other considerations like broader access to economic opportunities, quality health services, availability of recreation activities, and safety from environmental risks are also relevant in an urban setting (Galster & Sharkey, 2017). These considerations extend to geographies beyond the immediate impact areas of the close-grained mixed-income housing policies like inclusionary housing to city and sub-city levels, spreading across political jurisdictions and the metropolitan region (Andersson & Musterd, 2010; Galster & Sharkey, 2017). Strategies at those broader levels can also encourage mixing of different income groups and create inclusive and diverse areas at the city and sub-city level through a variety of deliberate interventions:

(1) removing barriers like *exclusionary zoning* practices that restrict the building of low-income housing in high-income areas (Orfield, 2005; Serkin & Wellington, 2014);
(2) requiring accommodation of housing needs of all income groups through *fair-share housing goals* (Basolo & Scally, 2008; Calavita & Mallach, 2010);
(3) reserving pockets of *residential zones for geographically dispersed low-income housing* (Santoro, 2019); and
(4) leveraging public land and financial resources to require a greater share of low-income housing development in large-scale *public-private partnership* (PPP) projects (Okechukwu Onatu, 2010).

The existing literature on mixed-income or social mix housing models does not adequately factor in the question of scale and level of intervention (Arthurson, 2010a; Chapple, 2015). Approaching integrated and inclusive development at larger scales allows cities to tackle existing challenges in the spatial distribution of opportunities without forcefully redeveloping existing housing stock, as with public housing redevelopment efforts. It also helps guide future growth by facilitating the balance between integrating different social classes and preserving the sense of social belonging within each group while providing equitable access to opportunities. Those efforts may include city-level initiatives like removing barriers to affordable housing production as noted above, although without appropriate sub-city changes, enclaves of affluence and poverty can still persist (Serkin & Wellington, 2014). Efforts may also include infrastructure upgrades and income mixing at the sub-city scale or intermediate level through transit-oriented-development, zoning that encourages low-income housing, and leveraging public lands for affordable housing development so that residents "share important civic and commercial spaces and transportation facilities" (Tach et al., 2014, p. 10). The intermediate level is also a scale at which a natural balance between social integration and a desired amount of clustering may be facilitated within different parts of the city.

As this paper will show, strategies at these different levels are critical in rapidly growing Indian cities that have experienced widening gaps in income and living standards. The next section provides an overview of those place-based policies at different scales issued by India's federal government. The sections that follow discuss their implementation success at the local level.

National policies for low-income housing: Strategies for income mixing and inclusive development in India

Starting in 2005, the Indian national government took a keen interest in urban development and housing policy issues. A series of national policies were issued that promote low-income housing production and *slum* redevelopment while prioritizing private participation through project-based funding (Yap, 2016). Three main programs, *Jawaharlal Nehru National Urban Renewal Mission* (2005–2013), *Rajiv Awas Yojana* (2009–2014), *and Pradhan Mantri Awas Yojana* (2015-current), were created as conditional grant programs that required state and local governments to enact a series of urban reforms in order to receive funding. Scholars and international agencies have written extensively about these policies from the low-income housing and *slum* redevelopment perspectives. However, these initiatives have important policy components for income mixing and integrated development that were underexplored in previous studies. This paper expands the literature by studying low-income housing initiatives funded under the three federal programs since 2005 and the accompanying strategies for income mixing and integrated development.

Two federal schemes, *Jawaharlal Nehru Urban Renewal Mission* and *Rajiv Awas Yojana*, mandated the adoption of inclusionary housing policy reforms (coined as "earmarking of land/housing for pro-poor housing") through conditional grants for land sub-divisions and housing developments, respectively (Jawaharlal Nehru National Urban Renewal Mission, 2006; Ministry of Housing and Urban Poverty Alleviation, 2013). *Rajiv Awas Yojana* also encouraged state and local property rights legislation to treat all informal households in a city to be legal and be marked as a residential zone in the city's comprehensive or master plan. However, the program that succeeded it, *Pradhan Mantri Awas Yojana*, has diluted both inclusive planning norms and inclusionary housing policy reforms and instead mainly focused on financial subsidies for PPP projects under the *Affordable Housing in Partnership* component. Under this component, private builders are compensated for including a minimum of 35% of the units for affordable housing in a mixed-income development in this PPP mode (Ministry of Housing and Urban Poverty Alleviation, 2016).

A careful review of federal housing policies in India revealed that each policy promoted a combination of income mixing and inclusive development initiatives that prominently targeted the delivery of low-income housing units by private developers. Policy interventions promoted inclusionary housing programs that were predominantly small-scale initiatives, while PPPs could either be small or large-scale projects depending on the size of land parcels involved in the process. There were some requirements under *Rajiv Awas Yojana* for government-led city-level initiatives on ending exclusionary zoning and offering protection for *slums* as residential zones for a limited period. Yet, the existing academic literature has largely focused on discrete examples of inclusionary housing (Mishra & Mohanty, 2017; Mishra & Sen, 2020) and PPPs (Mahadevia et al., 2018; Parashar, 2014; Sengupta, 2013). What is lacking is a clear understanding of how federal mixed-income policy initiatives were translated into local-level implementation efforts and stakeholders' response to these initiatives.

Research methodology and context

This study examines four mixed-income housing models promoted under India's three federal housing programs operating since 2005 in Vijayawada, located in Andhra Pradesh. The aim is to examine how federal housing initiatives have interacted with local efforts and actors to produce mixed-income housing in Vijayawada and to evaluate possible opportunities for intervention.

Vijayawada is the commercial capital of the southern state of Andhra Pradesh. It is located in a rich river-delta region with excellent road and rail connectivity to the rest of the country. The new capital of Andhra Pradesh, Amaravati, is under construction and within 20 km distance to Vijayawada with the intent to function as part of the larger urban agglomeration. Vijayawada is highly dense, with a total population of one million (according to the 2011 census) living in 61.88 square kilometers of the municipal area (Vijayawada Municipal Corporation, 2018). The acute land shortage resulted in the growth of informal settlements on canal bunds and hillslopes. A quarter of the city's population (about 227,000) is below the national poverty line, and a majority of them live in the 105 *slums* located within the municipal limits (Vijayawada Municipal Corporation, 2018). Vijayawada serves as a good site for examining mixed-income housing models, given its successful engagement with all three federal programs since 2005 through award-winning housing initiatives that are often showcased in federal government reports on best practices. Three of the four models included in this study were based on these reports. The fourth model was selected based on interviews with the key informants.

Document analysis, interviews, and site visits were conducted in an iterative process that helped continually inform the data collection and analysis process. All the interviews and field visits for the study were conducted between December 2018 and September 2019.

A total of 270 documents, including government policy documentation, executive orders, intergovernmental communications, evaluation and progress reports, newspaper articles, and government press releases, were analyzed. A manual content analysis of the documents was conducted, paying attention to the definition of terms, actors and agencies involved, specifics of the policy design, and project progress. Content analysis also helped construct the historical timeline of mixed-income efforts and provided the framework for the stakeholder interviews.

Six key informants in different institutions at the federal, state, and local levels involved in the program design and implementation of the three federal housing programs helped identify other stakeholders through snowball sampling. A total of 61 interviews of planners, policymakers, housing activists, and developers provided the *thick descriptions* around policy choices and implementation realities. On average, each interview lasted between 45 and 60 minutes. Interviews were recorded, transcribed, and coded using Dedoose software based on the overarching themes. Themes were drawn inductively from the data relating to different policy and project specifics: formulation/design process, roles, impressions, primary barriers, and feasibility assessment. These themes were further categorized based on different stakeholder groups and analyzed using a constructionist approach to thematic analysis focusing on the realities of data (Braun & Clarke, 2006). Direct quotes from the interviews are followed by numbers in square brackets that denote the identification number assigned to the specific interviewee to ensure confidentiality.

Field visits were possible only for three of the four mixed-income housing models evaluated as part of this study. The author visited each of the three field sites on two separate occasions. The second visit was within a month of the first visit to the site. On each visit, the author spent approximately 4 hours walking around the site, observing, and informally conversing with different actors present. Only one of the three sites was inhabited while the other two sites were in various stages of construction with an opportunity to observe the visitors and families who were already allotted units. Site visits helped contextualize how plan documents translated on the ground and provided a sense of the transportation access to the project site, the desirability of the living conditions, and the amenities available on site.

Four models of mixed-income housing efforts in Vijayawada city

This study evaluates the impact of federal mixed-income housing initiatives by examining Vijayawada's experience. Vijayawada Municipal Corporation is actively involved in *slum* rehabilitation and low-income housing development programs supported by the federal government. The following are some prominent examples of Vijayawada's experience with federal mixed-income housing policies since 2005. While each of the cases are carried out due to federal mixed-income housing initiatives, their local implementation resulted in the expansion of implementation to larger scales at the city and sub-city level. Model 1 was a response to federal inclusionary housing mandates. Models 2 and 3 were carried out at a larger scale as part of the *slum* rehabilitation and PPP efforts in urban expansion areas. Model 4 is also a PPP-funded project integrated as part of a comprehensive plan for a greenfield city. There are no implementation examples for Model 1. Three different sites for models 2, 3, and 4 are depicted in Figure 1.

Model 1: The inclusionary housing efforts

In response to the inclusionary reform mandates at the federal level under *Jawaharlal Nehru National Urban Renewal Mission* (2007), land-based reservations were first introduced in 2011 through state-level regulation in Vijayawada for layouts (or subdivisions) proposed in an area greater than 4000 sq m. This requirement was repealed in less than a year due to widespread developer opposition. Instead, inclusionary zoning requirements were applied to multi-unit developments as per *Rajiv Awas Yojana* requirements (Ministry of Housing and Urban Poverty Alleviation, 2013). Twenty-five percent of the total housing units proposed in a land area greater than 5 acres (around 20,000 sqm) were to be reserved for low-income housing, while those in the area ranging from 3,000 sqm to 5 acres were only required to financially compensate in the form of opt-out fees called shelter fees (also known as fees-in-lieu in other

Jakkampudi PMAY-AHP Project (Model 3)

Amaravati PMAY Housing (Model 4)

Jakkampudi JNNURM Housing Colony (Model 2)

Figure 1. Project location sites in the Vijayawada Metropolitan Region (adapted from Google maps, pictures by author).

country contexts). These mandatory inclusionary housing requirements were revised to become voluntary provisions in 2017 under the *Pradhan Mantri Awas Yojana* with an option to pay a fee-in-lieu for even those developments in an area greater than 5 acres.

The actual implementation of inclusionary zoning stipulations is hard to assess due to the absence of appropriate monitoring systems and awareness. Multiple town planning officials from Vijayawada Municipal Corporation—both past and present—confirmed that no layout approvals were issued during the years 2011 and 2012 that would have required land reservations for low-income housing [interviews 10, 18, 20]. They also explained that there were no private large-scale housing developments in areas exceeding five acres, even in Vijayawada's metropolitan region that would trigger inclusionary units before 2015. While some projects prompted inclusionary housing requirements after 2015, due to the policy change in 2017, all qualifying developments opted to pay the fees instead of providing low-income housing units [7][55]. Mostly, inclusionary housing policies in Vijayawada appear to have failed to produce any actual housing or land for low-income housing needs.

Model 2: Jakkampudi land pooling scheme under Jawaharlal Nehru National Urban Renewal Mission

The Jakkampudi land pooling scheme is hailed as one of the best practices of inclusive planning and successful innovative land-sharing practices in India (Mishra, 2017). Funded under *Jawaharlal Nehru National Urban Renewal Mission*, contingent on the passing of inclusionary zoning requirements in Vijayawada, Jakkampudi is a township development on a *60:40 land-sharing model*. In land sharing or readjustment models, the government aggregates disparate parcels of land from the landowners and returns a predetermined percentage of their land as developed lots after planned development with infrastructure access and land use permissions at little or no cost (Turk, 2008).

In 2007, when the Vijayawada Municipal Corporation could not find viable public land close to the city as part of a *slum* rehabilitation effort, it approached landowning farmers about 7 kilometers outside the city limits of Vijayawada who agreed to a land-sharing model [10]. After pooling the land with the power of a tailored executive order for this project alone, in the *60:40 land sharing model*, the government developed the land and handed over 60% of their initial holdings to the landowners. A certain portion of the remaining 40% of the land after infrastructure provision was used for constructing low-income housing. A total of 226.54 acres were pooled from farmers from the villages of Jakkampudi and Gollapudi. Mohanty (2014) estimates that a full land acquisition effort for approximately 90 acres would have cost the government nearly INR 529 million (approximately US$7.2 million) at the rate of INR 5.8 million per acre (about US$800,000).[3] However, the development of trunk infrastructure at the cost of INR 460 million (US$6.3 million) and the conversion of agricultural land to urban use resulted in an almost three-fold increase in land value for the farmers and a savings of INR 69 million (about US$940,000) in land acquisition costs to the government (Mohanty, 2014).

Jakkampudi Jawaharlal Nehru National Urban Renewal Mission township, named after the federal program, is locally referred to as *Jakkampudi JNNURM colony*. Today, it is a thriving housing development with inbuilt social infrastructure like a school, community hall, post office, parks, and playground, as well as well-connected trunk infrastructure, additional facilities such as bus bays, a sewage treatment plant, and solar power panels. However, this site was not well-connected to the city when the project was proposed in 2007. As a local developer remarked, Jakkampudi was known as the "*adda* [den] of pickpockets and thieves" and that it is "no wonder that the landowners were willing to part with their land back then" [41]. The township is now "well-connected to the railway station and the city center and has good bus service access, thanks to government intervention and the growth of the city" [10].

Site visits revealed that the developed land returned to the farmers for higher-income housing was located three kilometers away from the township. In place of a high-income thriving version of the colony, there was a barren skeleton of sunken roads with teetering streetlight poles and overgrown weeds cutting off road access. The planner initially responsible for the housing project's design hesitantly disclosed that landowners "did not want to be located adjacent to the low-income housing development with shared amenities and access roads" [10]. As a result, land developed for higher-income housing remains vacant with crumbling infrastructure due to lack of use. Others noted that the landowners had gained immensely from the conversion of agricultural land to urban residential use with "no cost or hassle," and the rapid growth of the city would ensure a "twenty-fold increase in land value for future development" [58]. Therefore, while the land pooling model helped secure land for low-income housing, the mixed-income aspect of the development failed as an integration effort. Nevertheless, Jakkampudi is a definite win from the government's perspective for its ability to secure land for low-income housing while providing access to necessary infrastructure within the development and to the city at large.

Model 3: Jakkampudi funded under the PPP model—Pradhan Mantri Awas Yojana-affordable housing in partnership

About six kilometers further away from the Jakkampudi Jawaharlal Nehru National Urban Renewal Mission land pooling project, Vijayawada Municipal Corporation again proposed about 28,000 low-income housing units on 265 acres under the *Pradhan Mantri Awas Yojana-Affordable Housing in Partnership* component during the period 2017–2020. It is one of the largest developments sanctioned in the country that envisions PPP developments to encourage private-sector participation in the affordable housing sector (Ministry of Housing and Urban Affairs, 2017).

Discussions in the field revealed that the Andhra Pradesh state had altered the *Affordable Housing in Partnership* model to construct 100% low-income housing without involving private developers [16][49]. They also created a new organization called Andhra Pradesh Township and Industrial Development Corporation (APTIDCO), responsible for the planning, approval, 24/7 video surveillance construction monitoring, and maintenance of the *Pradhan Mantri Awas Yojana* projects.

Officials note that the organization had applied the lessons learned from *Jawaharlal Nehru National Urban Renewal Mission* by ensuring high-quality construction through shear-wall technology, provision of the trunk and social infrastructure, and employment opportunities [46]. The state government is, therefore, completely embedded in the entire lifecycle of the project.

The site was originally a hill surrounded by mango orchards, paddy fields, and a lake. At the time of field visit, the massive hillside was being blasted and leveled to create buildable land. Additionally, the site is embroiled in several legal and practical problems. The project was initially proposed as mixed-income housing and mixed-use development. However, negotiations for land pooling with the surrounding landowners failed due to extremely high market demand for land, and the project, as of 2019, caters only to the low-income families with some light industry.

Further inquiry revealed that during the initial setup phases in 2016, APTIDCO had planned to implement the *Affordable Housing in Partnership* component in the manner envisaged by the federal government. However, the state government chose not to accede to the incentives that the developers had requested: an increase in state subsidy contribution, several fee waivers, transferrable development rights, and relaxations of parking requirements. Instead, the state government adopted a model that gave them the control and resources to develop housing *en masse* and show "political favoritism" in determining who gets the housing and where [52].

In essence, *Pradhan Mantri Awas Yojana*-Jakkampudi is a replica of the large-scale low-income public housing projects located in city peripheries that the *Pradhan Mantri Awas Yojana-Affordable Housing in Partnership* guidelines hoped to change through PPP models and integrated development. However, the high-quality and speed of construction, in addition to the pressure from extremely skewed land markets in Vijayawada, appear to have aided the government effort at this stage.

Model 4: Comprehensive plan for a greenfield city—Amaravati

Amaravati is the new capital city being built in the metropolitan region of the Vijayawada-Guntur-Tenali. The ambitious capital-building process started in 2015, for which a total of 217 square kilometers of agricultural land was assembled through a land pooling scheme by convincing 28,181 farmers to handover their land to the government (Andhra Pradesh Township and Industrial Development Corporation, 2019). In addition to obtaining 25% of land in reconstituted land parcels, farmers also received 10-year annuities. The land pooling mechanism adopted as part of the Amaravati Master Plan (comprehensive plan) is different from that of the *Jawaharlal Nehru National Urban Renewal Mission* Jakkampudi project. While the government initiated the Jakkampudi land pooling process through an executive order for that single initiative, in Amaravati, the process was determined in legislation explicitly passed to create the capital city. The Andhra Pradesh Capital Region Development Authority Act (2014) sets statutory provisions for the reservation of 5% of the land pooled using this scheme for low-income housing.

When the development authority created the master plan for the new capital, it also reserved land for the poor. However, this mainly came out of the land pooling process, which itself experienced severe opposition from some villages (Ramachandraiah, 2016). The Amaravati city master plan is the only master plan in Andhra Pradesh—perhaps in the country—that included designated land parcels for low-income housing in different residential zones [5]. The development authority allocated land in ten different locations in the capital city region, where landless families from five villages are clustered on sites reserved for low-income housing. Under the *Pradhan Mantri Awas Yojana*, construction of a total of 5,024 units has been proposed (Andhra Pradesh Township and Industrial Development Corporation, 2019). Many of these have already been grounded, and some were closer to completion during the site visits.

According to one of the planners interviewed in this study, the actual implementation resulted in about 3% set-asides against the 5% requirement stipulated in the Andhra Pradesh Capital Region Development Authority Act (2014) [55]. The Capital Development Authority planners also said that these set-asides were a one-off case and that there were no plans to reserve any land parcels for low-income housing in the future. Additionally, the revision of inclusionary housing mandates in 2017 means that developers may choose to pay a shelter-fee instead of building low-income housing units in any future housing developments. Therefore, once fully developed, Amaravati and its surrounding areas could ultimately become like every other Indian city where the poor are forced to make their own space through informal means and land occupation.

Federal policies and local low-income housing initiatives: Where is the disconnect?

Overall, federal reforms that prioritized small-scale mixed-income initiatives like inclusionary housing policies and PPPs, which shift the onus of low-income housing provision to private developers, have failed in Vijayawada, as examined under models 1 and 3. The city-level initiative, as discussed under Model 4 in Amaravati, was an isolated effort. Overall, in the state of Andhra Pradesh, suggestions for inclusive development at the city level through comprehensive planning initiatives, such as reservation of residential zones for low-income housing, had no impact. Some protection was being offered to informal settlements by conferring property rights or a level of security of tenure on a case-by-case basis [5][4][21]. The only initiatives that appear to have succeeded in their implementation were large-scale low-income housing projects in urban extension areas under Models 2 and 3. While these were developed under the PPP component encouraged by the federal government, they deviated from the federal intent, being neither delivered by private developers nor provided on private lands. More importantly, they were not mixed-income housing. Instead, they were primarily led by the state and local governments on public land where possible or by pooling land when necessary, and exclusively provided for low-income families. Insights into the disconnect between federal policies and local implementation through local actors' perceptions can help explain the barriers and possibilities for policy reception. The following discussion is grouped by major place-based initiatives.

Comprehensive plans do not respond to equity concerns

Master planning (or comprehensive plan) processes in India are disconnected from realities on the ground and have consistently disenfranchised poor people with impractical building standards (Bhan, 2013; Mishra & Mohanty, 2017). Therefore, housing activists are justifiably skeptical of planners' ability to cater to low-income housing needs. Other measures, like the setting of fair-share goals through comprehensive plans, are also partial and unreliable efforts. Most master plan-enabling legislation requires a housing needs estimation for different income groups based on population projections. However, such projections are mostly far-removed from the reality of the growth patterns experienced by Indian cities (Ahluwalia et al., 2017), and these projections rarely translate into zoning stipulations [23].

Local town planners are also resistant to incorporating residential zones for low-income housing at the city level. While some claimed it was an impractical initiative [7][10][14], others objected to the principle. One town planner explained, "I can't get the developers to accept a low value for their lands because I decided to shade [color coding on zoning map] their land for low-income housing. It is not for environmental concerns" [51].

Another town planner felt that equity-based concerns had no room in land use planning; "Any policy efforts that try to link urban poverty and town planning are just conceptualizing wheels within wheels" [3]. Therefore, when federal government reforms required master plans to incorporate reservations for low-income housing, planners conveniently passed these requirements on to the developers through inclusionary zoning mandates for private sector-led new housing developments instead of making city-level changes.

One planner who was sympathetic to planning for equity explained that even though equity objectives are important in planning processes, there is very little they could do in the already built-up areas of the city. He said that it is easier to incorporate equity measures when "we are building from scratch" [5]. Model 4 in Amaravati is a clear example of this process, where residential land was reserved for the lowest-income group through the land pooling legislation as a greenfield city was built. However, initiatives to build new towns are very few, and most of the urban growth occurs in the existing cities.

Inclusionary housing policies are "too close for anybody's comfort" and financially unviable for developers

Developers during the author's fieldwork were very critical of planning norms like inclusionary housing policies that were redistributive in intent. This sentiment is perhaps understandable from developers, given the perception of public officials discussed above. Developer resistance resulted in repeated amendments and dilution of inclusionary housing norms. Private developers stated, "We don't want to do this [inclusionary housing] as a charity" [43]. Policies that require them to give up the most expensive commodity in India—urban land—developers argue, are "unfair" and implausible [6]. Government functionaries were also clear that inclusionary housing policies were not a priority at present and that there were no plans to modify the incentive structure to accommodate developer concerns.

One developer laughed at the idea of housing extremely poor people in a mixed-income development and said disparagingly, "Do you think people from the *slums* would know how to use the community swimming pools? They will likely wash their clothes in them" [6]. Housing very poor people adjacent to high-income families within one project, sharing the same amenities was "too close for anybody's comfort," according to another developer [57]. While entertaining the idea of mixed-income housing, another said the idea of "servant quarters" might be a selling point for high-income flat owners who may be interested in buying low-income units for housing their "drivers and other household help" in close proximity for "convenience" and "making sure that they remain 'loyal' and reliably available" [42]. Many planners and activists agreed with the developers that the most significant selling point to the idea of mixed-income housing would be to market the idea of servant quarters given the socioeconomic fabric in India. This notion clearly underscores the innate class differences and their acceptance in the Indian context. One housing activist clarified their position, "Poor people don't have a square foot space to call their own in our cities, to stop their evictions and to protect their right to stay is itself an uphill battle, how can we even think of social integration when basic needs are not being met?" [38]. The highest priority, other activists concurred, should be protecting and encouraging incremental development of existing informal housing and extending these rights to informal settlements in the future as well. Another activist responded to the researcher's prodding regarding inclusionary housing policies with a frustrated sigh: "If the government that has a clear responsibility to provide for the poor people won't do anything on their own, it is laughable to think private developers would cut their profit margins to house poor people" [8].

When asked about the possibility of providing low-income housing directly to low-income families, builders concurred that it was "impossible" for them to offer price points for people in the lowest income quartile in their developments, even if inclusionary housing policies were designed with better incentive structures. Experience from the United States also suggests that inclusionary housing policies mainly cater to workforce housing, rather than low-income families served by public housing (Thaden & Wang, 2017). Therefore, inclusionary housing policies' ability to realize close-grained social integration in India is hampered by both developers' financial concerns and the deeply embedded notions of class segregation by all the actors involved.

Private developer participation in PPPs for low-income housing: Why they don't and what they want

In federal low-income housing policies that envisioned delivery of low-income housing units by private developers, PPPs received the maximum attention and financial thrust. While inclusionary housing policies were favored as conditional reforms, their actual implementation relied heavily on local and state interest and compliance (Mahadevia & Datey, 2012). On the other hand, PPPs are designed and funded directly by the federal government with a continuous upward revision of financial subsidies since the *Affordable Housing in Partnership* scheme's introduction in 2007. Scholars have pointed out that PPP projects were mainly prevalent only in states where the government could offer public land for the development of affordable housing (Bhan et al., 2014). Where private lands were involved, they were located in far-flung areas with poor connectivity and infrastructure, resulting in very poor occupancy rates (Deb, 2016).

Discussing their disinterest in PPP projects under the *Pradhan Mantri Awas Yojana-Affordable Housing in Partnership*, developers in Vijayawada revealed that urban land management and planning processes at the local level were major deterrents. They explained that government subsidies and any additional revenue from the sale of market-rate units through cross-subsidization "does not adequately compensate" for the issues inherent in dealing with "multiple stages of bureaucratic mess, let alone toward the high land costs in urban areas" [43][57]. They also stated that they would not be able to cater to the housing needs of people with informal jobs and that "it is a segment best served by the government" [58]. Overall, developers concur that the biggest attraction to leveraging private land in large PPP projects is the easy access to trunk infrastructure and planning permissions for their land parcels with government support. Financial incentives offered by the government, they said, though a welcome sign, are "minuscule when compared to the value appreciation" their lands acquire from the connectivity [42]. This aspect indicates a high potential for the government to bargain for at least moderately low-income units in urban expansion areas. Additionally, they argued that with its large-scale low-income housing construction, as shown in Model 3, the state government of Andhra Pradesh has "completely taken over the low-income housing segment" and that it is difficult for developers to offer competitive pricing options [41].

Builders, planners, and housing activists argued that government would never truly engage private sector in the affordable housing sector due to "vote-bank politics" [10][43]. Public housing developments, called *housing colonies*, have been hotbeds for vote extraction for decades now. Many still bear the symbol of the political parties and statues of the leaders under whose aegis the development took place. Therefore, local governments with institutional and strategic advancements are more drawn to mass-housing projects with a high proportion of the shelter-poor population with voting rights.

Large-scale low-income public housing may be an inescapable reality

Examining the four models for low-income housing provision in Vijayawada and discussions with different stakeholders indicates the prominent role state and local governments play in housing the poor. This centralization of government initiative and investments in large-scale public housing projects in India coincides with global trends in rapidly developing countries (Buckley et al., 2016b; Sengupta et al., 2018).

Governments may be unwilling or unable to entirely rely on private developers for low-income housing production for various reasons. As discussed in the earlier sections, these reasons may range from "vote-bank politics" to the private sector's disinterest. An important factor underlying these reasons is the massive housing shortage for the lowest-income group in Indian cities. Primarily, 96% of India's 18.78-million-unit urban housing shortage is for families earning up to 600,000 INR (about US$8,200) per annum (Ministry of Housing and Urban Poverty Alleviation, 2012). Of these, 60% of the housing shortages apply to the lowest income group earning up to 300,000 INR (about US$4,100) per annum. These families are mainly employed in the informal sector and reside in informal settlements. It is also the income group national affordable housing policies attempt to target, and that the private commercial developers do not reach. Support for self-help housing and *slum* upgradation projects, on the other hand, has been conservative (Buckley et al., 2016a). Instead, large-scale public housing delivery appears to have emerged as a preferred solution at the implementation level, citing the massive housing shortages, the need for deep affordability, and "big plans" [3].

However, such large-scale projects also require large parcels of land that are hard to find within the city limits. This shortage makes building large-scale public low-income housing in the urban peripheries a "tough reality that implementation agencies have to contend with on the ground" [46]. Models 2, 3, & 4 examined in this study suggest cautious success in urban extension areas and may provide some lessons on what can be done to ensure the success of such initiatives.

Opportunities for integrating housing initiatives and urban development in urban extension areas

Models 2 and 4 (and to some extent, model 3) suggest how local implementation agencies adapt federal policies and funding stipulations to work within local conditions and strategic priorities. Instead of working within the confines of PPP and inclusionary housing policy frameworks, state and local governments in Vijayawada adopted land-sharing approaches to find appropriate land with potential for quick urban development and connectivity. A local planner explained their approach: "What is *around* the housing project is as important as what is *inside* the public housing project [added emphasis]" [20]. He suggested that the Jakkampudi JNNURM colony (model 2) was successful since they prioritized an "integrated environment" by enlarging the scope and considering infrastructure considerations and connectivity beyond the narrow focus on an individual low-income housing project. He agreed that the social integration component did not "play out as expected" but reiterated that planning for a wider area provided infrastructure investments and accelerated the city's growth toward the project site. More importantly, he suggested that the provision of plotted developments for higher-income groups helped uplift the area's development potential overall and brought more opportunities and connectivity to the low-income housing colony.

Unlike with model 2, under model 4 in Amaravati, vast expanses of land were pooled for a greenfield city, and low-income housing units were scattered across key sites instead of concentrating them in one location. While it is still early to speculate on the success of an ongoing project as the capital construction project is in itself on hold, model 4 may have increased options for social integration with other socioeconomic groups. On the other hand, it may lack supporting infrastructure provided exclusively for low-income families, such as skill development and training institutes, schools, market space, etc., in model 2. It requires careful experimentation and evaluation to find an appropriate balance between clustering and social-mixing to realize social integration objectives in the Indian context. However, at this time, land pooling appears to have worked as a successful strategy for models 2 and 4 in securing suitable land for new low-income housing development with the potential for rapid and planned urban integration. Yet, land pooling attempts were explicitly tailored as an individual initiative, rather than through a systemic mechanism using zoning regulations, in both these cases. Issues faced in model 3's implementation suggest a need for a sustained initiative that supports planned urban expansion through planning and zoning regulations with inbuilt mechanisms for reserving land for low-income housing. However, cash-strapped local planning and civic agencies charged with policy implementation can only afford to undertake large-scale infrastructure upgradation and planned expansion with federal financial support.

Ending the disconnect: Need for a multi-level approach

The current federal housing programs in India offer funding to subsidize the construction costs of low-income housing development but do not address the needs for integrated land development and planning (Tiwari & Hingorani, 2014). There was a clear disconnect between local strategies and federal intent for low-income housing delivery on the policy front. While local models relied on land-sharing mechanisms in the urban expansion areas, federal policies failed to recognize the need for a complementary regulatory reform for integrated development in the urban expansion areas.

Instead, federal policies encouraged small-scale, developer-led models for mixed-income housing "to allow a self-propelled market" in delivering low-income housing (Ministry of Housing and Urban Affairs, 2017, p. 9).

The biggest disconnect in the federal government's approach is that small-scale mixed-income strategies like inclusionary housing and PPP approaches were proposed as *low-income housing enabling mechanisms* that emphasize the participation of private developers, rather than as mechanisms for encouraging a social mix of different income groups. To truly encourage small-scale mixed-income initiatives that foster social integration, the federal government has to offer deeper subsidies, encourage ownership and rental models for a mix of income thresholds, and require local governments to offer better incentives for inclusionary housing policies.

Another aspect that needs particular attention in federal policy is evaluating and eliminating existing barriers to inclusive and integrated urban development. Incorporating social equity objectives into land-use planning and regulation regimes through the comprehensive planning process is a challenge given the planners' apparent resistance to it, as was observed in the author's fieldwork. At the city scale, housing initiatives and strategies need to be better integrated with urban development plans through fair-share goals that are then translated into zoning stipulations, especially in the area of place-based production strategies for low-income housing. Land use planning and other regulatory frameworks at the state and city levels should protect existing informal settlements by reserving them as residential zones for low-income housing. There is also a need for greater action to modify exclusionary planning norms and building regulations that create entry barriers for poor people in accessing formal housing markets. At a sub-city scale, project proposals for large-scale land-use change and the use or sale of public land should trigger land dedication requirements for low-income housing development. In the urban expansion areas, land readjustment schemes could be carried out to ensure planned urban growth that would meet the housing needs of all income groups.

Among those proposed efforts, the federal government needs to pay immediate attention to urban expansion areas. These areas have not received any attention in federal housing policies to date, yet they witness considerable activity through federally funded low-income housing projects. Lessons from Vijayawada suggest that low-income housing developments benefit greatly from planned infrastructure development in urban expansion areas, particularly those that cater to the needs of market housing development. Federal policies and support can help address the twin challenges of unplanned urban growth and low-income housing shortages by encouraging regulatory and zoning changes for planned development in urban expansion areas that include low-income housing needs. This approach would help local implementation agencies to leverage land readjustment and sharing tools in the urban expansion areas, not only to find viable land for low-income housing but also to build inclusive urban environments.

At these expanded scales, low-income housing provision through integrated development of land, infrastructure, and market housing for other income groups can help create *self-propelled* economic opportunities. If the Indian government continues to ignore location and infrastructure needs in those urban expansion areas where the government has more bargaining power and a relatively clean slate to create integrated housing options, the country's affordable housing crisis will deteriorate, further exacerbating urban inequalities and residential segregation to the point of no return.

Conclusion

Experience from the current federal approach to low-income housing provision in India shows a clear disconnect with local implementation challenges and preferences, and highlights how disengaged these efforts are from urban planning and development practices as well as the local regulatory framework. These efforts point to missed opportunities in bridging the extreme socioeconomic disparities and deeply embedded patterns of caste and income-based segregation in Indian cities.

This study offers suggestions for effective government intervention to connect policy objectives and implementation realities, and identifies priorities for intervention. In doing so, it has contributed to the existing literature on scale-based strategies for promoting social integration and socioeconomic development of low-income housing communities. It lends support to the argument that intermediate scales at the sub-city level may serve as areas for effective intervention for witnessing physical changes that can yield high policy impact. In the Indian context, it might also offer the path of least resistance at this time. However, over time, federal policies and local plans need to incorporate low-income housing and equity concerns at multiple scales to promote inclusive urban development. What these different scales mean may vary in different urban contexts based on population aggregates, densities, levels of development, and the growth rates of cities. However, charting planning strategies and housing initiatives at multiple levels offers clarity in assessing the conflicts that may arise when policies and implementation work at cross-purposes. We need more housing research that addresses urban segregation and inequalities at multiple scales in developing economies like India. Such research will help identify targeted government interventions that recognize the polarizing patterns of urban growth at large and in assessing government's own role in exacerbating them.

Large-scale expansions of low-income housing stock in Global South countries like India encounter difficult challenges but also present unique opportunities for making impactful decisions. This study argues that affordable housing policies, inclusive development goals, and social integration objectives should be pursued together under a unified objective, aided by both financial and land use planning and regulation framework. Such a unified effort will not only attend to low-income housing needs in a comprehensive manner but will help create a better and more integrated blueprint for an equitable urban future.

Notes

1. This paper uses the term *urban expansion areas* to mean urban peripheries and growth areas that are not currently part of the city administration limits but are either contiguous or in close proximity to the city limits.
2. The usage of the term *slum* is widespread in policy and other government documents in India. While the term is not often used in the same pejorative sense as in the Western countries, the author recognizes the adverse impact of the usage of the label. This paper uses an italicized form of the word to denote the original use of the term in government policy and programs in India. Where the author discusses issues outside of government terminology, the term *informal settlements* is used.
3. US$1 is equivalent to 73.4 INR (Indian Rupees) based on conversion rates as of October 19, 2020.

Acknowledgments

First, I would like to thank Lan Deng and Ana Paula Pimentel Walker, who have been generous with their time, support, and feedback as my advisors since the early stages of this paper. Thanks are also due in large part to the special issue guest editors—Anna Maria Santiago, Iris Levin, and Kathy Arthurson, as well as the journal managing editor, Andrew Kirby, for their critical feedback. I would like to thank Martin Murray, Jenna Bednar, Eric Bettis, Rachel Kantrowitz, Pavan Ankinapalli, and the three anonymous reviewers for their valuable inputs. Most importantly, I owe my gratitude to the many respondents who generously spared their time and shared their views with me.

Disclosure statement

No potential conflict of interest was reported by the author(s).

Funding

This work was supported by Barbour fellowship and the International Institute student fellowship at the University of Michigan.

ORCID

Naganika Sanga http://orcid.org/0000-0001-8018-1902

References

Ahluwalia, I. J., Kanbur, R., & Mohanty, P. K. (2017). *Urbanisation in India: Challenges, opportunities and the way forward* (Vol. 91). Sage Publications.

Andersson, R., & Musterd, S. (2010). What scale matters? Exploring the relationships between individuals' social position, neighbourhood context and the scale of neighbourhood. *Geografiska Annaler: Series B, Human Geography*, 92(1), 23–43. https://doi.org/10.1111/j.1468-0467.2010.00331.x

Andhra Pradesh Capital Region Development Authority Act No. 11 of 2014. Andhra Pradesh Legislature. http://www.bareactslive.com/AP/ap097.htm

Andhra Pradesh Township and Industrial Development Corporation. (2019, November 8). *GOI (Government of India) sanctions*. https://www.aptidco.com/GOI%20sanctions.html

Arthurson, K. (2010a). Operationalising social mix: Spatial scale, lifestyle and stigma as mediating points in resident interaction. *Urban Policy and Research*, 28(1), 49–63. https://doi.org/10.1080/08111140903552696

Arthurson, K. (2010b). Questioning the rhetoric of social mix as a tool for planning social inclusion. *Urban Policy and Research*, 28(2), 225–231. https://doi.org/10.1080/08111141003693117

Arthurson, K., Levin, I., & Ziersch, A. (2015). Social mix, '[A] very, very good idea in a vacuum but you have to do it properly!' Exploring social mix in a right to the city framework. *International Journal of Housing Policy*, 15(4), 418–435. https://doi.org/10.1080/14616718.2015.1093748

Basolo, V., & Scally, C. P. (2008). State innovations in affordable housing policy: Lessons from California and New Jersey. *Housing Policy Debate*, 19(4), 741–774. https://doi.org/10.1080/10511482.2008.9521654

Berube, A. (2006). Comment on Mark Joseph's "Is mixed-income development an antidote to urban poverty?" *Housing Policy Debate*, 17(2), 235–247. https://doi.org/10.1080/10511482.2006.9521568

Bhan, G. (2013). Planned illegalities. *Economic and Political Weekly*, 48(24), 59–70. https://www.epw.in/journal/2013/24/special-articles/planned-illegalities.html

Bhan, G., Anand, G., Arakali, A., Deb, A., & Harish, S. (2014). *India exclusion report 2013–14 (Issue January)*. Books for Change.

Bharathi, N., Malghan, D., Mishra, S., & Rahman, A. (2021). Fractal urbanism: City size and residential segregation in India. *World Development*, 141, 105397. https://doi.org/10.1016/j.worlddev.2021.105397

Bloom, N. D., Umbach, F., & Vale, L. J. (2015). *Public housing myths: Perception, reality, and social policy*. Cornell University Press.

Braun, V., & Clarke, V. (2006). Using thematic analysis in psychology. *Qualitative Research in Psychology*, 3(2), 77–101. https://doi.org/10.1191/1478088706qp063oa

Brophy, P. C. P., & Smith, R. N. R. (1997). Mixed-income housing: Factors for success. *Cityscape*, 3(2), 3–31. https://www.huduser.gov/periodicals/cityscpe/vol3num2/success.pdf

Buckley, R. M., & Kalarickal, J. (2005). Housing policy in developing countries: Conjectures and refutations. *The World Bank Research Observer*, 20(2), 233–257. https://doi.org/10.1093/wbro/lki007

Buckley, R. M., Kallergis, A., & Wainer, L. (2016a). Addressing the housing challenge: Avoiding the Ozymandias syndrome. *Environment and Urbanization*, 28(1), 119–138. https://doi.org/10.1177/0956247815627523

Buckley, R. M., Kallergis, A., & Wainer, L. (2016b). The emergence of large-scale housing programs: Beyond a public finance perspective. *Habitat International*, 54, 199–209. https://doi.org/10.1016/j.habitatint.2015.11.022

Calavita, N., & Mallach, A. (2010). *Inclusionary housing in international perspective: Affordable housing, social inclusion, and land value recapture*. Lincoln Institute of Land Policy.

Caldeira, T. P. R. (2017). Peripheral urbanization: Autoconstruction, transversal logics, and politics in cities of the global south. *Environment and Planning D, Society & Space*, 35(1), 3–20. https://doi.org/10.1177/0263775816658479

Chapple, K. (2015). *Planning sustainable cities and regions: Towards more equitable development*. Routledge.

Chaskin, R. J., & Joseph, M. L. (2011). Social interaction in mixed-income developments: Relational expectations and emerging reality. *Journal of Urban Affairs*, 33(2), 209–237. https://doi.org/10.1111/j.1467-9906.2010.00537.x

Chaskin, R. J., & Joseph, M. L. (2015). *Integrating the inner city: The promise and perils of mixed-income public housing transformation*. University of Chicago Press.

Chetty, R., Hendren, N., & Katz, L. F. (2016). The effects of exposure to better neighborhoods on children: New evidence from the Moving to Opportunity Experiment. *American Economic Review*, *106*(4), 855–902. https://doi.org/10.1257/aer.20150572

Coelho, K., Mahadevia, D., & Williams, G. (2020). Outsiders in the periphery: Studies of the peripheralisation of low income housing in Ahmedabad and Chennai, India. *International Journal of Housing Policy*. https://doi.org/10.1080/19491247.2020.1785660

Comandon, A., & Veneri, P. (2021). Residential segregation between income groups in international perspective. In M. van Ham, T. Tammaru, R. Ubarevičienė, & H. Janssen (Eds.), *Urban socio-economic segregation and income inequality: A global perspective* (pp. 27–45). Springer International Publishing. https://doi.org/10.1007/978-3-030-64569-4_2

Curley, A. M. (2010). Relocating the poor: Social capital and neighborhood resources. *Journal of Urban Affairs*, *32*(1), 79–103. https://doi.org/10.1111/j.1467-9906.2009.00475.x

Deb, A. (2016). Viability of public-private partnership in building affordable housing. In B. Frankel (Ed.), *Proceedings of the 2nd Annual International Conference on Urban Planning and Property Development (UPPD 2016)* (pp. 62–65). Singapore: Global Science and Technology Forum.

The Economic Times. (2016, July 21). 2.17 lakh houses made under Jawaharlal Nehru National Urban Renewal Mission, Rajiv Awas Yojna vacant. *The Economic Times*. https://economictimes.indiatimes.com/wealth/real-estate/2-17-lakh-houses-made-under-jnnurm-rajiv-awas-yojna-vacant/articleshow/53323944.cms?from=mdr

Fraser, J., Chaskin, R., & Bazuin, J. (2013). Making mixed-income neighborhoods work for low-income households. *Cityscape: A Journal of Policy Development and Research*, *15*(2), 83–100. https://doi.org/10.2307/41959112

Galster, G., & Sharkey, P. (2017). Spatial foundations of inequality: A conceptual model and empirical overview. *RSF: The Russell Sage Foundation Journal of the Social Sciences*, *3*(2), 1–33. https://doi.org/10.7758/rsf.2017.3.2.01

Goetz, E. G. (2000). The politics of poverty deconcentration and housing demolition. *Journal of Urban Affairs*, *22*(2), 157–173. https://doi.org/10.1111/0735-2166.00048

Imbroscio, D. (2016). Urban policy as meritocracy: A critique. *Journal of Urban Affairs*, *38*(1), 79–104. https://doi.org/10.1111/juaf.12262

Jawaharlal Nehru National Urban Renewal Mission. (2006). *Sample checklist for the "urban reforms agenda" under JNNURM*. Ministry of Urban Development, Government of India.

Kontokosta, C. E. (2014). Mixed-income housing and neighborhood integration: Evidence from inclusionary zoning programs. *Journal of Urban Affairs*, *36*(4), 716–741. https://doi.org/10.1111/juaf.12068

Kundu, A. (2014). Exclusionary growth, poverty and India's emerging urban structure. *Social Change*, *44*(4), 541–566. https://doi.org/10.1177/0049085714548538

Mahadevia, D., Bhatia, N., & Bhatt, B. (2018). Private sector in affordable housing? Case of slum rehabilitation scheme in Ahmedabad, India. *Environment and Urbanization ASIA*, *9*(1), 1–17. https://doi.org/10.1177/0975425317748449

Mahadevia, D., & Datey, A. (2012). *The status of pro-poor reforms in Indian states*. Centre for Urban Equity, Working paper 17. https://cept.ac.in/UserFiles/File/CUE/Working%20Papers/17CUEWP17_The%20Status%20of%20Pro-Poor%20Reforms%20in%20Indian%20States.pdf

Ministry of Housing and Urban Affairs. (2017). *Public private partnerships for affordable housing in India*. Government of India. http://mohua.gov.in/upload/uploadfiles/files/PPP%20Models%20for%20Affordable%20Housing.pdf

Ministry of Housing and Urban Poverty Alleviation. (2012). *Report of the technical group on urban housing shortage (TG-12) (2012–17)*. Government of India.

Ministry of Housing and Urban Poverty Alleviation. (2013). *Rajiv Awas Yojana (RAY) scheme guidelines 2013–2022*. Government of India. http://mohua.gov.in/upload/uploadfiles/files/RAYGuidelines.pdf

Ministry of Housing and Urban Poverty Alleviation. (2016). *Pradhan Mantri Awas Yojana (PMAY) guidelines*. Government of India.

Mishra, A. K. (2017). Is urban planning in India exclusionary? *Shelter*, *18*(2), 8–19. https://www.hudco.org/writereaddata/Shelter-oct17.pdf

Mishra, A. K., & Mohanty, P. K. (2017). Urban policy in Asia Pacific countries: A case for inclusionary zoning and housing. *Asia-Pacific Journal of Regional Science*, *1*(1), 191–215. https://doi.org/10.1007/s41685-017-0026-4

Mishra, A. K., & Sen, A. K. (2020). Cities and affordable housing in India—making land and housing market inclusive. *Shelter*, *21*(2), 8–19. https://www.hudco.org/writereaddata/Shelter-oct20.pdf

Mohanty, P. K. (2014). *Cities and public policy: An urban agenda for India*. Sage Publications.

Musterd, S., & Andersson, R. (2005). Housing mix, social mix, and social opportunities. *Urban Affairs Review*, *40*(6), 761–790. https://doi.org/10.1177/1078087405276006

Okechukwu Onatu, G. (2010). Mixed-income housing development strategy: Perspective on Cosmo City, Johannesburg, South Africa. *International Journal of Housing Markets and Analysis*, *3*(3), 203–215. https://doi.org/10.1108/17538271011063870

Orfield, M. (2005). Land use and housing policies to reduce concentrated poverty and racial segregation. *Fordham Urban Law Journal*, *33*(3), 877–936. https://ir.lawnet.fordham.edu/ulj/vol33/iss3/5

Parashar, D. (2014). The government's role in private partnerships for urban poor housing in India. *International Journal of Housing Markets and Analysis, 7*(4), 524–538. https://doi.org/10.1108/IJHMA-08-2013-0049

Ramachandraiah, C. (2016). Making of Amaravati: A landscape of speculation and intimidation. *Economic and Political Weekly, 51*(17), 68–75. https://www.epw.in/journal/2016/17/special-articles/making-amaravati.html

Roy, A. (2005). Urban informality: Toward an epistemology of planning. *Journal of the American Planning Association, 71*(2), 147–158. https://doi.org/10.1080/01944360508976689

Santoro, P. F. (2019). Inclusionary housing policies in Latin America: São Paulo, Brazil in dialogue with Bogotá, Colombia. *International Journal of Housing Policy, 19*(3), 385–410. https://doi.org/10.1080/19491247.2019.1613870

Satterthwaite, D., & Mitlin, D. (2014). *Reducing urban poverty in the global south.* Routledge. https://doi.org/10.4324/9780203104330

Schwartz, A., & Tajbakhsh, K. (1997). Mixed-income housing: Unanswered questions. *Cityscape: A Journal of Policy Development and Research, 3*(2), 71–92. https://www.huduser.gov/Periodicals/CITYSCPE/VOL3NUM2/unanswer.pdf

Sengupta, U. (2013). Inclusive development? A state-led land development model in New Town, Kolkata. *Environment and Planning C, Government & Policy, 31*(2), 357–376. https://doi.org/10.1068/c1103

Sengupta, U., Murtagh, B., D'Ottaviano, C., & Pasternak, S. (2018). Between enabling and provider approach: Key shifts in the national housing policy in India and Brazil. *Environment and Planning C: Politics and Space, 36*(5), 856–876. https://doi.org/10.1177/2399654417725754

Serkin, C., & Wellington, L. (2014). Putting exclusionary zoning in its place: Affordable housing and geographical scaling. *Urban Law Journal, 861*(2013), 1667–1696. https://heinonline.org/HOL/P?h=hein.journals/frdurb40&i=1697

Smets, P., & Salman, T. (2008). Countering urban segregation: Theoretical and policy innovations from around the globe. *Urban Studies, 45*(7), 1307–1332. https://doi.org/10.1177/0042098008090676

Steel, G., van Noorloos, F., & Klaufus, C. (2017). The urban land debate in the global South: New avenues for research. *Geoforum, 83*, 133–141. https://doi.org/10.1016/j.geoforum.2017.03.006

Tach, L., Pendall, R., & Derian, A. (2014). *Income mixing across scales. Rationale, trends, policies, practice, and research for more inclusive neighborhoods and metropolitan areas.* What Works Collaborative. https://tinyurl.com/y3tu9dh3

Thaden, E., & Wang, R. (2017). *Inclusionary housing in the United States.* Issue Working Paper WP17ET1. Lincoln Institute of Land Policy.

Thurber, A., Bohmann, C. R., & Heflinger, C. A. (2018). Spatially integrated and socially segregated: The effects of mixed-income neighbourhoods on social well-being. *Urban Studies, 55*(9), 1859–1874. https://doi.org/10.1177/0042098017702840

Tiwari, P., & Hingorani, P. (2014). An institutional analysis of housing and basic infrastructure services for all: The case of urban India. *International Development Planning Review, 36*(2), 227–256. https://doi.org/10.3828/idpr.2014.14

Tiwari, P., Rao, J., & Day, J. (2016). *Development paradigms for urban housing in BRICS countries.* Springer.

Turk, S. S. (2008). An examination for efficient applicability of the land readjustment method at the international context. *Journal of Planning Literature, 22*(3), 229–242. https://doi.org/10.1177/0885412207310283

Turok, I. (2016). Housing and the urban premium. *Habitat International, 54*(3), 234–240. https://doi.org/10.1016/j.habitatint.2015.11.019

Vale, L. J., & Shamsuddin, S. (2017). All mixed up: Making sense of mixed-income housing developments. *Journal of the American Planning Association, 83*(1), 56–67. https://doi.org/10.1080/01944363.2016.1248475

van Ham, M., Tammaru, T., Ubarevičienė, R., & Janssen, H. (2021). Rising inequalities and a changing social geography of cities. An introduction to the Global Segregation Book. In M. van Ham, T. Tammaru, R. Ubarevičienė, & H. Janssen (Eds.), *Urban socio-economic segregation and income inequality: A global perspective* (pp. 3–26). Springer. https://doi.org/10.1007/978-3-030-64569-4_1

Vijayawada Municipal Corporation. (2018). *Vijayawada municipal corporation.* Retrieved July 8, 2019, from http://www.ourvmc.org/general/aboutvmc.htm

Yap, K. S. (2016). The enabling strategy and its discontent: Low-income housing policies and practices in Asia. *Habitat International, 54*(3), 166–172. https://doi.org/10.1016/j.habitatint.2015.11.026

In the name of "social mixing": The privatization of public housing to non-governmental organizations

Yael Shmaryahu-Yeshurun

ABSTRACT
This paper explores the invocation of "social mixing" to camouflage the reduction of public housing through state-led gentrification processes. I focus on the use of social mixing in Israel to justify the privatization of public housing projects, transferring state assets to not-for-profit organizations. These organizations encourage middle-class families and students to relocate to disadvantaged neighborhoods. Exploring this practice reveals tensions between stakeholders regarding their perceptions of social mixing. Data for this study were drawn from interviews conducted with policymakers, NGO members, and public housing tenants, supplemented by analysis of press articles and policy and NGO documents. Findings highlight use of the social mixing discourse to contextualize benefits accrued via differential access to public housing stock. Such benefits are viewed specifically by long-term tenants as displacement and gentrification. This study further assesses the advantages and disadvantages of this policy, explicating the links between gentrification and social mixing.

Introduction

The physical degradation of public housing coupled with a high maintenance cost and affordable housing supply shortage (which has intensified worldwide since the 1980s), has promoted privatization of state public housing assets. Because of this process, housing ownership is largely transferred to developers, private companies, or nonprofit housing associations (Lees, 2008; Pawson et al., 2019). Some scholars argue that privatization can deliver benefits to tenants in terms of better management, delivery of services, and improvements to physical infrastructure (Jacobs et al., 2004; Pawson & Gilmour, 2010). Such privatization is often accompanied by the deliberate introduction of new tenants to public housing developments, a process described as "social mix" or "social mixing." Policymakers perceive social mixing as a useful tool for counteracting processes of segregation and urban decay, crime, unemployment, anti-social behavior, and the shortfall in quality education alternatives in homogenous public housing communities (Andersen, 2017; Arthurson et al., 2015; Bond et al., 2011). Social mixing is also presented as a fulcrum with which to improve the image and physical environment of public housing stock (Morris et al., 2012), as well as promote social inclusion and community cohesion (Doney et al., 2013).

However, a critical body of academic literature argues that using the term *social mixing* is a means of camouflaging the displacement of low-income populations from affected communities as a result of state-led gentrification (Arthurson et al., 2015; August, 2014, 2019; Bacque' & Fijalkow, 2011; Lees, 2008; Lees et al., 2011). It has been argued that policy makers embrace ostensibly neutral terms such as *diversity, mixed communities*, and *social mixing* to legitimize gentrification processes and deflect public resistance (Lees, 2008; Lees et al., 2011). Moreover, privatizing public housing stock for NGOs deprives working-class tenants of subsidized housing, leading to their displacement (Jacobs et al., 2004; Pawson & Gilmour, 2010; Pawson et al., 2019). Finally, these processes may lead to conflict and tense relationships between veteran tenants and middle-class newcomers (Arthurson, 2012; Atkinson & Kintrea, 2001; Lees, 2008).

The privatization of public housing in Israel is an ongoing process, one that began in the state's early years (Carmon, 2001). Over time, the state has sold off its public housing stock to its tenants; it also made decisions at a governmental level to transfer housing to private companies and redefine the government's housing company as a commercial entity (New Amidar n.d., Hananel, 2017). This trend of privatization, directed toward managing the costs of maintaining public housing, is a manifestation of New Public Management (NPM), the model driving privatization in many countries around the world (Laffin, 2019; Mullins et al., 2018; Pawson et al., 2019).

NGOs in Israel have played a crucial role in the local evolution of the privatization agenda. This study sought to ascertain whether the claims of displacement and tense relationships between tenant and newcomers are valid regarding the privatization of public housing to NGOs who are committed to social integration. Such privatization also does not involve physical displacement of tenants, but rather promotes middle-class relocation into public housing projects that had been formerly uninhabitable. In this case, the middle class will supposedly be motivated to integrate and volunteer with the local community; such motivations serve as the primary justification for their presence in the neighborhood. When privatization does not involve displacement and is not profit-motivated as in many other cases around the world, one may wonder about the tenants' attitudes toward this policy, and whether they accuse NGOs of displacing them. This study analyzes in depth the actuality of how tenants perceive this unique form of privatization in which tenants are not physically displaced.

This study focuses on manifestations of social mixing in Yeruham, a peripheral town in the Negev area of southern Israel. "The periphery" is a term used to describe socially and economically marginalized areas of Israel that often contain less concentrated Jewish populations vis-a-vis Arab and Bedouin minorities. Drawing data from 37 in-depth interviews with policymakers, local residents, and NGO members, together with an analysis of 150 policy, media, and NGO operational documents, I explore the understandings different stakeholders bring to the policy of social mixing, and the implications of these findings. I specifically examine the transfer of public housing stock to the Ayalim movement and Garin Torani, two NGOs operating in this town. Both NGOs were established to encourage young middle-class families and students to move into disadvantaged neighborhoods in Israel's socioeconomic periphery. Driven by a social agenda operating alongside a Zionist agenda, members of these organizations take part in activities that they claim strengthen the social fabric of their local communities (Shmaryahu-Yeshurun & Ben-Porat, 2018; Tzfadia, 2008).

Literature on the Garin Torani and Ayalim NGOs in Israel tends to emphasize the nationalistic agenda that feeds into privatization as an expression of Zionist discourse and Judaization of space (Shmaryahu-Yeshurun & Ben-Porat, 2020; Tzfadia, 2008; Tzfadia & Yacobi, 2015; Yiftachel & Avni, 2019). However, much less consideration has been given to the role these organizations have played in promoting social mix policy via privatization of public housing stock. While ethno-nationalism is a driving force, it does not explain the NGOs' settlement in public housing projects specifically. Below, I explain how NGOs propagate social mix policy via privatization through community integration.

This examination will further contribute to filling the gap in current literature on social mixing, which, as referenced by Arthurson et al. (2015), fails to consider the variety of perceptions espoused by various stakeholders on social mixing's implementations. In particular, I anticipate that this study will greatly strengthen our understanding of the role NGOs play regarding social mixing through privatization. The Israeli case is unique—privatization does not include displacement of tenants from the housing. Moreover, the organizations managing the privatization agenda have an explicit social agenda and commitment to social integration, alongside the Zionist agenda. Consequently, this case broadens our understanding of differing attitudes to social mixing and can illuminate whether these conditions cause displacement claims and local resistance, as in other cases (Arthurson et al., 2015; August, 2014; Bacque´ & Fijalkow, 2011; Lees, 2008; Lees et al., 2011).

Therefore, this research seeks to understand: (a) How the different stakeholders impacted by privatization of public housing stock understand and experience the policy, and (b) what features characterize the relationship between the public housing tenants and NGO members who move into such locales due to social mixing implementation. In the following section, I will review the literature on social mixing policy and will critically assess its negative consequences, as well as its connection to gentrification. I will then outline the case of public housing in the Israeli periphery and its privatization to NGOs. Afterward I will describe the methodology of this research. The findings portion will then present, in four different sections, the perceptions of stakeholders toward the policy. I will end with some concluding thoughts.

Social mix policy in public housing: Definitions and goals

The concept of social mixing is understood in a variety of ways, with definitions growing more ambiguous and controversial over time (Alves, 2019; Galster & Friedrichs, 2015). Broadly speaking, social mixing can be defined in terms of diverse social groups sharing a neighborhood having in common economic wherewithal, ethnicity, nativity, household structure, or type of tenure (Galster & Friedrichs, 2015).

Given the lack of clarity associated with this construct, this article uses the phrase "social mix" or "social mixing" to describe initiatives directed toward striking a balance in the socioeconomic and ethnic demographic composition of a spatially defined area, as referred to by Andersson et al. (2010): "Public policies that 'explicitly' but not necessarily exclusively aim to affect the demographic, social or ethnic composition of residential districts in such a way that cities become 'less segregated' than they would have been had such measures not been taken" (p. 238).

The dominant policy tool for promoting social mixing in disadvantaged areas is the privatization of public housing to developers, private companies, or nonprofit housing associations (Jacobs et al., 2004; Pawson & Gilmour, 2010). This is often accompanied by the deliberate introduction of new middle-class tenants to public housing developments. In the United States, the privatization of public housing stock is commonly perceived as a neo-liberal strategy to generate economic profit (August, 2019; Lees, 2008). However, studies of public housing privatization to NGOs and nonprofit housing associations in Australia, Britain, France and the Netherlands (Mullins et al., 2018; Pawson et al., 2019; Laffin, 2019 (conceptualize it as an expression of a new public management model (NPM). NPM uses privatization to streamline public services, provide a more cost-effective strategy for managing public housing, and improve the physical condition of housing stocks and neighborhoods. This conceptualization nods at an "enabling state" model, in which public infrastructure and services are predominantly provided by non-state actors rather than directly by governments (Pawson et al., 2019). In this model, there exists a partnership between the state and the private and third sectors: Either management of the housing is privatized while ownership remains with the state, or there is a complete privatization of the housing provision.

The dysfunctionality of homogeneous public housing estates can be explained by the absence of social mixing (Cole & Goodchild, 2001). It has also been argued that the spatial separation of disadvantaged populations from wider society cuts them off from necessary services, employment opportunities, and social networks that accompany stronger degrees of social and spatial integration (Galster & Friedrichs, 2015; Massey et al., 2013; Santiago et al., 2014). The presumption here is that social mix policies promote social inclusion and community cohesion (Doney et al., 2013)—reducing crime, unemployment, anti-social behavior, and the lack of quality education alternatives, as is commonly the case in homogenous public housing communities (Arthurson, 2012; Arthurson et al., 2015; Bond et al., 2011).

Finally, social mix policies serve to improve the image and physical environment of public housing stock. The most tangible outcome of deliberate social mix policies is the improvement to housing quality and general appearance of the area (Morris et al., 2012). These can be seen by improvements to quality-of-life indices such as increased space, green areas, and the general esthetic image of the neighborhoods (Morris et al., 2012). Broadly speaking, it is accepted that social mix policies can improve the reputation of neighborhoods dominated by social housing, lessening the stigma often appended to them (Arthurson, 2013; Keene & Padilla, 2010; Raynora et al., 2020).

Social mix policy in public housing: Unexpected outcomes?

Contrary to the declared goals and intentions of social mix policies, a critical body of academic literature emerging over the last decade has highlighted the negative consequences of such policies. This literature suggests that these consequences are similar to those resulting from gentrification processes (Arthurson, 2012; Goetz, 2011; Kleinhans & Varady, 2011; Lees et al., 2011). In fact, Arthurson (2012) claims that many of the assumptions made by practitioners in relation to the social mixing ideal do not pan out on the ground.

In some cases, social contact between the veteran and new residents in managed social mix settings was negligible; residents in these neighborhoods lived alongside each other, but not together (Arthurson, 2012; Atkinson & Kintrea, 2001). As Lees (2008) claims, gentrification is an aggressive process designed to retake the inner city for the middle classes, who despite their desire for diversity are sometimes far from socially tolerant; consequently, they tend to self-segregate. One of the primary shortcomings of these social mix policies has been the accompanying reduction of affordable housing options for people with lower incomes—new public housing tends to be associated with higher costs and thus higher rents (Jacobs et al., 2004; Musterd & Ostendorf, 2012; Pawson & Gilmour, 2010).

The above implications have led critical scholars to argue that the ostensibly community-minded discourse behind social mixing conceals the motivation of municipal authorities to dismantle public housing as a cost-cutting measure, thereby promoting gentrification and the consequent displacement of lower-income populations from these areas (Arthurson et al., 2015; August, 2014; Bacque' & Fijalkow, 2011; Lees, 2008; Lees et al., 2011).

Gentrification involves, in parallel, introducing new residents of a higher socioeconomic status to an area, as well as changes to the built environment through reinvestment in fixed capital. Nowadays, gentrification is used as an urban policy strategy. Municipalities and governments encourage the "creative middle class" to move into these areas in order to strengthen the municipal tax base, generate growth, and rehabilitate urban spaces. However, as a result of this urban redevelopment, local working-class residents, unable to absorb the rising cost of living in such areas, are displaced (Lees et al., 2011; Smith, 2002).

To elude the accusation of displacement, neutralize the negative image that the process of gentrification bears, and to legitimize the process, policymakers use ostensibly neutral terms such as *diversity, mixed communities,* and *social mix*, describing the urban process as "urban renaissance," "urban revitalization," "urban regeneration," and "urban sustainability," thus avoiding the class connotations appended to the processes (Lees, 2008; Lees et al., 2011). For example, Wilson and Grammenos (2005) show how the gentrification of Chicago's Humboldt Park was presented as progressive, civically improving the culturally lacking neighborhood.

The use of language to obscure controversial implications of policy is not only related to descriptors like social mixing, but also aspects of gentrification. As Delgado and Swanson (2019) observe, "Rhetoric and language are powerful tools used to reshape controversial debates, and gentrification is no exception" (p. 4). While the term *gentrification* was initially associated with critiques of working-class displacement, it is now often framed as politically neutral and a positive icon of urban change (Arthurson et al., 2015; Delgado & Swanson, 2019). In many cases, gentrification has been presented in policy discourse as controlled and positive (Rose et al., 2013), or even smart (Dyson & Varady, 2018)—emphasizing its social inclusion aspect, while actively downplaying the negative consequences of the process (Arthurson et al., 2015).

Similarly, gentrifiers themselves justify gentrification and attribute positive or at least neutral connotations to their settlement. Typifying gentrifiers' attitudes toward agency, Kaddar (2020) distinguished between "Agonisers" and "Activists"—gentrifiers who feel moral discomfort about their role in the process, as opposed to "Shruggers" and "Upgraders," who are morally indifferent to gentrification. While the first gentrifier types express the "gentrifier's dilemma" (Donnelly, 2018), the last uphold solely positive outcomes of the processes, such as the improvement of infrastructure and spatial and social features. Stressing the benefits of gentrification for both the local community and the gentrifier, they engage in "reframing the outcomes" (Donnelly, 2018) in a way that justifies their interests. Language, therefore, becomes an instrument of action and power. The neutralizing language reshapes the symbolic value and meaning of discourse, helping powerful stakeholders pursue particular interests (Bourdieu, 1993).

Despite the contributions of the above-mentioned studies, analysis of the discourse and perceptions of social mixing remains incomplete with regard to the case of privatizing public housing to NGOs, whose members seek to integrate with the residents, which does not lead to the displacement of veteran tenants from the housing.

Public housing in the Israeli periphery: Establishment and privatization

When the state of Israel was established in 1948, 64% of the country's Jewish population was concentrated in the main cities of Tel Aviv, Haifa, and Jerusalem. Of this Jewish population, 80% were of European descent (Ashkenazi Jews), with only 20% from countries in the Middle East and North Africa (Mizrahim Jews[1]). This proportion changed dramatically during the first decade of the young state, following the migration of more than 900,000 Jews. Most of them were refugees from countries in the Middle East and North Africa relocating to Israel.[2] This flow of immigration was perceived as threatening, potentially causing massive congestion in the urban centers with a concomitant impact on existing physical infrastructure, labor markets, and social welfare provisions. Moreover, the development of areas in the north and south of the country, outside the metropolitan hubs, was a key political objective of nation building. These objectives, of "population dispersal," "decentralization," "immigrant absorption," and "integration of the exiles," were the central reasons behind the establishment of what came to be known as "development towns" (Lipshitz, 1998; Yiftachel & Tzfadia, 2004).

Consequently, 27 towns were established, mostly in the Negev and Galilee areas of northern and southern Israel—areas with sparse Jewish populations. Israeli citizens with a more established presence in the country, mainly Ashkenazi Jews, resisted resettlement to these inaccessible and underdeveloped areas. Thus, the state's "population dispersal" policy became, in fact, an immigrant dispersal policy. By the mid-1960s, about 200,000 immigrants had been steered to these development towns, often against their will. This immigrant dispersal policy led to the creation of what became known as "peripheral towns," harboring socially segregated and often homogeneous ethnic populations. These groups often face significant social and economic challenges; from the 1950s until the present day, residents of these development towns have contended with poor living conditions, limited access to employment opportunities, social isolation, and institutional neglect, leading to persistently high levels of unemployment and negative migration (Tzfadia, 2006; Yiftachel & Tzfadia, 2004).

Limited housing facilities existed for immigrants moved to the periphery: Public housing, or otherwise the tents of immigrant transit camps (*ma'abarot*) (Bernstein, 1981). The provision of public housing was facilitated through the establishment of public construction companies, owned by the State of Israel and the *Sochnut*, the Jewish Agency for Israel. The companies were tasked with building and administering the units designated for public housing. They created 10,000 dwelling units in 1949, 125,000 in 1958, and 200,000 in 1962. Most of these units were situated in development towns (Tzfadia, 2006). However, since the 1950s, the state has sold its public housing stock to current tenants. By the 1960s, about half of all the housing units that had ever been publicly owned had already been sold (Carmon, 2001).

Privatization was also implemented through both the transfer of public housing to Amigur, a private company belonging to the Jewish Agency in 1972, as well as a 1977 government decision to transfer management of public housing stock to the private sector (Government Decision No. 1543, 29 January). This decision sparked protests by some tenants and social change movements, leading to the establishment of the Public-Housing Forum (PHF). This coalition joined forces with some members of Israel's Knesset (parliament), headed by member Ran Cohen. Cohen proposed a new law—"The Public-Housing Act of 1998"—intended to enable tenants to buy their apartments at discounts of up to 85%, after which the state would build new apartments with sale proceeds (Hananel, 2017; Public housing law- Purchase Rights, 1998). Although in practice the government suspended the law, repeatedly postponing its implementation, between 1999 and 2011 around 37,500 apartments were sold. Contravening the spirit of the law, proceeds from these sales were not used to build additional public housing. Thus, by the end of 2011, the total number of public housing apartments had shrunk to 63,500. Conversely, demand for public housing was high; despite the stringent criteria which limited eligibility and shortened waiting lists, there were 2,500 eligible families and individuals on public housing waiting lists, many of whom had been waiting for allocation for substantial periods of time (Hananel, 2017; State Comptroller, 2013).

Significant expression of housing privatization in Israel occurred in later years, with the redefinition of the government housing company as a commercial enterprise, expected to generate profits. Similar to other countries that had struggled economically to maintain public housing and therefore adopted the model of New Public Management (NPM), in Israel a government housing company called Amidar formed a strategy designed to adapt the company's structure to existing needs. This plan promoted efficiency in the service system and located new growth engines and sources of income for the company. Thus, in 2016 the company was renamed "New Amidar"; in 2018, it was successfully launched on the Debt Exchange, thus becoming a reporting company on the stock exchange (New Amidar, n.d.; State Comptroller, 2013).

Privatizing public housing to NGOs in Israel

As part of the privatization process, 2,300 public housing units were leased by the state to a range of public organizations, which included local authorities, educational institutions, nonprofit organizations and others (State Comptroller, 2013). This was in line with Government Decision Number 3799 in 2008, which authorized the rental or sale of public housing stock to NGOs working to strengthen the community fabric through activities such as volunteering with the local community.

Acknowledging the entrenched gaps between center and periphery, the government has encouraged internal migration of middle-class populations—organized as NGOs named Garin Torani and Ayalim—to the development towns. This policy is also founded on the nationalist ideology of Judaizing peripheral areas (Shmaryahu-Yeshurun & Ben-Porat, 2020; Tzfadia, 2008). The state devised a number of incentives to encourage this internal migration, including the provision of subsidized public housing to new arrivals. Israeli NGOs who manage the privatized housing stock settle middle-class citizens driven by ethnonational and social ideology; these citizens seek to integrate in the neighborhoods and volunteer with local communities in the periphery.

Garin Torani is a Zionist group of religious families which settle in disadvantaged neighborhoods, mostly in Israeli development towns. The families' raison d'etre is a combination of the agenda of integrating Israeli society through volunteering with disadvantaged populations, and the ideological objective of the Judaization of space and dissemination of Zionist ideology among the general population. The first Garin Torani group was established in the late 1960s in Kiryat Shmona, a development town in northern Israel. Today, there are over 80 similar initiatives scattered around the country (Reichner, 2013).

The second NGO is the Ayalim movement. Ayalim was established in 2002 to strengthen Zionist settlement from the outside and encourage social involvement in the Negev and Galilee. Ayalim implements its mission by establishing "student villages," student campuses, and social housing apartments set up as distinct self-contained neighborhoods for both its religious and secular student members. These establishments are situated in disadvantaged neighborhoods within the local community. In such neighborhoods, the students repair and renovate the apartments and the area as whole. In return for a scholarship and subsidized accommodation, students agree to volunteer in the local communities. Ayalim founded 15 villages and eight alumni groups, reaching a membership of more than 1,200 students, all of them Jewish (over the years, there have been only a few non-Jewish participants) (Ayalim Association, n.d.).

The research literature on these NGOs emphasizes the nationalistic agenda behind the phenomenon, in terms of the expression of Zionist discourse and the Judaization of space (Shmaryahu-Yeshurun & Ben-Porat, 2020; Tzfadia, 2008; Tzfadia & Yacobi, 2015; Yiftachel & Avni, 2019). However, only a few studies have addressed issues relating to the relationship that ensues between the veteran population and the newcomers, or the resulting socioeconomic and ethnic differences between the populations (Gamzu & Motzafi-Haller, 2016; Shmaryahu-Yeshurun & Ben-Porat, 2018).

Data and methods

The current study explores how different stakeholders in Yeruham perceive housing policies implemented to support the work of two NGOs. The study includes a total of 37 in-depth interviews with 12 long-term public housing tenants from Yeruham, 12 members of Ayalim, seven members of Garin Torani, and six policymakers from the Yeruham municipality. The interviews, conducted face-to-face between 2013–2018 as part of my doctoral thesis research, lasted between 30 to 90 minutes and were audiotaped and transcribed. At their request, the names of some interviewees have been changed. In addition to the interviews, the study also analyzed 150 documents: Municipal, state, documents relating to the relevant organizations, and press articles. The documents were selected via recommendations by the interviewees, as well as a systematic internet search of key words focusing on the 2013–2018 period.

The sampling strategy combined quota sampling (to ensure sufficient representation from each group) and snowball sampling (to reach key participants involved in the process). After setting a quota of a minimum of 5 interviewees per sub-group (policymakers, newcomers, and tenants), I approached formal policymakers and activists in each group, asking them to refer me to other relevant stakeholders.

Interviewees included the current and former mayors of Yeruham, the deputy mayor, senior executives engaged in community development, and executives and members of the community housing association project. Finally, I interviewed long-term public housing tenants from Yeruham, including residents who lived there for more than 20 years.

After collecting the necessary data, I identified, analyzed, and reported dominant patterns (themes) and discourse within data ("Thematic Analysis," Clarke & Braun, 2016). In order to manage the vast amount of data collected, I used Atlas.TI8 software—a qualitative analysis software package designed for conducting large-scale thematic analysis. An example of such a pattern was the tendency of policymakers to describe public housing as a space of crime, disorder, physical dirt, and neglect; in terms of poverty and tenant passivity; and in relation to the economic burden of maintaining the buildings and their surroundings. Attributing these terms to public housing provides us with an understanding of the policymakers' motivations for promoting social mixing through privatization of public housing stock. Another example was some tenants' framing of the policy as "gentrification," "displacement," or "discrimination." This provides us with an alternative perspective regarding the policy and contextualizes the criticism of tenants to it.

Findings and analysis: Settling public housing in Yeruham

In the Israeli public consciousness, the town of Yeruham presents as a quintessential case study illustrating the construction of remoteness and perpetual neediness in Israel's desert periphery (Motzafi-Haller, 2018). Located in the Negev region of southern Israel, Yeruham was founded as a development town in 1951. Over time, the town transitioned from a *Ma'abrarah* (transit camp) for Romanian and North African migrants to a local council, then to an official town. As of 2019, it had

9,974 residents, 97% Jewish and 3% Arab. In common with other Israeli development towns, Yeruham's residents contend with high unemployment rates, low socioeconomic status, poor employment opportunities, and inadequate transport and public services (Central Bureau of Statistics, 2019). Both Garin Torani and Ayalim were inspired by the challenging circumstances faced by Yeruham's citizens to settle the town, particularly in disadvantaged neighborhoods largely comprising public housing stock. Of the 600 public housing units in Yeruham, around 50 units, uninhabited due to their poor physical condition, were transferred to the Garin Torani and Ayalim associations.

The Garin Torani group in Yeruham was founded in 1992. Composed of around 200 religious Zionist families, the group has established a range of educational and cultural institutes in Yeruham, including schools and a *Yeshiva*—a Jewish educational institution for young boys and men (Bnei-Akiva Yeruham Community web). In general, the community members do not live in one defined neighborhood, but rather across the town. However, some of the Yeshiva students live with their families in around 30–40 public housing apartments in the town's Yitzhak Sadeh and Bar Kochva neighborhoods.

The Ayalim group has managed two forms of "villages," home to around 50 students, in Yeruham since 2008. One village consists of a ten-caravan complex on a hill at the town's edge; the other located in the Giva'a (the Hill) neighborhood consists of 12 public housing apartments in a disadvantaged neighborhood. Each unit houses around 30 students. In 2015, Ayalim's contract was ended, and Ayalim left the public housing due to reasons which will be discussed below.

The national government: Space Judaization and NPM

In the national government discourse, settlement of Ayalim and Garin Torani members in Yeruham has a national importance in terms of Judaizing the Negev. Politicians have described their settlement in terms of "making the desert bloom," "pioneering" and "Judaizing the Negev," and the "renewal of Zionism." As Prime Minister Benjamin Netanyahu explained in a speech to Ayalim members:

> We want a Jewish and democratic state here. For that we had to ensure that we control the southern border ... The Galilee and the Negev are our state reserves, and this development is ultimately the real guarantee of our future. (Prime Minister Benjamin Netanyahu, Beer-Sheva, 27 December 2012, available at: https://www.gov.il/BlobFolder/news/eventayalim271212/he/mediacenter_speeches_documents_ayalimb271212_3.doc)

The privatization of public housing to these organizations serves as an incentive for Zionist ideologists, but also carries its own socioeconomic mission and goals. Amidar, the Israeli government housing company, has struggled in making the maintenance of public housing an economically viable task. Some public housing apartments in Yeruham were neglected and unsuitable for human habitation; moreover, the cost of renovation was too high. Other apartment units were located on high floors without an elevator, making them inadequate for disabled or elderly tenants; as a result, the apartments remained uninhabited. Therefore, social mixing through privatization of public housing to housing associations helped relieve the economic burden of maintaining the apartments; the NPM model was an efficient means of reusing of apartments by renting them to nonprofit organizations, as described by the deputy Minister of Construction and Housing:

> When they [NGO members] arrived, the apartments were closed because the cost of the renovation was expensive ... you have to remember that there was a problem ... we thought it was uneconomic to invest a large sum of money in them in order to return them to public housing. We needed to sell them, or to do something else with them. (Meeting of the State Audit Committee - July 12, 2016, available at: https://www.nevo.co.il/law_html/law103/20_ptv_346535.htm)

Beyond the motivation of transferring responsibility for apartment maintenance to NGOs, any economic profit derived from renting the apartments was intended for use in increasing the stock of public housing, As described by the Ministry of Construction and Housing and the government housing company:

> In this way we earn twice as much; apartments that had been out of the public housing inventory for decades, and were not in demand among eligible populations, generate income that can be used to purchase apartments in places where there is a shortage of public housing ... Furthermore, these organization members [newcomers]

from the fields of education, nursing, religion, etc. remain and strengthen the local community. (Ministry of Construction and Housing in: Mirowski, 2015)

Moreover, social mixing between veteran tenants and members of these organizations—the latter perceived as possessing the human capital necessary for instigating neighborhood redevelopment—is presented as a means of improving public service systems, especially in the fields of education, welfare and culture. They will do so, according to the ministry's claim, by both raising standards and expectations and contributing their expertise to professional and volunteering activities. As described in the report of the Ministry of Development of the Periphery, the Negev, and the Galilee regions in 2016:

> The activity of the NGOs in many cases complements public systems, and they are a significant auxiliary force for the public system. They contribute to strengthening ... disadvantaged neighborhoods, encouraging migration to the Negev and Galilee regions. They encourage social involvement and community activity ... They are building partnerships with the local community and are gradually becoming a source of public and community leadership. (The Ministry of the Periphery Development, the Negev and the Galilee, 2016, p. 11)

Finally, social mixing through privatization was also described as a tool for strengthening quality of life in the neighborhoods. Anticipated benefits included improving neighborhood visibility as well as the physical maintenance of public housing for newcomers. As described in the New Amidar (n.d.):

> They renovate the apartments of the elderly population and improve the image of public space in disadvantaged neighborhoods. The combination of young people who live in these neighborhoods alongside public housing residents leads to a significant improvement in living conditions in the neighborhoods, improving the atmosphere of the neighborhoods.

Thus, an ethno-national ideology, together with a shortfall in the resources necessary to maintain public housing stock, as well as the neglected state of public housing neighborhoods in the periphery, led the government to promote social mixing. The government did this through privatization of public housing stock to a population that was not the original target demographic. The transfer of responsibility for public housing neighborhoods from the government to NGOs was perceived, in the government discourse, as an efficient process that would benefit all tenants.

The local municipality: Social order, urban redevelopment, and social justice

In contrast to the national government discourse that emphasized national and economic goals, local municipality policymakers described the privatization of public housing in terms of social order, urban redevelopment, and social justice. While the homogeneity of its long-term working-class residents was perceived as a "problem" to the social order, social mixing through the entrance of NGO members was presented as promoting a safe environment and urban redevelopment in disadvantaged neighborhoods. For example, policymakers described how members of Garin Torani, living in public housing in the Yitzhak Sadeh neighborhood of Yeruham, had voluntarily initiated the establishment of building committees. They also renovated apartments and public gardens in poor physical condition, improved the physical infrastructure in the neighborhood, and promoted community safety. Avi, the executive in charge of the public housing redevelopment project, described its contribution to the neighborhood thus:

> It's good to have a social mix that allows a more pleasant, aesthetic, and safe environment in the old part of the town ... it is difficult to provide normal services to a street that is mostly populated by public housing tenants ... There's a police patrol there all the time, a lot of alcoholics. It's an unsafe environment ... and then the Garin Torani members started to rent there ... We started a redevelopment project by asking them to help us and get involved so we could finally also reach the rest of the residents ... And it worked, because they are not [caught] in a survival war.

Policymakers heard similar accounts in relation to the activities of Ayalim members in the Giva'a neighborhood. (Figure 1)

Therefore, local policymakers argued that whilst public housing is designated by law for disadvantaged populations, privatization approaches were justifiable because they contributed not only to social mixing but also to social order within the neighborhoods.

Another central meaning revealed by the discourse on social mix policy is the municipality's desire to prevent—or at least reduce—the ingress of more disadvantaged populations into public housing in the town. As noted by Tal Ohana, Yeruham's current mayor:

> The organization's members were not originally an eligible population for public housing, but their entry into public housing has revitalized the entire area ... There are dozens of people waiting for public housing, so you are constantly in a dilemma ... but if you are really quantifying and appreciating the contribution of these young people to the neighborhood, then you understand that it has to be done ... It is not possible to have such a large welfare population; you have to take care of the town's financial support, and this is the demographic way of doing it.

Presenting the transfer of public housing stock to NGOs as social mixing revealed this additional motivation: Preventing the allocation of public housing to disadvantaged populations, and thus reducing their numbers in the town. According to the municipality's policymakers, Yeruham bears a heavier burden in housing disadvantaged populations than other cities in Israel. As Avi explained:

> The center lacks public housing, and here we have it. So they send us public housing tenants from other towns. In Yeruham, 30% of the population is supported by welfare; we are carrying enough of the "social stretcher." It is harsh to overload [us with] more tenants.

Local policymakers justified the privatization of public housing to NGOs through a discourse of social justice between development towns and more affluent cities in the country. In their fight against institutional inequalities between the periphery and center, along with their strong desire to protect the town's economy, they used the term *social mix* to justify excluding public housing tenants from the town. While one might consider this discourse cynical, the complexity of dealing with institutional injustice when distributing public housing between cities is also revealed.

Newcomers: Social involvement, population diversity, and alienation

The Garinim Toranim and Ayalim organizations have two declared goals: (a) The nationalist-oriented goal of increasing Jewish presence in the Israeli periphery and contested cities, and (b) a social goal of strengthening disadvantaged towns and populations. In so-called "mixed" or contested Israeli cities, the organizations emphasize the importance of a Jewish presence in the face of an increasing Arab population, in what is described as "state-led ethno-gentrification" (Shmaryahu-Yeshurun & Ben-Porat, 2020). However, in peripheral towns defined by underprivileged Jewish populations, the organizations underscore promoting the social mix of different socioeconomic and ethnic populations. According to the organizations' discourse, social mix is a remedy for removing the stigma often appended to such neighborhoods. Gal, a member of Ayalim, observed:

> Before coming to Yeruham, I studied social work and thought I was going to change the world ... I wanted to live in an atmosphere of social change ... to strengthen disadvantaged communities, to bring young people to the Negev to reveal to them other sides of the Negev. The thing that is most harmful to the town is its image ... People living here have a consciousness of inferiority, of "We live in a bad place" ... we need to change it.

Another social goal referenced by members of both organizations was working to improve the ethnic and socioeconomic diversity of neighborhoods. As Assaf, a member of Garin Torani, described it:

> One of the things that is problematic in the development towns is that they are very homogeneously populated ... a mix of groups, of populations, is good for towns ... Garin attracted teachers, social workers, doctors to live here. It contributes to the town ... When they bought these cheap houses and moved here, it gave some of the long-term residents a sense of trust in the place.

Figure 1. Ayalim's urban renewal project in the Giva'a neighborhood. Sources: Oded Melamed; bottom right: the author.

Here, the objective of social mix in public housing is presented as a tool capable of strengthening both the neighborhood and its residents. However, despite their good intentions, the organizations' members acknowledged the difficulty of integrating with long-term residents of the town; socio-economic and ethnic differences between the populations obstructed the goal of social integration. Ayalim members, in particular, noted an additional challenge. While they were all students, young and mostly single, the older residents were mostly middle-aged families with children. As Hadassah, an Ayalim member described it:

> Who lives in our neighborhood? Mainly families with children or the Moroccan elderly population... On the one hand, it is very natural that no connection will be formed. On the other hand, we pass through the community garden, see the same group of women sitting every day, and have no conversation with them... There really is a gap in the worlds we come from.

As discussed by Lees (2008), tension manifests between the desire for diversity and a natural tendency for self-segregation. When recounting obstacles to integration, newcomers frequently mentioned some residents' resistance to their arrival. These long-term residents framed their discourse in exclusionary terms, describing the newcomers as foreign residents and refusing to accept their presence as Yeruham residents. As Hadar, an Ayalim member, observed:

> There are arguments that do not make one want to stay here... even racist statements such as "This 'Ashkenazi' pretending to save the place," or "those rich [people] who come from outside"... They [long-term residents] don't give you the chance to say, "I just came to live here"... Why do you care why I came here, who my parents are, and where I came from?

The members depict a harsh experience, stemming from the failure to gain acceptance from the long-term residents, which made it difficult for them to forge a tangible sense of belonging to the town. Local resistance to the policy had a significant effect on Ayalim. In 2015, the organization decided to wind down the Yeruham project and move out of the public housing stock that had been allocated to them, and the units returned to Amidar. As Ori, the organization's manager, explained to me in 2013, 2 years before the organization moved out of the apartments:

> We need to think if it is the right move to let strong populations live in these apartments. Obviously, if there is someone who has no place to live, then we will be the first to leave the apartment for them. We started to move out of public housing in some cities we were living in before ... But you also have to look into this resident's claim in depth .... these apartments we moved into were empty before we came. I have never seen a homeless [person] in Yeruham ... So we do keep a finger on the pulse.

Trying to resolve this dilemma they were facing, the new residents justified their somewhat privileged access to public housing by explaining they would gladly vacate the apartments for more needy populations.

Unlike Ayalim members, who can be identified as "Agonizers" (Kaddar, 2020) due to their moral discomfort and ambivalent sense of belonging in the face of gentrification, Garin Torani members justified the gentrification, developing a strong sense of belonging similar to "Upgraders." Although some did understand the reasoning of the local resistance, they nevertheless underscored the social contribution of their redevelopment project as legitimization for their presence. As Elisha, a Garin Torani member, explained:

> So let's say gentrification theories are true. What do you suggest? To move us out of the town? ... Prevent new residents from coming? I'm not worried by the criticism because I feel we're doing something real here, and I'm sure that in the future things will change; it's first-generation difficulties, for starters ... Garin Torani is an excellent and blessed phenomenon. Revolutions are measured in decades, not in twenty years, and in my opinion, this is a tremendously positive revolution.

Overall, differences between the organizations can be explained in the fact that Garin Torani comprised young families who had lived in these apartments for several years. Some had already assimilated into local life, either through the education system or other means. On the other hand, Ayalim members were single students, living in Yeruham during their academic programs and leaving afterward (similar to the case of studentification in Beersheba; see: Avni & Alfasi, 2018). Finally, beyond the differences between the two organizations, there were also differences in Ayalim's mode of operation in different cities. While in contested cities Ayalim members remained in public housing despite local resistance (Shmaryahu-Yeshurun & Ben-Porat, 2020), in Yeruham they decided to leave. This difference reinforces the claim made earlier that settlement in Yeruham had not only ethnonational motivations, but also the social mission of integration with locals—forcing them to acknowledge, and thereby try and soften, local resistance.

Public housing tenants: The price of redevelopment

Long-term public housing tenants described the redevelopment project, and the arrival of new residents, in ambivalent terms. The most notable contribution observed by the residents was improvements to the neighborhood's physical environment following the arrival of the new residents. As Hana, a public housing resident in the Giva'a neighborhood of Yeruham, described the circumstances:

> Once, there were dirt and garbage here all over. There used to be fights and shouting here ... Since Ayalim got here, it has become quiet. No crime ... The neighborhood changed, progressed nicely ... I'll tell you the truth, I really love these students ... Thanks to them, this neighborhood is almost the best neighborhood in Yeruham today.

As has been noted in other circumstances (e.g., Morris et al., 2012), improvements to the physical environment of Yeruham neighborhoods were universally acknowledged. These were also described in terms of a change in the image of the neighborhoods, previously tagged as slum neighborhoods, as in other cases around the world (Arthurson, 2013; Keene & Padilla, 2010; Raynora et al., 2020). At the same time, long-term residents doubted these changes could actually improve their economic status. As Eliyahu, a resident, explained:

> Reputation and image are not the crucial problem of the town .... We need employment first. A factory hasn't been built here in decades ... Our youth leave, and I understand them. What future do they have here? ... The

state has always abandoned us … Yeruham will always remain without a father. Neither students nor professors can ever change Yeruham.

While social mix policy did succeed in rehabilitating the image of Yeruham neighborhoods, long-term tenants argued that it had no impact on their socioeconomic status. They affirmed that the entry of a wealthy population could not provide a solution to deeper structural problems, which the government was eluding rather than addressing.

Beyond this, some residents also noted that social mix policies actually caused displacement. Even though the new residents moved into units that had been abandoned due to their poor physical condition, residents still used terms denoting displacement and gentrification to describe the dynamic. As Rachel, one of the long-term residents, put it:

> The discourse of the government is that when a strong population is brought to the periphery, it will improve and leverage the place. I say that it is impossible to strengthen disadvantaged populations by having someone strong next to them, to serve as a model to them. You can't mix strong and weak and produce an average. It is not a chemical compound. What happens is that the weak are displaced! They are excluded from their cultural environment, home, and workplace.

The residents' discourse reveals the tension between ostensibly positive aspects of social mix policy and more troubling aspects of gentrification policy. Unlike the discourse of policymakers and the new residents, the use of the term *displacement* by long-term residents underscores their experiences. The use of this term can be understood in two ways. The first is *indirect displacement* (Davidson, 2008)—the loss of community resources, identity, or former neighborhood cohesion, all of which contribute to displacement indirectly. As Meir, a long-term resident explained:

> Places are changing. That is right. There is gentrification in many places. So what? Does that mean it's fair? No … When someone says that his home, his safe place, where he feels belongs, is taken from him, I think it's wrong … there is a social and moral problem here.

Beyond indirect connotations, the use of this term can be further understood in terms of displacing a disadvantaged population denied public housing (August, 2019; Musterd & Ostendorf, 2012). Such residents are refused housing because it had been allocated to new residents, without building new units in their place as originally planned. Thus, although direct displacement did not occur, the experience testifies to the use of the term. As Rachel, a resident, explained:

> Why hasn't my friend, who is a single mother of two children and eligible by law for public housing, received it on the grounds that there is no apartment to give her—but a young student who comes from the center of the country to save us receives public housing at a ridiculous price? Even in the country's backyard, where all the Mizrahim were thrown away, we have no rights here either!

While the discourse of policymakers and NGO members presents the privatization of public housing stock as an act of social involvement and even social justice, some residents experienced it as reproducing a social inequality that they already knew well. Using the phrase "throwing away all the Mizrahim," Rachel encapsulated not only the class displacement but also its intersection with ethnicity, and its cultural implications by way of changing the identity of the neighborhood and weakening historical community bonds (Goetz, 2011; Wyly et al., 2010). Due to the apprehension of displacement, some residents organized to express resistance to the policy through publicizing their claims in media outlets and making representations to the municipality. In addition, as part of the *Public Housing Forum* and the *Distributive Justice Forum* established in 2012, residents have posed challenges to the policy of social mix and the consequent transfer of public housing stock. They did have some success in this respect; as noted earlier, Ayalim ultimately decided to withdraw from the initiative in Yeruham.

Figure 2 below summarizes the four attitudes toward the policy, according to which the interviewees from different positions were divided, as elaborately explained in this finding chapter.

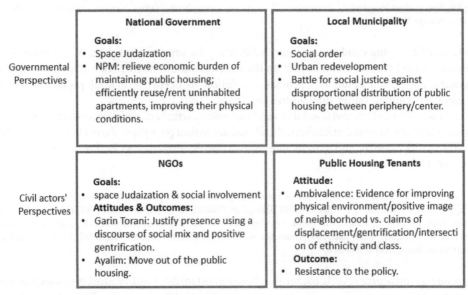

Figure 2. Stakeholders' attitudes toward social mix policy.

Conclusion

This study clarifies the relationship between the terms *gentrification* and *social mix* by elaborating on the perceptions of social mix stakeholders. More specifically, it elucidates various stakeholder perceptions wherein the privatization of public housing to NGOs did not involve displacing tenants. Instead, this privatization promoted middle-class entrance into public housing by motivating the tenants to integrate with the local community. While existing literature comments on tenants displaced from privatized housing, this situation is unique in that the newcomers were encouraged to assimilate with and improve the local community.

Consistent with previous research (Arthurson et al., 2015; August, 2014, 2019; Bacque´ & Fijalkow, 2011; Lees, 2008; Lees et al., 2011), the current study demonstrates how the neutralization of language helps reshape the symbolism of social mix in Yeruham's policy debate. This neutralization assists powerful stakeholders in pursuing their interests. Discourse mobilization is also used by veteran tenants, who resist the policy by employing terms like *displacement* and *gentrification* to describe their experiences. A unique contribution of this research is my analysis of many different actors in the social mix discourse. In response to Arthurson et al.'s (2015) call to examine the full spectrum of perceptions held by various stakeholders on social mix policies, the study identified differences and contradictions between stakeholders in their understanding and experiences.

At the national perspective, social mixing is described as Israel's mission of Judaizing the Negev. It is also viewed as a more cost-effective means of managing public housing, exemplifying the New Public Management model. National policymakers justified reallocating public resources intended to support the neediest in society. Such resources instead reached a population that was not an original target of public housing. These policymakers emphasized their intention to build new apartments with funds raised from housing rentals; however, this did not happen in practice, leading instead to the de facto reduction of public housing in Yeruham.

The privatization of public housing received further justifications in the local municipality discourse, which described the policy as promoting the neighborhood's physical redevelopment. Municipal leaders also claimed privatization encouraged social order and justice. In their fight against institutional inequalities between periphery and center, as well as their need to protect the town's economic viability and wellbeing, the term *social mix* was deployed to prevent more dependent populations from entering the town. The complexity inherent in issues of institutional injustice, that had not been previously well documented, becomes apparent.

Similarly, from the civil actors' perspectives, newcomers relied on this interpretation of the social mix discourse to justify the advantages accrued to them via privileged access to public housing. However, the tension between social mixing and gentrification becomes clear in conversations with the newcomers. One expression of this discrepancy can be detected in use of the term *gentrification*— acknowledging the inherent problem but defending it as a "tremendously positive revolution." The new residents are thereby caught between wanting to integrate into the neighborhood and facing the existing differences between two populations. This dilemma is exacerbated by the perceived illegitimacy of their presence. Thus, despite the lofty declarations and stated goals of social integration initiatives, social mix policy failed in practice to achieve meaningful integration between the populations. This study further enhances the emerging literature arguing that social mixing is not always beneficial to the community.

Finally, the above tension intensifies in the narratives of public housing tenants, with some claiming that social mix is a euphemism for social displacement. Although direct displacement from public housing is not observed in this case study, one can understand how using words such as *displacement* and *gentrification* express indirect displacement (Davidson, 2008). These words critique the changing cultural character of the neighborhoods and the fact that eligible populations were supplanted by newcomers for priority public housing (August, 2019; Musterd & Ostendorf, 2012).

This research successfully identified gaps between stakeholders' attitudes toward social mix policy and the actual relationship between residents and settlers. Such evidence supports the critique in current literature regarding use of the term *social mix* as a means of camouflaging state-led gentrification processes (Arthurson et al., 2015; August, 2014, 2019; Bacque´ & Fijalkow, 2011; Lees, 2008; Lees et al., 2011), even if the process is promoted by NGOs and community housing associations (Jacobs et al., 2004; Pawson & Gilmour, 2010; Pawson et al., 2019). As this study shows, despite the newcomers' commitment to social involvement and the fact that the privatization did not directly displace tenants from public housing, the policy faced resistance from veteran tenants and ultimately failed to achieve meaningful integration between the populations.

Notes

1. "Mizrahim"(Mizrahi in the singular) means "Orientals" or "Easterners," and refers to Jews who immigrated to Israel from countries in the Middle East and North Africa, and their descendants.
2. All quotes translated from the original Hebrew by the author.

Acknowledgments

The author wishes to thank Professor Guy Ben-Porat and the four reviewers for their helpful comments and suggestions.

Disclosure statement

No potential conflict of interest was reported by the author(s).

ORCID

Yael Shmaryahu-Yeshurun http://orcid.org/0000-0002-0297-5712

References

Alves, S. (2019). Nuancing the international debate on social mix: Evidence from Copenhagen. *Housing Studies*. https://doi.org/10.1080/02673037.2018.1556785

Andersen, H. S. (2017). Selective moving behavior in ethnic neighborhoods: White flight, white avoidance, ethnic attraction or ethnic retention? *Housing Studies*, 32(3), 296–318. https://doi.org/10.1080/02673037.2016.1208161

Andersson, R., Bråmå, Å., & Holmqvist, E. (2010). Counteracting segregation: Swedish policies and experiences. *Housing Studies*, 25(2), 237–256. https://doi.org/10.1080/02673030903561859

Arthurson, K. (2012). *Social mix and the city: Challenging the mixed communities' consensus in housing and urban planning policies*. CSIRO Publishing.

Arthurson, K. (2013). Mixed tenure communities and the effects on neighborhood reputation and stigma: Residents' experiences from within. *Cities*, 35, 432–438. https://doi.org/10.1016/j.cities.2013.03.007

Arthurson, K., Levin, I., & Ziersch, A. (2015). What is the meaning of 'Social Mix'? Shifting perspectives in planning and implementing public housing estate redevelopment. *Australian Geographer*, 46(4), 491–505. https://doi.org/10.1080/00049182.2015.1075270

Atkinson, R., & Kintrea, K. (2001). Disentangling area effects: Evidence from deprived and non-deprived neighbourhoods. *Urban Studies*, 38(11), 2277–2298. https://doi.org/10.1080/00420980120087162

August, M. (2014). Negotiating social mix in Toronto's first public housing redevelopment: Power, space and social control in Don Mount Court. *International Journal of Urban and Regional Research*, 38(4), 1160–1180. https://doi.org/10.1111/1468-2427.12127

August, M. (2019). Social mix and the death of public housing. In M. Moos (Ed.), *A research agenda for housing* (pp. 116–130). School of Planning, University of Waterloo. https://doi.org/10.4337/9781788116510.00015

Avni, N., & Alfasi, N. (2018). UniverCity: The vicious cycle of studentification in a peripheral city. *City & Community*, 17(4), 1248–1269.

Ayalim Association. https://www.ayalim.org.il/en/

Bacque', M. H., & Fijalkow, Y. (2011). Social mix as the aim of a controlled gentrification process: The example of the Goutted'or district in Paris. In G. Bridge, T. Butler, & L. Lees (Eds.), *Mixed communities: Gentrification by stealth?* (pp. 115–132). Policy Press.

Bernstein, D. (1981). Immigrant transit camps: The formation of dependent relations in Israeli society. *Ethnic and Racial Studies*, 4(1), 26–43.

Bnei-Akiva Yeruham Community. http://www.kehila-yerucham.org.il

Bond, L., Sautkina, E., & Kearns, A. (2011). Mixed messages about mixed tenure: Do reviews tell the real story? *Housing Studies*, 26(1), 69–94. https://doi.org/10.1080/02673037.2010.512752

Bourdieu, P. (1993). *Language and symbolic power*. Harvard University Press.

Carmon, N. (2001). Housing policy in Israel: Review, evaluation and lessons. *Israel Affairs*, 7(4), 181–208. https://doi.org/10.1080/13537120108719620

Central Bureau of Statistics. (2019). *Local Authorities in Israel, 2019, No. 1759*. https://www.cbs.gov.il/he/Pages/default.aspx

Clarke, V., & Braun, V. (2016). Thematic analysis. In E. Lyons & A. Coyle (Eds.), *Analysing qualitative data in psychology* (2nd ed., pp. 84–103). Sage.

Cole, L., & Goodchild, B. (2001). Social mix and the 'balanced community' in British housing policy: A tale of two epochs. *GeoJournal*, 51(4), 351–360. https://doi.org/10.1023/A:1012049526513

Davidson, M. (2008). Spoiled mixture: Where does state-led 'positive' gentrification end? *Urban Studies*, 45(12), 2385–2405. https://doi.org/10.1177/0042098008097105

Delgado, E., & Swanson, K. (2019). Gentefication in the barrio: Displacement and urban change in Southern California. *Journal of Urban Affairs*. https://doi.org/10.1080/07352166.2019.1680245

Doney, R. H., McGuirk, P. M., & Mee., K. J. (2013). Social mix and the problematisation of social housing. *Australian Geographer*, 44(4), 401–418. doi:10.1080/00049182.2013.852500.

Donnelly, K. (2018). The gentrifier's dilemma: Narrative strategies and self-justifications of incoming residents in Bedford-Stuyvesant, Brooklyn. *City & Community*, 17(2), 374–393. https://doi.org/10.1111/cico.12296

Dyson, R., & Varady, D. P. (2018). Using housing vouchers to create stable mixed-income gentrifying neighborhoods: A case study of Over-the-Rhine, Cincinnati, OH. *Journal of Community Practice*, 26(3), 257–282. https://doi.org/10.1080/10705422.2018.1475315

Galster, G. C., & Friedrichs, J. (2015). The dialectic of neighborhood social mix: Editors' introduction to the special issue. *Housing Studies*, 30(2), 175–191. https://doi.org/10.1080/02673037.2015.1035926

Gamzu, S., & Motzafi-Haller, P. (2016). The face of development aid: Volunteers and their hosts in southern Israel. *Development in Practice, 26*(7), 876–891. https://doi.org/10.1080/09614524.2016.1211092

Goetz, E. (2011). Gentrification in Black and White: The racial impact of public housing demolition in American cities. *Urban Studies, 48*(8), 1581–1604. https://doi.org/10.1177/0042098010375323

Government Decision Number 1543 of the 14th Government. *Opening the management of the apartment inventory to competition.* (29/01/1997).

Government Decision Number 3799 of the 31st Government. *Allocation of public housing apartments in the Negev and Galilee for the purpose of accommodating students contributing to the community.* Retrieved July 17, 2008, from https://www.gov.il/he/departments/policies/2008_dea3799

Hananel, R. (2017). From central to marginal: The trajectory of Israel's public-housing policy. *Urban Studies, 54*(11), 2432–2447. https://doi.org/10.1177/0042098016649323

Jacobs, K., Marston, G., & Darcy, M. (2004). 'Changing the mix': Contestation surrounding the public housing stock transfer process in Victoria, New South Wales and Tasmania. *Urban Policy and Research, 22*(3), 249–263. https://doi.org/10.1080/0811114042000269281

Kaddar, M. (2020). Gentrifiers and attitudes towards agency: A new typology. Evidence from Tel Aviv-Jaffa, Israel. *Urban Studies, 57*(6), 1243–1259. https://doi.org/10.1177/0042098020904252

Keene, D. E., & Padilla, M. B. (2010). Race, class and the stigma of place: Moving to "opportunity" in Eastern Iowa. *Health & Place, 16*(6), 1216–1223. https://doi.org/10.1016/j.healthplace.2010.08.006

Kleinhans, R., & Varady, D. (2011). A review of recent evidence on negative spillover effects of housing restructuring programs in the USA and the Netherlands. *International Journal of Housing Policy, 11*(2), 155–174. https://doi.org/10.1080/14616718.2011.573205

Laffin, M. (2019). Explaining reforms: Post-New Public Management myths or political realities? Social housing delivery in England and France. *International Review of Administrative Sciences, 85*(1), 45–61. https://doi.org/10.1177/0020852317746223

Lees, L. (2008). Gentrification and social mixing: Towards an inclusive urban renaissance? *Urban Studies, 45*(12), 2449–2470. https://doi.org/10.1177/0042098008097099

Lees, L., Butler, T., & Bridge, G. (2011). Introduction: Gentrification, social mixing and mixed communities. In G. Bridge, T. Butler, & L. Lees (Eds.), *Mixed communities: Gentrification by stealth?* (pp. 1–14). The Policy Press.

Lipshitz, G. (1998). *Country on the move: Migration to and within Israel.* Kluwer Academic Publishers.

Massey, D., Albright, L., Casciano, R., Derickson, E., & Kinsey, D. (2013). *Climbing Mount Laurel: The struggle for affordable housing and social mobility in an American suburb.* Princeton University Press.

Mirowski, A. (2015, January 1). *340 apartments belonging to the public were sold in two days to religious institutions and yeshivas - without a tender.* TheMarker. https://www.themarker.com/realestate/1.2527163

Morris, A., Jamieson, M., & Patulny, R. (2012). Is social mixing of tenures a solution for public housing estates? *Evidence Base, 2012*(1), 1–21. doi:10.21307/eb-2012-001.

Motzafi-Haller, P. (2018). *Concrete boxes: Mizrahi women of the periphery of Israel.* Wayne State University Press.

Mullins, D., Milligan, V., & Nieboer, N. (2018). State directed hybridity? – The relationship between non-profit housing organizations and the state in three national contexts. *Housing Studies, 33*(4), 565–588. https://doi.org/10.1080/02673037.2017.1373747

Musterd, S., & Ostendorf, W. (2012). Inequalities in European cities. In S. J. Smith, M. Elsinga, L. F. O'Mahony, O. S. Eng, S. Wachter, & D. Clapham (Eds.), *International encyclopedia of housing and home* (pp. 49–55). Elsevier.

New Amidar (n.d.). *Housing for students.* https://www.amidar.co.il/wps/portal/amidar/service/article/student-housing

Pawson, H., & Gilmour, T. (2010). Transforming Australia's social housing: Pointers from the British stock transfer experience. *Urban Policy and Research, 28*(3), 241–260. https://doi.org/10.1080/08111146.2010.497135

Pawson, H., Milligan, V., & Martin, C. (2019). Building Australia's affordable housing industry: Capacity challenges and capacity-enhancing strategies. *International Journal of Housing Policy, 19*(1), 46–68. https://doi.org/10.1080/19491247.2018.1469108

Public Housing Law- Purchase Rights. 1998.

Raynora, K., Panzab, L., Ordóñezc, C., Adamovicd, M., & Wheelere, M. A. (2020). Does social mix reduce stigma in public housing? A comparative analysis of two housing estates in Melbourne. *Cities, 96*, 102458. https://doi.org/10.1016/j.cities.2019.102458

Reichner, E. (2013). *There of all places: The story of the social settlers.* Yediot Sfarim. (Hebrew).

Rose, D., Germain, A., Bacque, M. H., Bridge, G., Fijalkow, Y., & Staler, T. (2013). 'Social mix' and neighbourhood revitalization in a transatlantic perspective: Comparing local policy discourses and expectations in Paris (France), Bristol (UK) and Montréal (Canada). *International Journal of Urban and Regional Research, 37*(2), 430–450. https://doi.org/10.1111/j.1468-2427.2012.01127.x

Santiago, A., Galster, G., Lucero, J., Ishler, K., Lee, E. L., Kypriotakis, G., & Stack, L. (2014). *Opportunity neighborhoods for Latino and African American youth.* U.S. Department of Housing and Urban Development/Policy Development and Research. http://www.huduser.org/portal/publications/Opportunity_Neighborhoods.html

Shmaryahu-Yeshurun, Y., & Ben-Porat, G. (2018). "We came to change": Settlements groups in periphery towns. *Megamot, 52*(2), 195–222. (Hebrew).

Shmaryahu-Yeshurun, Y., & Ben-Porat, G. (2020). For the benefit of all? State-led gentrification in a contested city. *Urban Studies*, 004209802095307. https://doi.org/10.1177/0042098020953077

Smith, N. (2002). New globalism, new urbanism: Gentrification as global urban strategy. *Antipode*, 34(3), 427–450. https://doi.org/10.1111/1467-8330.00249

State Comptroller. (2013). *Public housing apartments that have not been rented to public housing* (Report No. 64A). https://www.mevaker.gov.il/sites/DigitalLibrary/Pages/Reports/408-16.aspx

The Ministry of the Periphery Development, the Negev and the Galilee. (2016). *Accountability of the Commissioner for Implementation of the Freedom of Information Law in the Ministry of Development of the Periphery, the Negev and the Galilee for 2016*. http://negev-galil.gov.il/mediacenter/tenders/documents/info2016.pdf

Tzfadia, E. (2006). Public housing as control: Spatial policy of settling immigrants in Israeli development towns. *Housing Studies*, 21(4), 523–537. https://doi.org/10.1080/02673030600709058

Tzfadia, E. (2008). New settlements in metropolitan Beer Sheva: The involvement of settlement NGOs. In Y. Gradus & E. Meir-Glitzenstein (Eds.), *Beer Sheva: Metropolis in the making* (pp. 105–123). Ben-Gurion University.

Tzfadia, E., & Yacobi, H. (2015). The privatization of space. In Y. Galnoor, A. Paz-Fuchs, & N. Zion (Eds.), *Privatization policy in Israel: State responsibility and boundaries between the public and the private* (pp. 405–440). Van Leer and Hakibutz Hameuhad (Hebrew).

Wilson, D., & Grammenos, D. (2005). Gentrification, discourse, and the body: Chicago's Humboldt Park. *Environment and Planning D: Society and Space*, 23(2), 295–312. https://doi.org/10.1068/d0203

Wyly, E., Newman-Schell, K., Schafran, A., & Lee, E. (2010). Displacing New York. *Environment and Planning A*, 42(11), 2602–2623. https://doi.org/10.1068/a42519

Yiftachel, O., & Avni, N. (2019). Privati-Nation—Privatization, nationalization. *Housing and Gaps. Planning*, 16(1), 225–247. (Hebrew).

Yiftachel, O., & Tzfadia, E. (2004). Between periphery and 'third space': Identity of Mizrahim in Israel's development towns. In A. Kemp, D. Newman, U. Ram, & O. Yiftachel (Eds.), *Israelis in conflict: Hegemonies, identities and challenges* (pp. 203–235). Academic Press.

Social mix in context: Comparing housing regeneration programs in Australia and Israel

Iris Levin, Nava Kainer Persov, Kathy Arthurson, and Anna Ziersch

ABSTRACT
During the past 30 years, social mix has been on the policy agenda of many countries as a tool for deconcentrating urban disadvantage and enhancing social inclusion. However, these projects often take diverse forms in different institutional and policy contexts. In this article, we compare two separate studies of current urban regeneration programs in Australia and Israel. The comparative analysis reveals major similarities and differences regarding the physical and social outcomes of social mix. Our findings suggest that although both projects did not declare to create socially mixed communities, the resulting resident makeup was mixed. Despite differences in the projects' physical designs, both resulted in two communities living side-by-side but not interacting meaningfully, and therefore not gaining from the possible benefits of social mix. We argue that international comparative studies of social mix policies in different contexts allow for a better understanding of the practicalities of social mix processes for policymakers and planners.

Introduction

Efforts to create social mix through housing have waxed and waned but date back to mid-nineteenth century, when utopian ideas about mixing different classes in new neighborhoods and towns were explored in England (Sarkissian, 1976). Discussions around social mix reappeared after the Second World War in social justice and egalitarian debates in the UK and the U.S. (Arthurson, 2012). The concept made another comeback in the 1990s, with policies and programs aiming to encourage social mix thriving in many countries through a process of policy transfer in a global climate of neoliberal governance (Darcy, 2010).

Over the past 30 years, social mix has been on the policy agenda of many countries as an intended aim of housing regeneration processes—used as a tool for deconcentrating urban disadvantage and enhancing social inclusion (Arthurson, 2010a). While the term social mix has been critiqued as slippery and vague (Galster & Friedrichs, 2015; Goodchild & Cole, 2001; Vale & Shamsuddin, 2017), Galster (2013) has proposed three main aspects of social mix: the social composition that forms the basis of the socially mixed community; the concentration of social mix and ideal ratio of groups; and the scale of social mix.

Housing regeneration programs that have included an aim to increase social mix have taken many forms in different institutional, planning and policy contexts. These include the State-led regeneration of public housing estates and the creation of mixed-tenure communities; the regeneration of inner-city neighborhoods and the in-migration of affluent residents to gentrified neighborhoods; and the privately led regeneration of private residential buildings in disadvantaged neighborhoods (Arthurson et al., 2015). Social mix has been criticized as being largely a policy justification for redevelopment projects of public housing estates and urban renewal projects in inner-city neighborhoods—which have led to the displacement of disadvantaged communities due to gentrification (Bridge et al., 2012; Lees, 2008) and the substantial loss of social housing units and communities (Morris, 2019). The debates around social mix, the social engineering the term implies, and its effectiveness in creating new mixed communities, are still ongoing.

This article presents a comparative study of two housing regeneration programs in two countries with very different housing systems, Australia and Israel. Crucially, the programs differ in their design: the Australian program utilizes private funding to rebuild public housing, while the Israeli program utilizes private money to rebuild (mostly) private housing. Despite this difference, the programs share many similarities, not least in the unintended consequences of social mix. The article's purpose is to contribute to these debates through a critical analysis of social mix in different institutional and policy settings. The central question investigated is what can be learned about social mix from comparing two approaches of housing regeneration in two countries with different policy contexts?

In the next section, we discuss previous research on the physical and social outcomes of housing regeneration programs through social mix followed by comparative international research. We then describe the two case studies before presenting the policy contexts and details of the programs. Then, we present the physical and social consequences of social mix, concluding with a discussion of the lessons learned and suggestions for future research.

Theoretical background

Physical and social outcomes of housing regeneration programs

Research on the physical outcomes of housing regeneration programs through social mix has focused on the extent of physical similarity of housing categories, maintenance, spatial configuration and public spaces (Bolt & Van Kempen, 2013; Camina & Wood, 2009; Joseph & Chaskin, 2010; Kearns et al., 2013; Tiesdell, 2004). Findings suggest that satisfaction with the neighborhood and the level of social mixing was highest in areas where different tenures share similar style, size and quality of buildings (Camina & Wood, 2009). Additionally, maintenance of the buildings is crucial for the appearance and livability of the buildings (Joseph & Chaskin, 2010). Spatial configurations differ between segregated, segmented/clustered or integrated/pepper-potted designs, and spatial configuration can influence the extent of social interaction between residents (Kearns et al., 2013; Tiesdell, 2004). Research suggests that integrated designs are the most effective way to encourage social interactions between the different groups. Research has also found that the design of public spaces influences the degree of social interaction between residents (Bolt & Van Kempen, 2013), with mixed evidence regarding the effectiveness of communal facilities to facilitate social interaction (Bond et al., 2011).

Research on the social outcomes of housing regeneration programs through social mix has highlighted a number of major issues. Previous studies suggest that public participation of the existing community in the design of its future mixed-income redevelopment has often been lacking (Camina & Wood, 2009; Chaskin et al., 2012). Social cohesion is frequently considered a major policy aim of socially mixed developments at the neighborhood level (Bolt et al., 2010), but research suggests this is often not achieved. For example, in a consolidation of six reviews of primary studies of UK social mix programs, Bond et al. (2011) found no improvements in social interaction and cohesion, and, in fact, found some evidence of negative effects such as tensions between tenures (see also, Joseph & Chaskin, 2010). Community development investment is imperative for creating a cohesive community yet is often absent from social mix programs (Camina & Wood, 2009).

Besides these issues, a key criticism of housing regeneration programs sees them as advancing neoliberal gentrification processes at the expense and displacement of the urban poor (Lees, 2008; Morris, 2019; Slater, 2006; Watt, 2008). The literature further points out that the "neighborhood effects" thesis is flawed as it focuses on the neighborhood as the cause of urban poverty instead of focusing on life chances and capital accumulation that dictate where people live in cities and neighborhoods (Slater, 2013).

Studies have found varied evidence regarding improved stigma in mixed communities (Arthurson, 2010b, 2013; Bond et al., 2011). Arthurson (2013), in her study of three Australian neighborhoods, found that while neighborhood stigma appeared to have improved, a more localized stigma around housing tenure stigma still existed. Often, social mix programs improve external stigma but can create stigma toward the preexisting community from new residents (Joseph & Chaskin, 2010).

Benefits of international comparative studies on social mix through housing

One of the benefits of international comparative studies is that shifts in contemporary meanings and practices attached to the idea of social mix can be examined across countries in light of wider global changes, such as the 2008 economic crisis (Costarelli et al., 2019) or a neoliberal global trend (Rose et al., 2013). Cross-country analysis thus offers an opportunity to examine if a given condition in one society is influential elsewhere or not, and to examine how similar social mix policies are enacted differently in practice. For example, Posthumus and Lelévrier (2013) explored neighborhood satisfaction with displaced public housing tenants after forced relocations in the Netherlands and France. They concluded that the Dutch context, where tenants had greater options for alternative dwellings, resulted in a more positive experience of forced relocation and was thereby preferable to the French one. Such studies help explain why different contexts can generate different experiences, providing clues about which contextual factors are important to improving these experiences (e.g., Kleinhans & Varady, 2011; Marom & Carmon, 2015; Stal & Zuberi, 2010; Vesselinov et al., 2018).

Methods

While the literature points to the benefits of international (or cross-national) comparative studies, there are some methodological requirements specific to this kind of inquiry. These include ensuring that theories are relevant in each context, methods are translatable between cultures, and units of analysis are compatible in order to establish comparability at each stage of the research process (Buil et al., 2012; Seixas et al., 2018). These considerations are particularly important when the research is policy-focused and there are linguistic, cultural, professional and philosophical differences between the countries involved (Martinus & Hedgcock, 2015). For example, difficulties can arise from dealing with different cultural understandings of ethics, recruitment practices of participants, data collection and the "insider" knowledge needed for achieving these tasks. Furthermore, intercultural perceptions, interactions and power relations during interviews, inadvertently influence the fieldwork process as well as the analysis and writing stages. Researchers engaged in international comparative research need to recognize and name these uncertainties toward establishing a rigorous research process (Martinus & Hedgcock, 2015; Mullings, 1999).

In contrast to most international comparative research referenced above, this article draws on data from two separate studies in Australia (Arthurson et al., 2015; Levin et al., 2014, 2018; Ziersch et al., 2018) and Israel (Kainer Persov, 2008, 2017; Kainer Persov & Carmon, 2020) that were not designed as one research project but undertaken by local housing academics who were familiar with the local contexts. Nevertheless, similarities in research design and outcomes enabled us to compare the two case studies and draw some conclusions. As Seixas et al. (2018) argue, international comparisons can contribute to public policy research through providing better understandings of the distinct ways in which particular issues may be addressed. It also provides a more comprehensive understanding of the issues addressed by policy design as well as useful insights on appropriate responses.

Table 1 highlights the key features of the two projects. Despite not being part of a single study, both research projects were undertaken at a similar time, shared similar interests, and used multi-method designs.

The Carlton study commenced in 2011 after the completion of Stage 1 of the regeneration project. This study focused on Stage 1 only which included a replacement of eight old public housing walk-ups

Table 1. Comparison of the two research projects.

Characteristics		Carlton regeneration study	Green Ono regeneration study
Research aims		Investigate relocation experiences of public housing tenants and the socially mixed community	Investigate equity impacts of the project and the socially mixed community
Dates of research project		2011–2014	2014–2016
Methods		Community observations Semi-structured interviews Planning policies	Community observations Structured interviews Architectural plans and records
	Interviews with	Public tenants: 31 Private residents: 10 Service providers: 10 Total: 51	Long-term residents: 17 (incl. 2 public housing tenants) New residents: 34 Planning professionals: 10 Total: 61
	Survey	200 local residents	N/A

(128 apartments) with three new apartment blocks comprising a mix of public (84 apartments) and private housing units (98 apartments). The study ended in 2014. Similarly, the Green Ono evaluation was conducted between 2014 and 2016 with the aim of examining the equity impacts of the regeneration project. The study took place after the completion and occupation of 10 buildings (with 480 apartments) and during the construction of the last building (with additional 50 apartments).

As seen in Table 1, both studies employed similar data collection methods: the Carlton project interviewed a total of 51 participants, including public housing tenants, private housing residents, and service providers; the Green Ono project interviewed a total of 61 participants, including long-term residents, new residents, residents' committee representatives and planning professionals. In both studies, observations were conducted during various time of the days and days of the week (the average number of observation hours in both studies was 50 hours). Both projects' architectural and planning documents were examined to identify the aims and the spatial configuration of the projects. In the Carlton study, researchers completed a survey of 200 residents living in the neighborhood to gather information about attitudes regarding regeneration of public housing and social mix. Although the studies had somewhat different aims, they both explored the physical and social outcomes of social mix in the neighborhoods as a result of housing regeneration.

Context: Regeneration in Australia and Israel

Urban regeneration policies in Australia and Israel have been prominent since the 1990s in response to global concerns around sustainable planning practices and recognition that planning strategies need to allow for land preservation and densification (Newton & Thomson, 2017; Orenstein & Hamburg, 2009). In both countries, major sites of urban regeneration have been dilapidated, large or medium-density housing estates built during the 1960s. The key difference is that in Australia (likewise UK and the U.S.) these are mostly public housing estates; in Israel most of these housing units were built as public housing but over the years have been sold to sitting residents and are currently owned primarily by private homeowners (Hananel, 2017).

Australian cities typically have very low densities in contrast to Israeli cities which have high densities, comparable to European cities. Since Israel is much smaller in area than Australia, there is little space for cities to further expand. Hence, several national plans in the 1990s determined that future housing stock in Israel should be built within the boundaries of existing cities. In this way, open land would be preserved (Orenstein & Hamburg, 2009). While Australia has plenty of space beyond existing cities, policymakers have likewise encouraged local councils to build within the boundaries of their cities, in high-value brownfield sites (e.g., post-industrial sites, docklands, or train station precincts), with small-scale "knockdown and rebuild" of private housing units (Wiesel et al., 2013) and construction of larger-scale apartment blocks in place of low-density private housing to increase density (Easthope & Randolph, 2009).

In Australia, policies of urban regeneration of public housing estates were evolved to address social exclusion through the deconcentration of urban poverty and improvement of housing stock. Yet in reality, these projects have been driven by neoliberal objectives through a discursive strategy that includes the problematization of public housing tenancy and the generation of binary narratives around community life (Darcy, 2010, 2013; Shaw et al., 2013). Governments have realized that public housing land in inner-city locations possess an "untapped equity," which provides incentives for large renewal projects involving private developers and a focus on public housing regeneration in Australian capital cities (Pawson & Pinnegar, 2018, p. 311).

Since 1998, the goal of the main regeneration program in Israel (*Demolition and Redevelopment*) has been to increase the housing stock by adding new housing units as well as making better use of existing infrastructure (physical and social). The regeneration program is promoted through governmental incentives by way of building rights and reduced taxes. It also requires a financial agreement between a developer and the homeowners. Long-term homeowners sell their rights to their old apartment and receive in return "an apartment for an apartment"—a new, larger apartment in the same location—without the need to pay for regeneration of their homes and neighborhoods (Kainer Persov & Carmon, 2020). The developer profits from the sales of new additional apartments at market rate. Currently, there are 51 Demolition and Redevelopment projects in different stages of implementation, mostly in the Tel Aviv metropolitan area, which has the highest land value in Israel.

In both countries, the programs utilize private sector funding and delivery due to a global neoliberal trend of shrinking public investment in housing. Dependency on private sector funding has resulted in urban regeneration projects taking place in high land value areas, concentrated mostly in major capital cities in the Australian case (Pawson & Pinnegar, 2018) and in the Tel Aviv metropolitan area in the Israeli case (Margalit & Alfasi, 2016).

However, regeneration projects in Israel use housing estates mostly owned by homeowners while in Australia, housing estates are mostly owned by the government. In both countries, however, public housing stock has been shrinking since the 1990s. In Australia, declining funding and a shift to rental assistance by the federal government resulted in a decrease from 5.2% of social housing stock in 1996 to 4.8% in 2011 (Groenhart & Burke, 2014), and in 2016, only 3.5% of the Victorian's housing stock was social housing (Parliament of Victoria, 2017). Similarly, public housing stock in Israel comprises only 2.5% of the total housing stock and since 1991, hardly any public housing units have been built (Hananel, 2017).

The Australian case study: Carlton

The Australian case study focused on the regeneration of a public housing estate in the affluent inner-city neighborhood of Carlton in Melbourne, Victoria's capital city. In 2016, Carlton had 19,001 residents (Australian Bureau of Statistics, 2020). Located two kilometers from the central business district (CBD), the area is well-serviced by public transport, hospitals and two university campuses.

The Carlton regeneration project commenced in 2006 and at the time was the largest private–public partnership project in Victoria (Department of Human Services, 2009). The project was designed over nine stages and was due to be completed in 2017. In 2020, however, it was still unfinished although all public housing buildings have been completed. The project included three sites: two with public housing clusters, Lygon and Elgin, and one, Keppel, without public housing. Originally the Lygon and Elgin sites had a number of high-rise buildings (4 and 2, respectively) and low-rise apartment blocks (dubbed "walk-ups," with 4–5 floors without elevators; 8 and 4, respectively). The Keppel site was a defunct public hospital. The project focused on the demolition of the 12 public housing walk-ups while keeping the high-rise buildings. It also included the development of 14 new apartment buildings (three public housing buildings—one on each site—and 11 private housing buildings), an aged-care facility, new public parks and landscaping, and the gradual renovation of apartments in the six existing public housing high-rises on the sites. Public housing tenants left the sites in 2006 and only a few returned after 2011 with the completion of Stage 1 of the regeneration. Most tenants stayed in their

Figure 1. Carlton Estate's three sites (Stage 1 is marked with the number 1). Sources: Department of Human Services (2009, p. 3).

Figure 2. Housing before (left) and after (right) regeneration at Carlton. Sources: Department of Human Services (2009, p. 5); Photograph: Iris Levin, 2011.

temporary units choosing not to return, and in their place other public housing tenants moved into the buildings. Private residents (homeowners and renters) also started moving into the private buildings after 2011 (see Figures 1 and 2).

Prior to regeneration, the estate was occupied only by public housing tenants. After regeneration, the estate comprised two groups of residents divided according to tenure: public housing tenants, including those who stayed living in the high-rise buildings and those who returned to the new public housing buildings, and new middle-income residents (homeowners and renters) who moved into the new private buildings.

The Israeli case study: Green Ono

The Israeli case study focused on the regeneration of the Green Ono project, formerly the King Shaul neighborhood, in Kiryat Ono, which was the first housing cluster in Israel to undergo demolition and reconstruction as part of the national urban regeneration policy (Kainer Persov, 2008, 2017).

Figure 3. Green Ono's site. Source: https://www.govmap.gov.il/?c=187418.2,662839.63&z=9&b=1

The project was in Kiryat Ono, a middle-class town with 40,000 residents (in 2018), located in the Tel Aviv metropolitan area (Central Bureau of Statistics [CBS], 2020). Like the estate in Carlton, the old King Shaul neighborhood, located near the center of town, was considered rundown and neglected (Globes, 2012). The regeneration project was focused, much like in Carlton, on 174 apartments in 10 walk-up buildings (2–3 story buildings without elevators) which were quickly built during the 1960s. The 10 buildings were occupied by a majority of homeowners (61%) private renters (25%), and a minority of public tenants (14%), all mixed within the buildings (see Figures 2 and 3).

In 2003, after several years of uncertainty regarding the regeneration project, long-term homeowners signed an agreement with a developer and shortly thereafter, the residents vacated their apartments. The long-term homeowners received a monthly rental payment from the developer that allowed them to rent an apartment elsewhere. In contrast, private renters living in the buildings had to leave without any assistance and relocate elsewhere; they did not return to the neighborhood after the project's completion.

The project focused on the demolition of the 10 existing buildings and the development of 11 new high-rises (11–14 buildings with 530 units) built around a public playground and landscaping. Upon completion of the buildings, long-term homeowners received an "apartment for apartment" as part of the regeneration contract (Kainer Persov, 2017). Public housing tenants could purchase their unit at a subsidized rate and be subject to the same conditions as the long-term homeowners (four households did so before the project began), relocate permanently to another public unit elsewhere, or return to a new public housing unit. The rest of the new apartments were sold at market rate to homeowners, mostly middle-income young families. The last building was completed in 2016.

Prior to regeneration, the housing cluster comprised low to low-moderate income households. After regeneration, it included three groups of residents, divided according to tenure and income: long-term low-income homeowners who returned to the new buildings, long-term public housing tenants who also returned, and new middle-income residents (homeowners and renters) who moved into the new buildings.

See Table 2 for a comparison of the major features of the two regeneration projects.

Similarities and differences in the design of the programs

The program development plans at Carlton and Green Ono shared similar objectives focused mainly on improving the housing stock and increasing densities, consistent with neoliberal drivers to maximize profit for private developers (Shaw et al., 2013). At Carlton, objectives were to integrate the site with the

Table 2. Comparison of the regeneration projects in Israel and Australia.[a]

Characteristics	Carlton Estate, Melbourne, Australia	Green Ono, Kiryat Ono, Israel
Decade originally built	1960s	1960s
Aims of the regeneration project	To integrate the site with the local community and improve housing and neighborhood design	To use land efficiently, improve housing conditions and add units
Partners	Private developer State Housing Authority	Private developer Homeowners
Regeneration project – Years in construction	2006–present	2003–2016
Dwellings before regeneration	192	174
Community before regeneration	Public housing tenants (100%)	Private homeowners (61%) Private renters (25%) Public housing tenants (14%)
Dwellings after regeneration	1,093	530
Mixed community after regeneration	Public housing tenants (23%) Private housing residents (77%)	Long-term homeowners (29%) Public housing tenants (4%) New private housing residents (67%)

Sources: Department of Human Services (2009), Kainer Persov (2017).
[a]In both projects, we did not have access to financial information regarding government expenditures and private sector's investments and gains.

local neighborhood, improve urban and building design, and ensure the development contributes to addressing community needs (Department of Human Services, 2009, p. 9). In Green Ono, objectives were to regenerate the area and increase housing densities (Hashimshoni, 2003). In both policy documents, the words *social mix* were not used and there was no mention of the social consequences of such regeneration projects. However, in Australia, the notion of social mix has been central to the public discourse around public housing regeneration in all Australian cities (Darcy, 2010, 2013; Shaw et al., 2013). In Israel the debate around social mix is still relatively new with scholars calling for planning authorities to consider the social aspects of urban regeneration projects (e.g., Padan, 2014). Both projects focused on the physical aspects of renewing rundown and dilapidated housing.

The programs also focused on a similar scale: the estate or the housing cluster scale, both located in inner-city neighborhoods. The Green Ono project was part of a national plan of urban regeneration while the Carlton program was focused only on one site. However, the Carlton project was part of a long-term agenda of public housing urban regeneration in Victoria, leading to the launch of another large public housing regeneration program in 2017 (Kelly & Porter, 2019).

A key difference between the two programs lies in their target communities and the nature of social mix. While the Carlton project introduced private middle-income residents into an existing public housing community, the Green Ono project introduced private middle-income residents into an existing community of low-income and mostly older private homeowners, with a minority of public housing tenants before and after regeneration. In Carlton, the preexisting community included 100% public housing tenants. In Green Ono, the preexisting community included 14% public housing tenants.

Another difference lies in the mechanisms of initiating the projects. In Australia, the project was a private–public partnership (PPP) involving the government selling public land to a consortium of private companies. In Israel, the national plan empowered private developers to initiate projects in neighborhoods that had been designated for urban regeneration. As a result, the project was led by a private developer who signed contracts with homeowners in the neighborhood. Yet, in both case studies, the private sector yielded a lot of power in the negotiation and implementation of the projects.

Findings: The outcomes of the two programs

We identified two major areas for comparison regarding the outcomes of the programs in Australia and Israel: the physical outcomes of social mix and the social outcomes of social mix, both of which are discussed below.

Figure 4. Housing before (left) and after (right) regeneration at Green Ono. Photographs: Nava Kainer Persov, 2005; 2018.

The physical outcomes of social mix

Neighborhood physical changes

The physical changes the two estates underwent during regeneration were quite similar in many respects (see Figures 3 and 4). In Carlton Stage 1, the housing composition changed from eight, 4–5 story walk-up buildings dispersed across the estate with open spaces between them to a much denser complex of three attached buildings (with 4 or 8 stories) and a communal garden between them. Similarly, in Green Ono, the housing composition changed from 10 dispersed walk-up buildings surrounded by open space between them, to 11 buildings (between 11 and 14 stories each) facing an oval-shaped public area with a playground, trees and benches. In both of the regeneration projects, the housing densities increased by three- and four-fold, providing financial incentives for developers. Table 3 summarizes the physical characteristics of the projects.

Housing condition and size changes

Housing conditions improved significantly in both projects for returning residents, changing from old, rundown apartment buildings without elevators, to new, well-equipped apartment buildings with elevators, lobbies, carparks, and in the Israeli case, storerooms and community rooms. In Carlton,

Table 3. Comparison of physical characteristics of the projects.

Characteristics	Carlton Estate, Melbourne, Australia	Green Ono, Kiryat Ono, Israel
Scale of project	Housing clusters (3 sites 7.5 ha)	Housing cluster (3 ha)
Dwellings before regeneration	192 Units in total Public housing units Private housing units: 0	174 Units in total Private housing units (149, 86%) Public housing units (25, 14%)
Dwellings after regeneration	1,093 Units in total Public units (in 3 sites) (246, 23%) Private units (847, 77%) Total: 1,093	530 Units in total Long-term private units (153, 29%) Public units (21, 4%) Private market-rate units (356, 67%)
Units location after regeneration	Separate buildings: 3 buildings for public housing and 8 buildings for private residents.	Mixed buildings: 11 buildings mixed with long-term residents, public housing tenants and new residents
Number of dwellings Before/After ratio	1/4.4	1/3
Housing condition change	Before: 12 × 4–5 story walk-ups without elevators (Stage 1: 8 walkups) After: 14 (varied no. of stories) buildings with elevators and carparks (Stage 1–3 buildings)	Before: 10 × 2–3 story walk-ups without elevators After: 11 (11–14 stories) buildings with elevators, storerooms, community rooms and carparks
Housing size change	Before: 3-bedroom apartments After: A mix of 1–4 bedroom apartments	Before: 1- to 2-bedroom apartments After: mostly 3.5 bedroom apartments

public housing buildings also included environmental features to reduce tenants' electricity costs. In both case studies, residents appreciated these physical features of their new and improved housing. This is supported by previous research showing that residents in mixed communities were more satisfied when the architecture and design of housing were of high quality (Camina & Wood, 2009; Joseph & Chaskin, 2010).

The size of the apartments changed too. In Carlton, instead of three-bedroom apartments in all the demolished public housing buildings, the new building in Stage 1 has a mix of apartment sizes with a majority of one- and two-bedroom units (76%) and only a minority of three- and four-bedroom units (24%), to cater for the more diverse needs of current public housing tenants in Victoria. A major critique of the Carlton regeneration program was that although there has been an increase in the number of public housing units across the three sites, from 192 to 246 units (an increase of about 28%), the number of actual bedrooms (and therefore, the number of people that can be housed) decreased from 576 to 444 (a decrease of about 30%) (Kelly & Porter, 2019). In Green Ono, the average size of the apartments doubled, from 60 square meters to 120 square meters. Additional service areas were added to the new buildings, increasing the built-up area six times in terms of built space.

In Carlton, the two private buildings are managed by an external private company while the public housing building is managed by the housing authority. This was a cause for some tensions among private homeowners who felt they were expected to conform to rules which were not adhered to in the public building. In Green Ono, long-term and new residents share the same building, and therefore share the same maintenance company. The change in the quality of the housing brought with it rising costs of building maintenance and municipal taxes for the long-term residents who previously cleaned their buildings themselves. The new residents were uncertain if the long-term residents will be able to pay, leading to tensions between the two groups. These findings support Joseph and Chaskin's (2010) conclusion that the maintenance of the buildings is crucial for their appearance and livability.

The physical design of social mix: Segregated or clustered?

Prior to regeneration, there were only public housing buildings on the Carlton estate. After regeneration, Stage 1 of the Carlton project included one public housing building and two private housing buildings. This configuration of housing mix has been termed *segregated* (Tiesdell, 2004, p. 205). Although the public and private buildings were in close proximity to each other, their distinct nature was reinforced by separate entrances, lobbies, elevators and car parks (see Levin et al., 2014 for a discussion of the estate's design). Moreover, there are no common areas for residents to interact. While there is an enclosed communal garden in the middle of the three buildings, our interviews revealed that it is accessible only to private residents and not to public tenants. Outside of this space, residents can interact only on the sidewalks and playground on the estate.

Prior to regeneration, there were only walk-ups with long-term residents in Green Ono. After regeneration, the new buildings included a mix of three social groups: long-term, low-income homeowners who returned to the site, new middle/high-income residents, and public housing tenants. The three groups share their buildings but are divided according to floors, with long-term homeowners and public tenants on lower floors. This configuration of housing mix has been termed *clustered* (Tiesdell, 2004, p. 205) or *segmented* (Kearns et al., 2013, p. 398). The agreement between the developer and the long-term homeowners granted them the opportunity to return to new apartments only on lower floors—one floor above the location of their original apartment, allowing the developer to sell higher apartments at a market price.

In Green Ono, residents of all groups share the building's lobby, storeroom, community room and parking. However, we observed that long-term residents (including public housing tenants) and new residents did not use the community room for joint activities across the groups. Long-term residents used it primarily to host their extended families on holidays, while new residents used it for children's birthday parties and a parenting lecture series. The outdoor area, located at the center of the complex, includes a playground that is used mainly by the new residents who have younger children. During interviews in Green Ono, we learned that at the beginning of residency in the development the shared responsibility of the common areas had caused tension between the groups of long-term and new residents. While new residents saw long-term residents as people who may damage the public areas due to their behavior and use, long-term residents saw themselves as the ones that made the regeneration project possible and had to go through all its stages of renewal.

As in previous studies, the spatial configuration of the buildings is important as it may encourage or discourage social interaction between the different groups within the mixed community (Joseph & Chaskin, 2010; Kearns et al., 2013; Tiesdell, 2004), and the degree of social interaction between residents depends on the design of public spaces (Bolt & Van Kempen, 2013). Although there are more physical spaces to interact in Green Ono compared to Carlton, interactions between groups have been minimal, and residents perceive themselves as two separate groups that live side-by-side, despite the more encouraging physical design of the complex. These findings are consistent with the lack of evidence regarding the effectiveness of communal facilities in facilitating social interaction (Bond et al., 2011).

The social outcomes of social mix

Community participation in the planning process

The planning process in both programs did not include a meaningful consultation process. In Carlton, tenants were not consulted but only informed of changes to their living environment during regeneration. They were invited to the monthly meetings of the Community Liaison Committee (CLC), which was a formal mechanism for participation that felt out of reach for public housing tenants (see Arthurson et al., 2015). This resembles the public consultation experiences in three mixed-income developments in Chicago, which were not designed for residents' special needs (Chaskin et al., 2012). Similarly, despite homeowners signing a contract with the developer in Green Ono, there was no meaningful consultation with the community in the planning process. Residents were informed occasionally by the developer about the project progress. In both case studies, then, participation of the preexisting community in the design process of the renewed area was not encouraged or supported by planning authorities or other stakeholders. Additionally, despite the literature highlighting the role of community development in facilitating social cohesion (Camina & Wood, 2009), neither project paid much attention to this. In Carlton, the government-funded position of the community development worker ceased to exist after most tenants moved in. In Green Ono, neither the developer nor the local council provided any community development assistance for the mixed community.

Relocation and return of the preexisting community

A major difference between the two programs was the process of relocating existing residents in each site before regeneration. In Carlton, relocation of public housing tenants was managed sensitively, with the housing authority relocating public housing tenants according to their preferences as much as possible. Tenant requests to move out of the neighborhood to a public housing property further away or to stay nearby were accommodated. Unoccupied properties in the high-rises on the estate or other properties on neighboring smaller estates were kept vacant until tenants moved into them. Tenants moved to three-bedroom properties that were comparable to the ones they had left and were promised the ability to return to the redeveloped building if they wished after project completion (Levin et al., 2018).

In Green Ono, long-term private renters who had rented low-priced apartments in the neighborhood had to find themselves another apartment to rent elsewhere with no assistance in an increasingly unaffordable rental market. Long-term homeowners received monthly rental payments from the developer for their temporary apartments and could choose where they wanted to rent. When regeneration was completed, they received a new apartment and moved back to their bigger and newer apartment. Long-term public housing tenants could either buy the old apartment they lived in (at a subsidized price) and become homeowners, relocate to another public housing unit elsewhere, or return to a new public housing apartment in the new project.

The process of return had mixed consequences in both projects. In Carlton, when tenants were due to return to the new building after five years away (and in some cases longer, if tenants relocated early in the process), they were told they would be reassessed by the housing authority, and consequently many were offered smaller units of one or two bedrooms only. Tenants told us they were frustrated and disappointed that they had not been told this prior to moving out of their old units (Levin et al., 2018), and some decided not to return because they felt they needed more bedrooms to accommodate family members (e.g., visiting children of divorced parents, grandchildren) or carers (in the case of tenants with disabilities), even if they technically lived alone. As a result, only about 20%[1] of the previous residents returned to the redeveloped public building (Stage 1) and other public housing tenants moved in instead. This is consistent with other studies documenting low levels of return by public housing tenants, with around 10–13% returning residents only in the U.S. context (Joseph, 2008; Jourdan et al., 2013).

As part of the regeneration contract in Green Ono, all long-term homeowners were offered a new and larger apartment in the new buildings. Yet almost two-thirds of the long-term residents who had lived in the housing cluster prior to regeneration in 2003, did not live in the new housing cluster in 2016. All long-term private renters were displaced (approximately 25%) as a result of regeneration. Interviews with residents indicated that about 30% of long-term private homeowners sold or rented their apartment after regeneration and five (out of 25, 20%) public housing households did not return to the neighborhood. Some of the long-term homeowners immediately sold their new apartments and relocated to another neighborhood while others lived in their new apartment for several years and then decided to rent it out, mostly because of high maintenance costs and municipal taxes. Four public housing tenants were able to buy their old apartment prior to regeneration and became the owners of new apartments in the regeneration project (Kainer Persov, 2017).

Social cohesion in the mixed communities
The two new socially mixed communities are very different in their group composition (Galster, 2013), and duration—how long the community remained socially mixed (Vale & Shamsuddin, 2017). In Carlton, the new socially mixed community is made up of public housing tenants and middle-income private residents (who are either owners or private renters), housed in separate buildings. This mix of public and private tenants will always remain, meaning the "duration" of this level of mixing is ongoing. If public housing tenants move out of their units, they will be replaced by other public housing tenants.

In Green Ono, the new community is made up of long-term low-income residents (including public housing tenants) and new middle- and high-income residents. The original plan for the new housing cluster designated a third of the apartments for long-term homeowners and public housing tenants, and two-thirds of the apartments for market rate sales. However, the duration of the mixed-community in Green Ono only seems to be short-term: after 10 years of residents living in the new project, long-term residents who moved to the first completed buildings in the project (in 2006) composed only 19% of the apartment tenants instead of the designated 33% (Kainer Persov, 2017). Given the tenure structure, the mixed community in Carlton will remained mixed while in Green Ono long-term homeowners can sell their apartments to new residents and therefore the mixed community will not remain mixed. This suggests that the area is gentrifying and low-income households are being pushed out, supporting findings from other studies that consider social mix programs as State-led gentrification efforts in disguise (Davidson, 2008; Lees, 2008).

In Carlton, there were few strong ties between the two groups that make up the socially mixed community. Community members lead different lifestyles: private residents were comprised primarily of young professionals or students sharing an apartment, were working or studying full time and spending most of their days at work or university. When they leave and return, they usually enter their apartments through the main entrance or the car park and do not interact with other neighbors. In contrast, most public housing tenants in Australia are welfare recipients (including age and disability pensions) (Groenhart & Burke, 2014) and in 2006, only about 27% of the Carlton public housing estate participated in the workforce (Department of Human Services, 2009). Our interviewees from both groups noted they have nothing in common with the other, although most did not object to getting to know their neighbors (Arthurson et al., 2015). Some interviewees noted they wanted to use the communal garden and were disappointed not having access. There was no community development work encouraging social cohesion (Camina & Wood, 2009).

Although the socio-economic gap between the two major groups in Green Ono is less pronounced that it is in Carlton and the residents in Green Ono live in mixed buildings and not in separate buildings as in Carlton, we identified through our interviews only one social relationship between a young, new family and older, long-term homeowner. Most of the interviewees from the three groups felt they belonged to two separate groups, long-term or new, with different lifestyles and social statuses. Our interviews in Green Ono suggested that many of the long-term homeowners were single or couple empty nest households who had retired from the labor force (Kainer Persov, 2017). These findings support previous research finding little evidence of positive effects of mixed tenure on social interaction and cohesion (Bond et al., 2011; Joseph & Chaskin, 2010).

Improvements in stigma and empowerment of old communities

Both projects experienced a decrease in the stigma of the area due to regeneration (Kainer Persov, 2017; Ziersch et al., 2018). In Carlton, prior to regeneration, the public housing estate had been socially separated from the rest of the neighborhood by visible boundaries. The public housing walk-ups were very different from the neighboring houses and tenants reported in interviews that negative stigma was very strong. After regeneration, the new public and private buildings look almost identical and their architectural treatment is similar, except for the different number of stories. Tenants felt the stigma attached to the estate has decreased significantly. Some tenants even noted that visitors cannot tell they live in a public housing building (Levin et al., 2018).

Similarly, in Green Ono, the project has reduced the stigma that was attached to the old, rundown housing cluster. We found that 90% of the long-term interviewees believed that the stigma change was due to the arrival of new residents with higher socioeconomic status and not just a result of the physical changes and design of the new buildings. In addition, long-term residents received larger apartments in place of their smaller older apartments which improved their economic status and their social standing (Kainer Persov, 2017). These findings regarding improvements in stigma and public attitudes support previous studies that found social mix improved broader perceptions of neighborhood stigma, although Arthurson (2013) found that housing tenure stigma has persisted.

A major difference between the programs is that while the economic benefits for long-term residents in Green Ono have been profound, there were no major economic benefits for public housing tenants in Carlton. In Carlton, public housing tenants improved their living environment and possibly reduced their cost of living. They moved into newer and nicely designed apartments with better insulation and an environmental program to help them keep their electricity costs down. However, these apartments are publicly rented and are not owned by the tenants. In contrast, Green Ono long-term homeowners received, as part of the regeneration contract, an apartment double in size and triple in value. They could realize financial gain if they sold their apartments. This has been an empowering result for the generally low-income, long-term homeowners in Green Ono.

One of the main critiques toward the Victorian Government was that it sold public land to private developers to regenerate Carlton (Darcy, 2013; Kelly & Porter, 2019; Shaw, 2013). Although we were not able to access both in Australia and Israel financial data of government expenditures and private investments and gains, in both projects it seems that developers have benefited from the projects.

Discussion and conclusions

By comparing two different approaches of social mix and housing regeneration, we were able to identify some characteristics that contributed to different experiences in each of the programs (Posthumus & Lelévrier, 2013). Three issues were identified: the unintended consequence of mixed community; the link between physical outcomes and the resulting social mixing; and whether the program has benefited the disadvantaged group. We conclude with lessons that can be learned from this comparison, the limitations of this research and avenues for further research.

The unintended consequence of social mix

Both the Australian and Israeli programs did not explicitly describe social mix as part of their objectives when designing their respective regeneration processes. Although low-income communities lived on both sites prior to regeneration, the aims of both regeneration projects emphasized the physical improvement of the existing housing stock. Despite this, both programs resulted in mixed communities and gentrified neighborhoods that were comprised of a minority of long-term residents returning to the sites and larger numbers of new middle-income residents. There were some local variations: the Carlton program also aimed at integrating the site with the rest of the neighborhood while the Green Ono program aimed at increasing densities as part of a national plan. However, similar to findings reported from other international comparative studies (e.g., Costarelli et al., 2019; Rose et al., 2013), both projects reflect similar neoliberal governance trends which have led to limited government investment in housing in both countries over the past 30 years. As a result, housing regeneration programs relying heavily on private sector investment, such as the programs examined here, incorporate market-rate housing to meet the profit requirement of the private sector (Marom & Carmon, 2015; Rose et al., 2013).

According to Galster's (2013) framework of composition, concentration and scale, the two projects shared somewhat similar characteristics. The composition of the socially mixed community divided both case studies along an income measure, although in Carlton, tenure was most evident and less so in Green Ono, where age was more salient as a dividing factor. Although both programs did not explicitly aim to create social mix, they inevitably resulted in socially mixed communities. The scale of both projects was at the housing cluster level yet researchers argue that social mix is likely to be less effective at this level than at the neighborhood scale (Arthurson, 2010b; Jupp, 1999). Nonetheless, regeneration projects resulting in social mix in both Australia and Israel are undertaken at the housing cluster level because of the availability of public land in Australia (Pawson & Pinnegar, 2018) and the presence of dilapidated housing estates in Israel (Margalit & Alfasi, 2016).

The link between physical design and the resulting social mixing

Despite the omission of the term social mix from the two programs' objectives, both resulted in the actual physical mix of different social groups living side-by-side on each estate. While in Carlton public tenants and private residents live in separate buildings, in Green Ono the three groups live in the same buildings and share public spaces but are clustered by floor or segmented. Therefore, as suggested in the literature, their chance for social interaction with the other group is higher than that of the Carlton's community (Joseph & Chaskin, 2010; Kearns et al., 2013; Tiesdell, 2004). Nevertheless, in both estates the social groups who comprise the socially mixed communities do not meaningfully interact with one another. Although the Carlton estate community does not have any shared communal spaces for interaction, Green Ono residents can interact in public spaces in their buildings (lobbies, elevators, community rooms). However, interviewees reported that they are two separate groups that coexist but have little meaningful interaction. This suggests that the prospect of genuine social mix outcomes are limited even if the physical design allows for interaction and underscores the need for community building and intentional and ongoing efforts to create a cohesive community

(Bond et al., 2011; Camina & Wood, 2009; Joseph & Chaskin, 2010). Even where social mix may not be the explicit aim of a program, the mix of residents likely to occur as a result of the changes must be acknowledged, and comprehensive efforts made to ensure social cohesion.

Has social mix benefited the disadvantaged group?

A critical aspect that should be examined when assessing programs of social mix through housing regeneration is whether the program has benefited the disadvantaged group that lived in the area prior to regeneration (Arthurson, 2012). In our case studies, the two programs differ on this aspect. In both projects, residents from the preexisting communities who returned benefited from a revitalized living environment with better apartments and facilities. Nevertheless, in both projects some community residents did not fare as well. In Carlton, many public housing tenants did not return to the development because they were offered smaller apartments that did not meet their needs. In Green Ono, private renters were not part of the agreement and therefore were displaced at the beginning of the project. Although in Green Ono long-term homeowners received a new apartment and benefited financially, in both projects the preexisting community became a minority in the socially mixed community, and had no influence on the physical and social planning of the community (Chaskin et al., 2012).

An interesting similarity, despite the contextual differences of the two programs, was that while the stigma attached to the physical appearances of both places may have diminished with the construction of new housing and renewed landscape, the stigma attached to poverty remained. In this sense, the poverty of public housing tenants or low-income residents is constructed as a disadvantage in itself (Darcy, 2010).

What can be learned from comparing two vastly different social mix and housing programs?

The first lesson to be learned from this comparative exercise is that a community with a socially mixed composition can be the unintended outcome of housing regeneration programs of different kinds even if there is no explicit intention (or declaration) to create a socially mixed community. Despite major differences in the housing tenure of preexisting communities in the two case studies, the unintended outcome seems to be very similar—a physically mixed community in terms of its physical characteristics, made up of two/three social groups that live in close proximity but do not meaningfully interact with one another. This means that integration with the wider community, which was an objective in Carlton, might have been achieved physically but not socially. This resembles findings from other studies of socially mixed communities (Chaskin et al., 2012; Joseph, 2008), although researchers have noted that many urban residents may be satisfied with casual and flexible local relationships in their community (Chaskin & Joseph, 2011).

The second lesson is that in the neoliberal policy climate, despite differences in the management and implementation of the programs, both projects were structured in a way that gave a lot of power to the private sector. This power can be used to the detriment of the more disadvantaged group and increase their vulnerability (Ruming, 2018), such as the public housing tenants in Carlton who either returned to smaller units or did not return at all and displaced private, low-income renters in Green Ono.

Finally, there are positive aspects to be learned from both programs. The Carlton program handled relocation of public housing residents in a sensitive manner by addressing most tenants' requests at the onset as part of the regeneration contract but failed to do so during the return stage of the project. The Green Ono program empowered long-term homeowners by providing them financial stability (tripled their housing value). This aspect of engaging homeowners can be adopted in other countries if public housing stock becomes limited.

There are three important limitations to this study, which future research will need to address. The first is that the two programs of social mix operate in diverse housing systems, and as a result the specific programs are inherently different in their means of achieving social mix (rebuilding public and private housing in one while rebuilding mostly private housing in the other) and the resulting social mix they promote. Nevertheless, as shown we believe there are still important lessons to be learned from this comparison. The second is that the two case study samples on which the findings are drawn are relatively small and not representative of the communities, limiting our analyses to exploratory, suggestive findings. The third limitation is that the study was not designed as a comparative case study but as two separate studies, and therefore the methods were slightly different as well as the focus of interview questions. Despite this, the main areas of research in both studies were similar. Future research can design a comparative study that engages with some of the questions and others we raised from the design stage by exploring two or more programs of social mix through housing in different policy and institutional contexts.

This article highlights the importance of understanding the physical and social outcomes of housing regeneration programs resulting in socially mixed communities even if they do not initially intend to create such communities. It also emphasizes the benefits of international comparative research on housing regeneration programs that can highlight the significant impact of policy and contextual factors on social mix outcomes.

Note

1. Information received verbally from a Carlton Housing officer in 2011.

Acknowledgments

We would like to thank our participants in both studies for their generosity. We are also grateful to the reviewers for their insightful comments. The Australian work was supported by the Australian Research Council Grant LP100100526. Dr Nava Kainer Persov would like to thank Professor Naomi Carmon, her PhD supervisor.

Disclosure statement

No potential conflict of interest was reported by the author(s).

Funding

The Australian component of this work was supported by the Australian Research Council [LP100100526].

ORCID

Iris Levin http://orcid.org/0000-0002-5176-4903

References

Arthurson, K. (2010a). Questioning the rhetoric of social mix as a tool for planning social inclusion. *Urban Policy and Research*, 28(2), 225–231. https://doi.org/10.1080/08111141003693117
Arthurson, K. (2010b). Operationalising social mix: Spatial scale, lifestyle and stigma as mediating points in resident interaction. *Urban Policy and Research*, 28(1), 46–63. https://doi.org/10.1080/08111140903552696
Arthurson, K. (2012). *Social mix and the city: Challenging the mixed communities consensus in housing and urban planning policies*. CSIRO Publishing.
Arthurson, K. (2013). Mixed tenure communities and the effects on neighbourhood reputation and stigma: Residents' experiences from within. *Cities*, 35, 432–438. https://doi.org/10.1016/j.cities.2013.03.007
Arthurson, K., Levin, I., & Ziersch, A. (2015). Social mix, '[A] very, very good idea in a vacuum but you have to do it properly!' Exploring social mix in a right to the city framework. *International Journal of Housing Policy*, 15(4), 418–435. https://doi.org/10.1080/14616718.2015.1093748
Australian Bureau of Statistics. (2020). *2016 census QuickStats: Carlton*. https://quickstats.censusdata.abs.gov.au/census_services/getproduct/census/2016/quickstat/206041117?opendocument
Bolt, G., Phillips, D., & Van Kempen, R. (2010). Housing policy, (de)segregation and social mixing: An international perspective. *Housing Studies*, 25(2), 129–135. https://doi.org/10.1080/02673030903564838
Bolt, G., & Van Kempen, R. (2013). Introduction special issue: Mixing neighbourhoods: Success or failure? *Cities*, 35, 391–396. https://www.sciencedirect.com/science/article/abs/pii/S0264275113000474?via%3Dihub
Bond, L., Sautkina, E., & Kearns, A. (2011). Mixed messages about mixed tenure: Do reviews tell the real story? *Housing Studies*, 26(1), 69–94. https://doi.org/10.1080/02673037.2010.512752
Bridge, G., Butler, T., & Lees, L. (Eds.). (2012). *Mixed communities: Gentrification by stealth?* Policy Press.
Buil, I., De Chernatony, L., & Martínez, E. (2012). Methodological issues in cross-cultural research: An overview and recommendations. *Journal of Targeting, Measurement and Analysis for Marketing*, 20(3), 223–234. https://doi.org/10.1057/jt.2012.18
Camina, M. M., & Wood, M. J. (2009). Parallel lives: Towards a greater understanding of what mixed communities can offer. *Urban Studies*, 46(2), 459–480. https://doi.org/10.1177/0042098008099363
Central Bureau of Statistics. (2020). *Kiryat Ono 2018*. https://www.cbs.gov.il/he/publications/doclib/2020/local_authorities18_1797/308_2620.pdf
Chaskin, R., Khare, A., & Joseph, M. (2012). Participation, deliberation, and decision making: The dynamics of inclusion and exclusion in mixed-income developments. *Urban Affairs Review*, 48(6), 863–906. https://doi.org/10.1177/1078087412450151
Chaskin, R. J., & Joseph, M. L. (2011). Social interaction in mixed-income developments: Relational expectations and emerging reality. *Journal of Urban Affairs*, 33(2), 209–237. https://doi.org/10.1111/j.1467-9906.2010.00537.x
Costarelli, I., Kleinhans, R., & Mugnano, S. (2019). Reframing social mix in affordable housing initiatives in Italy and in the Netherlands. Closing the gap between discourses and practices? *Cities*, 90, 131–140. https://doi.org/10.1016/j.cities.2019.01.033
Darcy, M. (2010). De-concentration of disadvantage and mixed income housing: A critical discourse approach. *Housing, Theory and Society*, 27(1), 1–22. https://doi.org/10.1080/14036090902767516
Darcy, M. (2013). From high-rise projects to suburban estates: Public tenants and the globalised discourse of deconcentration. *Cities*, 35, 365–372. https://doi.org/10.1016/j.cities.2012.10.010
Davidson, M. (2008). Spoiled mixture: Where does state-led 'positive' gentrification end? *Urban Studies*, 45(12), 2385–2405. https://doi.org/10.1177/0042098008097105

Department of Human Services. (2009). *Carlton housing redevelopment—Report No 1 baseline survey*. Victorian Government.

Easthope, H., & Randolph, B. (2009). Governing the compact city: The challenges of apartment living in Sydney, Australia. *Housing Studies, 24*(2), 243-259. https://doi.org/10.1080/02673030802705433

Galster, C. G. (2013). Chapter 15: Neighborhood social mix: Theory, evidence, and implications for policy and planning. In N. Carmon & S. S. Fainstein (Eds.), *Policy, planning, and people: Promoting justice in urban development* (pp. 307-335). University of Pennsylvania Press.

Galster, G. C., & Friedrichs, J. (2015). The dialectic of neighborhood social mix: Editors' introduction to the special issue. *Housing Studies, 30*(2), 175-191. https://doi.org/10.1080/02673037.2015.1035926

Globes. (2012). *A successful example of demolition and regeneration in Kiryart Ono*. [Hebrew]. https://www.globes.co.il/news/article.aspx?did=1000010453

Goodchild, B., & Cole, I. (2001). Social balance and mixed neighbourhoods in Britain since 1979: A review of discourse and practice in social housing. *Environment and Planning D: Society and Space, 19*(1), 103-121. https://doi.org/10.1068/d39j

Groenhart, L., & Burke, T. (2014). What has happened to Australia's public housing? Thirty years of policy and outcomes, 1981 to 2011. *Australian Journal of Social Issues, 49*(2), 127-149. https://doi.org/10.1002/j.1839-4655.2014.tb00305.x

Hananel, R. (2017). From central to marginal: The trajectory of Israel's public-housing policy. *Urban Studies, 54*(11), 2432-2447. https://doi.org/10.1177/0042098016649323

Hashimshoni, T. (2003). *Green Ono local development plan No. 285A*. [Hebrew]. https://apps.land.gov.il/IturTabotData/takanonim/telmer/5004511.pdf

Joseph, M. L. (2008). Early resident experiences at a new mixed-income development in Chicago. *Journal of Urban Affairs, 30*(3), 229-257. https://doi.org/10.1111/j.1467-9906.2008.00394.x

Joseph, M. L., & Chaskin, R. J. (2010). Living in a mixed-income development: Resident perceptions of the benefits and disadvantages of two developments in Chicago. *Urban Studies, 47*(11), 2347-2366. https://doi.org/10.1177/0042098009357959

Jourdan, D., Van Zandt, S., & Tarlton, E. (2013). Coming home: Resident satisfaction regarding return to a revitalized HOPE VI community. *Cities, 35*, 439-444. https://doi.org/10.1016/j.cities.2013.03.006

Jupp, B. (1999). *Living together: Community life on mixed housing estates*. Demos.

Kainer Persov, N. (2008). *The meaning of home in a transition process: Constancy and change in dwelling during the process of urban regeneration in the way of 'Pinuy-Binuy'* [MSc thesis]. Faculty of Architecture and Town Planning, Technion - Israel Institute of Technology. [Hebrew].

Kainer Persov, N. (2017). *Housing regeneration strategies: Evaluation from a social equity point of view* [PhD dissertation]. Faculty of Architecture and Town Planning, Technion - Israel Institute of Technology. [Hebrew].

Kainer Persov, N., & Carmon, N. (2020). Circles of influence of urban regeneration: An evaluation of 'clearance & redevelopment' and its consequences, from a social point of view. *Planning - Journal of the Israel Association of Planners, 17*(1), 148-179. [Hebrew]. https://www.aepi.org.il/loadedFiles/907.pdf

Kearns, A., McKee, M. J., Sautkina, E., Cox, J., & Bond, L. (2013). How to mix? Spatial configurations, modes of production and resident perceptions of mixed tenure neighbourhoods. *Cities, 35*, 397-408. https://doi.org/http://dx.doi.org/10.1016/j.cities.2013.03.005

Kelly, D., & Porter, L. (2019). *Understanding the assumptions and impacts of the Victorian Public Housing Renewal Program. Final report of a research project with Cities of Moreland, Darebin and Yarra*. Melbourne: RMIT University Centre for Urban Research. https://cur.org.au/cms/wp-content/uploads/2019/05/understanding-the-assumptions-and-impacts-of-the-phrp-final-report-28-5-19.pdf

Kleinhans, R., & Varady, D. (2011). Moving out and going down? A review of recent evidence on negative spillover effects of housing restructuring programmes in the United States and the Netherlands. *International Journal of Housing Policy, 11*(2), 155-174. https://doi.org/10.1080/14616718.2011.573205

Lees, L. (2008). Gentrification and social mixing: Towards an inclusive urban renaissance? *Urban Studies, 45*(12), 2449-2470. https://doi.org/10.1177/0042098008097099

Levin, I., Arthurson, K., & Ziersch, A. (2014). Social mix and the role of design: Competing interests in the Carlton Public Housing Estate Redevelopment, Melbourne. *Cities, 40*, 23-31. https://doi.org/10.1016/j.cities.2014.04.002

Levin, I., Arthurson, K., & Ziersch, A. (2018). Experiences of tenants' relocation in the Carlton public housing estate redevelopment, Melbourne. *Urban Policy and Research, 36*(3), 354-366. https://doi.org/10.1080/08111146.2018.1502661

Margalit, T., & Alfasi, N. (2016). The undercurrents of entrepreneurial development: Impressions from a globalizing city. *Environment and Planning A: Economy and Space, 48*(10), 1967-1987. https://doi.org/10.1177/0308518X16651872

Marom, N., & Carmon, N. (2015). Affordable housing plans in London and New York: Between marketplace and social mix. *Housing Studies, 30*(7), 993-1015. https://doi.org/10.1080/02673037.2014.1000832

Martinus, K., & Hedgcock, D. (2015). The methodological challenge of cross-national qualitative research: Comparative case study interviews in Australia and Japan. *Qualitative Research Journal, 15*(3), 373–386. https://doi.org/10.1108/QRJ-07-2013-0046

Morris, A. (2019). 'Communicide': The destruction of a vibrant public housing community in inner Sydney through a forced displacement. *Journal of Sociology, 55*(2), 270–289. https://doi.org/10.1177/1440783318815307

Mullings, B. (1999). Insider or outsider, both or neither: Some dilemmas of interviewing in a cross-cultural setting. *Geoforum, 30*(4), 337–350. https://doi.org/10.1016/S0016-7185(99)00025-1

Newton, P., & Thomson, G. (2017). Urban regeneration in Australia. In P. Roberts, H. Sykes, & R. Granger (Eds.), *Urban regeneration* (pp. 2–25). SAGE Publications.

Orenstein, D. E., & Hamburg, S. P. (2009). To populate or preserve? Evolving political-demographic and environmental paradigms in Israeli land-use policy. *Land Use Policy, 26*(4), 984–1000. https://doi.org/10.1016/j.landusepol.2008.12.003

Padan, Y. (2014). *Social aspects in planning urban regeneration*. Bimkom - Planners for Planning Rights.

Parliament of Victoria. (2017). *Victoria's social housing supply requirements to 2036*. https://www.parliament.vic.gov.au/images/stories/committees/SCLSI/Public_Housing_Renewal_Program/QON/VPTA-QON-Victorias_social_housing_supply_reqs_to_2036.pdf

Pawson, H., & Pinnegar, S. (2018). Regenerating Australia's public housing estates. In K. Ruming (Ed.), *Urban regeneration in Australia: Policies, processes and projects of contemporary urban change* (pp. 311–332). Routledge.

Posthumus, H., & Lelévrier, C. (2013). How local contexts influence the neighbourhood satisfaction of displaced tenants in the Netherlands and France. *International Journal of Housing Policy, 13*(2), 134–158. https://doi.org/10.1080/14616718.2013.789751

Rose, D., Germain, A., Bacqué, M.-H., Bridge, G., Fijalkow, Y., & Slater, T. (2013). 'Social mix' and neighbourhood revitalization in a transatlantic perspective: Comparing local policy discourses and expectations in Paris (France), Bristol (UK) and Montréal (Canada). *International Journal of Urban and Regional Research, 37*(2), 430–450. https://doi.org/10.1111/j.1468-2427.2012.01127.x

Ruming, K. (2018). Urban regeneration and the Australian city. In K. Ruming (Ed.), *Urban regeneration in Australia: Policies, processes and projects of contemporary urban change* (pp. 1–23). Routledge.

Sarkissian, W. (1976). The idea of social mix in town planning: An historical review. *Urban Studies, 13*(3), 231–246. https://doi.org/10.1080/00420987620080521

Seixas, V. B., Smith, N., & Mitton, C. (2018). The qualitative descriptive approach in international comparative studies: Using online qualitative surveys. *International Journal of Health Policy and Management, 7*(9), 778–781. https://doi.org/10.15171/ijhpm.2017.142

Shaw, K. (2013, November 26-29). *Public housing estate redevelopments in Australian inner cities and the role of social mix* [paper presentation]. The 6th State of Australian Cities Conference, Sydney, Australia. http://www.soaconference.com.au/wp-content/uploads/2013/12/Shaw-Governance.pdf

Shaw, K., Raisbeck, P., Chaplin, C., & Hulse, K. (2013). *Evaluation of the Kensington redevelopment and place management models: Final report* (amended version). University of Melbourne.

Slater, T. (2006). The eviction of critical perspectives from gentrification research. *International Journal of Urban and Regional Research, 30*(4), 737–757. https://doi.org/10.1111/j.1468-2427.2006.00689.x

Slater, T. (2013). Your life chances affect where you live: A critique of the 'cottage industry' of neighbourhood effects research. *International Journal of Urban and Regional Research, 37*(2), 367–387. https://doi.org/10.1111/j.1468-2427.2013.01215.x

Stal, G. Y., & Zuberi, D. M. (2010). Ending the cycle of poverty through socio-economic integration: A comparison of Moving to Opportunity (MTO) in the United States and the Bijlmermeer Revival Project in the Netherlands. *Cities, 27*(1), 3–12. https://doi.org/10.1016/j.cities.2009.10.005

Tiesdell, S. (2004). Integrating affordable housing within market-rate developments: The design dimension. *Environment and Planning B: Planning and Design, 31*(2), 195–212. https://doi.org/10.1068/b2998

Vale, L. J., & Shamsuddin, S. (2017). All mixed up: Making sense of mixed-income housing developments. *Journal of the American Planning Association, 83*(1), 56–67. https://doi.org/10.1080/01944363.2016.1248475

Vesselinov, E., Lennon, M. C., & Le Goix, R. (2018). Is it all in the eye of the beholder? Benefits of living in mixed-income neighborhoods in New York and Los Angeles. *Journal of Urban Affairs, 40*(2), 163–185. https://doi.org/10.1080/07352166.2017.1343633

Watt, P. (2008). The only class in town? Gentrification and the middle-class colonization of the city and the urban imagination. *International Journal of Urban and Regional Research, 32*(1), 206–211. https://doi.org/10.1111/j.1468-2427.2008.00769.x

Wiesel, I., Freestone, R., & Randolph, B. (2013). Owner-driven suburban renewal: Motivations, risks and strategies in 'knockdown and rebuild' processes in Sydney, Australia. *Housing Studies, 28*(5), 701–719. https://doi.org/10.1080/02673037.2013.758243

Ziersch, A., Arthurson, K., & Levin, I. (2018). Support for tenure mix by residents local to the Carlton Housing Estate, Melbourne, Australia. *Housing Studies, 33*(1), 58–76. https://doi.org/10.1080/02673037.2017.1344201

Re-scaling social mix: Public housing renewal in Melbourne

Ruby Capp, Libby Porter, and David Kelly

ABSTRACT
Social mix is a widely used component of urban housing policy in post-welfare states. Problematizing homogenous areas of disadvantage, social mix policies purportedly aspire to increase socioeconomic diversity within defined areas. In Melbourne, Victoria, Australia, a major program of public housing renewal has been underway since the early 2000s, justified by a social mix agenda. This paper investigates the discursive and scalar mechanisms used to justify and advance this policy scheme. First, the paper examines the discursive framing of social mix, demonstrating how this conceals both the commercial real estate drivers and continued government withdrawal from public housing. We then quantify the social mix outcomes of redevelopment, showing that estate renewal actually decreases mix at the neighborhood scale. In the midst of a serious housing crisis in Melbourne, the paper questions the purported social goals of public housing estate renewal and contributes to ongoing debates about social mix and public housing.

Introduction

Despite its reputation as "an intrinsically vague, slippery term" (Galster, 2013, p. 308), social mix has become a widely deployed housing policy tool (Lees, 2008; Rose et al., 2013). Founded on the problematization of homogenous areas of poverty and disadvantage through the neighborhood effects thesis, social mix policies purportedly aspire to increase socioeconomic diversity within defined areas. Such policies are commonly advanced through urban renewal programs that target disadvantaged populations, in particular public housing estates. The underlying assumption is that public housing estates are ghettoes of disadvantage, and that by living in proximity to private owners and higher income earners public housing tenants will experience upward mobility. The policy fix breaks up existing communities seen as disadvantaged and intentionally introduces private tenures to housing estates to create more "mixed" communities. Despite an abundance of studies demonstrating that this approach is "largely unsupported by the research evidence" (Bricocoli & Cucca, 2014, p. 80; see also Atkinson, 2005, 2006), such policies continue to be advanced in cities around the world.

Melbourne, Australia is no exception to this trend, where social mix is central to public housing estate regeneration schemes. In Australia, social housing is an umbrella term that includes both public and community housing (Legal and Social Issues Committee [LSIC], 2018): public housing is exclusively owned and managed by the state; community housing is owned and/or managed by nonprofit non-government housing associations. The regeneration approach widely used in Australia adopts a public-private partnership model that not only sells the public land to fund the redevelopment (Arthurson et al., 2015) but also transfers low-income housing from the public sector to community housing organizations (CHOs). Public housing estate renewal has been underway in Melbourne since the early 2000s, piloted in two large redevelopments at Kensington (2001–2012) and Carlton (2006–present). Kensington and Carlton have paved the way for a more extensive social mix-led renewal strategy, the Victorian government's Public Housing Renewal Program (PHRP), which will redevelop 11 inner-city public housing estates with a mix of private and social housing. The official justification for the PHRP is characterized by two common discourses: that residents' homes and therefore lives are stigmatized and in a state of disrepair; and that the estates are ghettoes of disadvantage. Social mix is an explicit policy aim of the PHRP and achieving that mix involves the displacement of low-income residents and introduction of higher-income residents to each site (Kelly & Porter, 2019).

In this paper, we critically examine this renewal agenda and its potential consequences for actually delivering the social mix it purportedly seeks. We focus on four inner-Melbourne public housing estates: Kensington and Carlton as the precursors to the PHRP, and North Melbourne and Northcote, two of the first estates being redeveloped under the PHRP. We find that the policy rationale relies on mischievously deployed narratives that obscure decades of strategic disinvestment and quietly advance the displacement of low-income people from inner-city neighborhoods. This is achieved by situating the social mix aspiration to the site scale, rather than the more appropriate neighborhood scale, and by discursively framing public housing estates as derelict and dysfunctional, with social mix-led renewal as the necessary solution. To examine the social mix claims made by the policy program, we "step inside" the site-scale policy framing and model the extent to which the proposed renewal would actually achieve its purported aims if taken on its own terms. We find that redevelopment results in a weakening of diversity and social mix and intensifies the class restructuring of inner Melbourne.

In the next section, we critically examine the concept of social mix, its underlying assumptions and its deployment as a tool in housing policy around the world. We then provide an overview of the public housing context in Melbourne and Australia and the methods used. The findings and discussion are set out in two main sections: the first critically examines the discursive deployment of social mix, and the second measures the actual or likely social mix outcomes.

Social mix: Roots and contours of a problematic concept

Social mix is rooted in class warfare and ideals of the privileged (Sarkissian, 1976). Often presented as a utopian aspiration, born from the principle that neighborhoods should reflect the socioeconomic diversity of broader society (Ziersch et al., 2018), diversity is conceived either broadly, such as Galster and Friedrichs' (2015, p. 176) definition as "a combination of diverse shares of social groups in a neighborhood"; or in relation to specific sociodemographic indicators such as housing tenure, age, ethnicity, class and income (see Arthurson, 2010; Morris et al., 2012).

By facilitating mix, poor communities will, in theory, share in the resources of other more affluent groups, reducing class-based and racial anxiety. The idea was central to early colonial socio-spatial arrangements in Australia, although at the exclusion of Indigenous peoples, who were profoundly segregated and excluded using a raft of racist policy and regulatory tools.

Contemporary applications of social mix are grounded in the neighborhood effects thesis, which states that concentrations of disadvantage exacerbate negative social outcomes because such concentrations compound that disadvantage (Morris et al., 2012). Social mix is advanced as a policy fix to this problem (Galster & Friedrichs, 2015). Internationally, the idea of neighborhood effects has been repeatedly challenged (Manley et al., 2012; Tyler & Slater, 2018; Watt & Smets, 2017). Central to these critiques is concern at the moralizing agenda of "role modelling via propinquity ... as a means of changing the behavior of social housing residents" (Doney et al., 2013, p. 404) through a normalizing process whereby attitudes, actions, values and beliefs of middle-class people transfer via proximity. Such narratives assert that public housing residents might remedy their disadvantage by forming new relations to the social norms of more advantaged populations, thereby reconstituting systemic disadvantage as individual responsibility.

By locating different socioeconomic classes in closer proximity, proponents also argue that this creates the conditions for interaction between classes—also known as social mixing. Shaw et al. (2013, p. 79) define *social mixing* as "encounters that are more meaningful than simply passing in corridors." This kind of interaction is the mechanism by which positive neighborhood effects, such as increased employment opportunities and social capital, can be actualized (Groenhart, 2013; Kearns & Mason, 2007). Recent empirical research, however, observes social interactions between ethnically and economically diverse residents as being "limited to ... neither positive nor negative interactions" (Bektaş & Taşan-Kok, 2020, p. 1). While some research does demonstrate that positive intra-group interactions may reduce the level of stigma higher-income residents project onto social housing residents (Raynor et al., 2020), a refined focus on race and ethnicity within social mix scenarios directly questions whether social interaction can meaningfully unfold when the terrain of interaction is determined by dominant, whiter tenures (Mele, 2019; Ruiz-Tagle, 2016; Schuermans et al., 2016). Indeed, the framing of interaction, mixing and mix within the housing policy and research paradigm can reveal divergent, conflicting and complicit understandings of socio-spatial relations.

The inherent slipperiness in the concept of social mix that Galster (2013) identified is revealed in the different ways social mix comes to be applied. Tunstall and Fenton (2006) and Kleinhans (2004) illuminate three areas where this slippage in definition takes place: composition, concentration and scale. *Composition* concerns the characteristics of social groups that make up socially mixed populations. It implicitly refers to class or socioeconomic status through the specific metrics of income and tenure, though there is wide variation in application. Considerable debate in the literature exists about the extent to which crude categories such as tenure can adequately represent the diversity notionally sought through social mix. Nonetheless, tenure mix has become a primary policy tool for advancing social mix programs, as is the case in the PHRP, perhaps because it is one of the few levers available to operationalize social mix by deliberately bringing wealthier residents to low-income areas such as social housing estates. The mix of tenures is presumed to deliver a range of social goods including "inclusive" and "sustainable" communities (see Bricocoli & Cucca, 2014; Morris et al., 2012; Ziersch et al., 2018). However, research finds considerable ambiguity in the results of social mix and a complete absence of correlation between tenure mix and social outcomes in multiple public housing redevelopments in the U.S., UK and Europe (Arbaci, 2007; Graham et al., 2009), particularly the HOPE VI program in the U.S. which resulted in wide-scale resident displacement (Goetz, 2013) and the dilution of community organization (Tach, 2009).

Concentration refers to the ratio of social mix implemented; in other words, the proportion of different population groups in relation to each other. Morris et al. (2012) note that there is no consensus around an ideal ratio. The discursive operation of concentration, however, is always deployed as a means of deconcentrating disadvantage, marked as socio-economic status and often overtly targets ethnic and racial mix (Bolt et al., 2010). Social mix is fundamentally about deconcentration and is always explicitly concerned with dispersing poverty and notably never with deconcentrating affluence (see for example, Kearns & Mason, 2007). In addition, it disproportionately impacts racially targeted groups (Somerville & Steele, 2002).

Scale refers to the spatial boundaries for measurement of social mix. It is perhaps the most slippery in conceptualizing social mix, in part due to the ambiguity around sites and methods of evaluating where mix is achieved (Arthurson, 2010). Given that the roots of social mix lie in the neighborhood effects thesis, the neighborhood is surely an important scale at which to consider or measure the potential impacts of social mix policies (Galster & Friedrichs, 2015). The neighborhood is the scale that organizes and represents people's sense of place or belonging, the scale at which everyday life is largely lived, and the scale of local service delivery (Manley et al., 2012; Ruming et al., 2004). However, the neighborhood is itself a concept that defies singular definition (Kearns & Parkinson, 2001). Experiences of a neighborhood are radically diverse (see Ruming et al., 2004), and so its deployment as a term and scale of analysis deserves sustained critique. As Atkinson (2005) demonstrates, the factors mediating individual or household outcomes are extremely complex and cannot be reduced either to tenure status, or to the level of neighborhood social mix, given the wider structural issues at play.

We do not wish to advance a thesis that the neighborhood scale "solves" the social mix problem, for as we will demonstrate here, the framing of social mix is inherently problematic in itself. However, it is clear that the importance of neighborhoods in creating the conditions for social mixing would suggest it is a far more useful scale at which to consider and apply social mix than the individual site or building (see Costarello et al., 2019). Whilst projects may concentrate on the renewal of smaller sites, larger scales are preferred to evaluate social mix in the "wider tenure form pattern of the city, across different scales" (Wimark et al., 2020, p. 215). Indeed, a policy brief produced by the Australian Housing and Urban Research Institute (AHURI) titled *Public housing renewal and social mix* asserts that "The spatial scale for any consideration of social mix is the neighborhood (4,000–8,000 people), not small-scale public housing developments or individual apartment blocks" (AHURI, 2020, para. 11). Even at the lower end of 4,000 people, this definition is considerably larger in scale than the Northcote and North Melbourne estates, which contained 87 and 112 dwellings respectively.

Despite these slippery categories and little evidence that social mix achieves its stated objectives, the concept has been advanced through a range of diverse instruments including new build construction, inclusionary housing policies, de-ghettoization practices, ethnic quotas, and large-scale urban renewal, especially of social housing estates (see Bolt et al., 2010; Bridge et al., 2012; Holmqvist & Bergsten, 2009; Lupton & Fuller, 2009; Münch, 2009; Musterd & Ostendorf, 2008). Indeed, social mix policies have been shown to catalyze economic and social exclusion (Shaw & Hagemans, 2015) such that Groenhart (2013, p. 97) argues social mix is "gentrification rebranded as a public policy tool."

Social mix-led renewal in Australia

In the Australian context, social mix "is firmly implanted as an assumed policy fix for social exclusion" (Doney et al., 2013, p. 15), carrying the strong patronizing presumptions of aspiration and betterment from its policy forbears in UK housing policy and obscuring the structural logics that result in impoverished environments and poor services. As a nation of homeowners, bred from a violent settler-colonial structure that uses settler creation of private property to legitimize the perpetual dispossession of Indigenous lands, private property ownership is held as a pinnacle of social achievement. Public housing is a thoroughly residualized welfare-net form of housing that has always been stereotyped as disadvantaged (Ruming, 2015).

The policy orthodoxy this breeds is that proximity to poverty leads to the entrenchment of disadvantage over time. For example, Australia's primary housing governance instrument negotiated between the federal and state governments, the National Affordable Housing Agreement, states an aspiration to create "mixed communities that promote social and economic opportunities by reducing concentrations of disadvantage that exist in some social housing estates" (COAG, 2007, p. 7; as cited in Pawson & Pinnegar, 2018, p. 315). This policy document provides a national justification for the restructuring of urban neighborhoods identified as having a concentration of disadvantage by displacing existing residents to enable wealthier residents to take their place.

This replacement process is advanced through tenure restructuring via the "renewal" of public housing estates. The aspiration is that redeveloped estates will have a social-private tenure ratio of approximately 30:70. Examples include the Bonnyrigg, One Minto and Airds Bradbury estates in New South Wales (NSW) and the Carlton estate in Victoria. While this tenure mix ratio has been the default policy of many redevelopment agents in Australia, the formula lacks any strong basis in evidence (Pawson & Pinnegar, 2018, p. 317). Indeed, the evidence points to real estate viability as the key driver, where the 30:70 ratio secures the best rate of return for commercial investment (Kelly & Porter, 2019).

The Public Housing Renewal Program has arrived in the midst of a crisis in the public housing sector in Victoria (Victorian Auditor-General's Office [VAGO], 2017). Nationally, the social housing system "fails to decently and affordably accommodate people on low incomes or facing other forms of disadvantage," as a direct result of long-term underfunding and neglect from policy makers (Flanagan et al., 2019, p. 2). As a proportion of overall stock, public housing in Victoria has been declining since the early 1990s and is currently around 2.5% of stock. This is in part because public housing is being transferred, in title and/or management, to CHOs. CHO stock portfolios have been expanding year-on-year while the total amount of public housing in Victoria has declined (Productivity Commission, 2019). Meanwhile, the waitlist for low-income housing continues to grow unabated. Victoria has the worst-performing public housing sector nationally, prompting two audits since 2012 by the Victorian Auditor-General's Office (VAGO). The most recent audit found a lack of long-term vision and a strategy for public housing that is "disjointed, poorly communicated and lacking in a comprehensive understanding of asset performance" (VAGO, 2017, p. viii). To date, the Victorian public housing system still has no asset management strategy or ongoing property condition assessment framework and has an endemic restriction on the flow of information.

In response, redevelopment of public housing estates has become a policy mainstay. The Kensington Estate was the first mixed-tenure estate renewal in Victoria, with works commencing in 2002. It was completed in 2012 and piloted the model where public land is sold to a developer to fund the redevelopment (Shaw et al., 2013). The redevelopment resulted in 453 social housing dwellings and 497 private dwellings, with a social–private ratio of 48:52 (DHHS, 2018a, p. 39). Victoria's second major mixed-tenure renewal, and its largest public-private-partnership (PPP) redevelopment project to date, was the Carlton Estate Redevelopment Project. Commenced in 2009, this nine-stage project concluded in 2020, with most stages completed between 2011 and 2015 (DHHS, 2018b). Comprising three sites across Carlton, the project delivered 246 public and roughly 800 private units, resulting in a social-private housing ratio of approximately 24:76 (LSIC, 2018). While Kensington employed the "pepper-potting" approach, where different tenures are distributed within the same building, Carlton employs a "block-by-block" approach, where each building is comprised solely of one tenure.

The latest advancement of public housing renewal in Victoria is the Public Housing Renewal Program (PHRP). Targeting nine estates across inner and middle-suburban Melbourne (plus two more funded under a different scheme, making 11 in total), each estate will be decanted, demolished and rebuilt through a PPP approach with a mix of social and private dwellings (LSIC, 2018). In 2018, it was announced that estates Northcote, and North Melbourne would be in the first tranche for renewal with the announcement of a partnership between private developer MAB Corporation and CHO HousingFirst (VHHSBA, 2018). A key departure from the Kensington and Carlton model was that the newly constructed social housing will be owned and/or managed by a CHO rather than the state, meaning there will no longer be any public housing on the sites (LSIC, 2018). As of March 2021, all residents at these estates have been relocated and demolition is now complete.

Methodology

The research utilized a case study approach with both qualitative and quantitative methods to address different dimensions of social mix-led renewal. Our four case study sites are Kensington and Carlton—the two mixed-tenure renewal projects to have occurred in Melbourne prior to the PHRP—and Northcote and North Melbourne, the first estates set to be renewed through the PHRP (VHHSBA, 2019a, 2019b) (Figure 1). We position Kensington and Carlton as key policy piloting sites, and Northcote and North Melbourne as sites where renewal policy undergoes refinement. All four are inner-Melbourne public housing estates with a similar number of dwellings, renewed by the state government using a mixed-tenure PPP model providing a strong basis for comparison.

Social forces such as economic and institutional power shape patterns of language use (Johnston, 2017) and this has been shown to be consequential for the stigmatization of public tenants through housing policy in Australia (Ruming, 2015). Given that there is remarkably little evidence used to apply social mix concepts, much of the meaning and momentum of large-scale renewal projects is driven by how government frames the policy interventions.

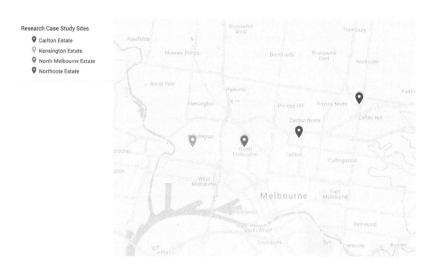

Figure 1. Case study sites.

We therefore used a discourse analysis to interrogate the corpus of policy documentation supporting and organizing estate renewal at these sites. A total of 19 documents were analyzed, including press releases, site master plans, community pamphlets, legislative reports, parliamentary debates and background feasibility studies commissioned by government. This comprised of three steps: firstly, key claims made by the government in relation to social mix were extracted and the assumption underpinning each claim identified. Claims were then compared to existing literature to determine whether they are grounded in any known evidence. Finally, we investigated patterns in language used to describe public housing tenants and the benefits of renewal or social mix, with a focus on mention of spatial scale. Our analysis sought to understand how the concept of social mix is operationalized in the PHRP, at what scale and with what evidence in support.

As discussed earlier, we are critical of the use of crude quantitative indicators, such as tenure, to drive social mix-led renewal. At the same time, there is little evaluation undertaken of the outcomes of estate renewal, with the exception of insightful qualitative evaluations (Arthurson, 2010; Hulse et al., 2004; Jama & Shaw, 2017; Shaw et al., 2013). Given the weight placed by policy proponents on achieving statistically articulated ratios of tenure mix, the lack of any evaluation based on these criteria is important to address. Therefore, for the second stage of our research we stepped "inside the frame" of the social mix agenda we have fully problematized and examine the outcomes on the terms set by the Victorian government.

Given that interaction between socioeconomic groups is contingent on socioeconomic diversity being present in the first place (Arthurson, 2010; Galster & Friedrichs, 2015; Jama & Shaw, 2017; Morris et al., 2012) we first analyzed the extent of socioeconomic diversity within each neighborhood to indicate whether such opportunity exists. We used the Australian Bureau of Statistics' Socio-Economic Index for Areas (SEIFA), which ranks the relative level of socioeconomic advantage and disadvantage of geographical areas. Using scores from the Index of Relative Socioeconomic Advantage and Disadvantage (IRSAD), which are derived from a range of variables (ABS, 2013), we created maps on the Australian Urban Research Infrastructure Network (AURIN) portal to visualize these sites, confirming each as islands of disadvantage in neighborhoods of relative affluence.

Noting evidence that social mix is best measured and implemented at the neighborhood scale (AHURI, 2020; Galster & Friedrichs, 2015), we compared site scale outcomes with neighborhood scale outcomes. To do so, we defined neighborhoods as a geographical urban area containing approximately 4,000 residents, following the methodology advanced in AHURI (2020), noting that this was key advice deployed in the justification of the PHRP. Neighborhoods were created by combining Statistical

Area Level 1s (SA1s), the smallest geo-statistical unit used in Australian census data with an average population of 400 (ABS, 2016), By working outward in spatially concentric rings around each case study estate, we systematically added SA1s until the total population reached between 4,000 and 5,000 people.

We then refined these boundaries by identifying the location of shops, parks, public transport and other essential services, as these are where social mixing between tenures is most likely to take place and are the geographical context that international evidence shows is where people experience their neighborhood in everyday life (Arthurson, 2010; Curley, 2010; Hulse et al., 2004; Ruming et al., 2004). Noting that what is included in any one neighborhood is always contested, our goal was not to conclusively define the "correct" neighborhood for each estate. Our neighborhoods are artificial, as are all neighborhoods derived in this manner. Rather, they present one conceivable boundary with a population size indicative of broadly accepted definitions of a neighborhood. This provides the necessary basis to apply the logic advanced by social mix proponents to examine the outcomes of the PHRP on its own terms. This is vitally important, given the claims in the PHRP that the program will "create more diverse communities" (VHHSBA, 2019a, 2019b) while "increasing tenure mix" (DHHS, 2018a, p. 33). To measure the social mix outcomes, we calculated tenure configurations for the four cases by combining census data with data in government planning documents and evaluation reports to examine the actual outcomes at Kensington and Carlton and the likely outcomes at Northcote and North Melbourne.

Our occupation with scale is relevant on a methodological level, but also speaks to applied policy terrains. The PHRP clearly targets defined public housing estate sites; the redevelopment is intensive and confined to the boundaries that define each estate. Yet the rationale offered in the policy discourse—that the estates embody concentrated disadvantage—is inherently relational and only applicable when broader scales, such as the neighborhood, are incorporated into an understanding of what diversity might mean. The next section unpacks this discourse to examine the framing of social conditions between public housing estates and their neighborhoods.

The discursive framing of social mix

> an opportunity to replace the isolated, segregated and inward-facing public housing estates of the past with mixed, inclusive communities that are home to public housing tenants, private renters and homeowners, and are integrated with their wider neighbourhood. (DHHS, 2018a, p. 6)

Public housing estates and residents in Australia, and around the world, are subjected to deep stigma. While there is significant evidence about how stigma "sticks" and with what effects (cf. Jacobs & Flanagan, 2013), our use of it here is to draw attention to the role of housing policy itself in the creation and sustenance of stigma. As Raynor et al. (2020) note "in Australia, social housing is largely viewed by the population *and policy makers* as a failed system" (p. 3 our emphasis).

Contributing to long-standing research about the construction of the housing "problem" through policy narratives, our analysis focused on the key claims and assumptions of the textual PHRP policy agenda. We uncovered a discursive framing of public housing estates as dysfunctional and "not fit for purpose" where estates are depicted as failing to connect with their surrounding neighborhoods and social issues are compounded by concentration of disadvantage. At the same time, social mix is depicted as an intrinsic public good that will deliver benefit to public housing residents by virtue of their proximity to greater affluence. This strong binary discourse of public housing estates as deviant and disconnected, and socially mixed neighborhoods as virtuous and beneficial runs throughout the PHRP agenda.

Our interrogation of key claims and assumptions revealed four discursive claims that drive this binary narrative: that current estates are isolated therefore social mix will deliver integration; that social mix can be designed in; that mix is required to deliver economic return; and that renewal delivers an uplift in social dwellings. Our analysis found that these claims are not supported by any apparent evidence. In the government's response to a parliamentary inquiry into the PHRP, which stands as a significant defense of the renewal policy, only one source is cited to justify the site-specific social mix model: the AHURI policy brief, published after the PHRP was developed, titled *Public housing renewal and social mix*, which contradicts the PHRP model by stating that "the spatial allocation of social, affordable and private housing should be considered at the neighborhood scale'[1] (AHURI, 2017 [updated in 2020]). In turn, the AHURI policy brief cites only one scholarly study to advance the neighborhood effects thesis: Galster and Friedrichs (2015, p. 183), who state that disadvantaged households are 'harmed by the presence of sizeable disadvantaged groups concentrated in their neighbourhoods.' As discussed earlier, place-based disadvantage on the scale that Galster and Friedrichs" work examines is not present in the Victorian PHRP context. The estates here are small islands of poverty in otherwise affluent, well-serviced neighborhoods. The AHURI policy brief acknowledges that "the international research literature is difficult to interpret or transpose to the Australian context," yet advances it anyway in support of the social mix agenda. In other words, evidence from a context already specified as not applicable to the local circumstances is used, swiftly followed by a claim that contradicts the very policy model being deployed. In a completely circular move, the AHURI brief references the PHRP as a best practice case of social mix in Australia, and PHRP documentation references the AHURI brief as the justification for a social mix approach.

Interaction and integration

Our analysis of key terminology in government documents found that a pejorative discourse about existing public housing estates was promulgated. Public housing estates were framed as neglected and isolated while mixed-tenure estates were framed positively, emphasizing interconnectedness and diversity. The renewal process itself was framed as the driver of this integration; for example, the government's submission to the parliamentary inquiry into the PHRP stated that the program delivers "integrated mixed tenure communities, rather than homogenous estates of public housing alone" (Victorian Government, 2019, p. 16). When discussing renewed estates, the terms *integrated* or *integration* were by far the most common, along with *diverse* and *inclusive*. Synonymous terms such as *unified, connected,* and *welcoming* were used to describe post-renewal outcomes. These terms present the public-private renewal model in a positive light, inviting thoughts of a happy, interconnected community where public and private residents socialize in harmony, a common urban renewal discursive tactic. Across all 19 documents analyzed, no adjectives with negative connotations were used to describe the mixed-tenure estate model. This depiction is juxtaposed against the description of estates pre-renewal: *segregated, inward-facing,* and *rundown*. These adjectives reinforce stereotypes of dysfunction and feed the justification for renewal. The only positive reference made to pre-renewal sites was their proximity to neighborhood shops, services and public transit.

Tenants themselves were also depicted in stereotypically negative terms. Numerous claims were made about tenants being isolated and segregated from their wider communities, justifying the policy fix of "integration." This includes the government's stance that the PHRP is anticipated to result in: estates being "integrated with their wider neighbourhood" (DHHS, 2018a, p. 6); helping "to combat ... the separation of public housing estates and tenants from the surrounding community that they are a part of" (DHHS, 2018a, p. 16); and "encouraging a greater social mix in our communities to ensure that we don't end up with pockets of isolation" (then Victorian Housing Minister Martin Foley, as cited in Preiss, 2017). These assumptions are not derived from empirical evidence. At Kensington, Shaw et al. (2013, p. 84) found that "the existing diverse population share a sense of belonging and commitment to their community." This aligns with international research that demonstrates how policy rationales are largely incongruent with the perceptions of residents (Lucio et al., 2014).

Renewal is also advanced as necessary for better integration between social and private tenants through claims such as: the PHRP "will introduce a social-private housing mix for each Site to foster an integrated community" (VHHSBA, 2017, p. 12) and will create "mixed, inclusive communities" (DHHS, 2018a, p. 6) or "more diverse communities" (VHHSBA, 2019a, 2019b). This claim is in fact countered by the literature, which finds that social mix does not necessarily lead to mixing (Arthurson et al., 2015; Galster & Friedrichs, 2015; Jama & Shaw, 2017; Morris et al., 2012) and that interaction occurs at the neighborhood scale, not onsite (Barwick, 2018). This is reflected at Kensington post-renewal, where "there is little evidence... of social mixing between the different tenure groups" (Shaw et al., 2013, p. 12) and the movements of tenures at Carlton likened to "tectonic plates" (Jama & Shaw, 2017, p. 22).

Economic return and social trade-offs
The PHRP model is often framed in explicitly economic terms, suggesting that a strong driver of the social model is in fact economic return. In the PHRP Registration of Capability for Stage One documentation, the fifth policy objective is to "achieve 'value for money' by maximising the return from the sale of private dwellings and commercial developments" (VHHSBA, 2017, p. 10). This was a driving concern as stated by the government in their submission to the parliamentary inquiry (DHHS, 2018a) whereby "mixed communities also enable the government to obtain a return from the sale of private dwellings" (p. 6).

Economic return is also used as justification by the government in its response to the final report of the parliamentary inquiry. Here it is stated that "the final public-to-private housing ratio is determined by a number of factors including... negotiated outcomes with development partners" (p. 31). Within this response, there is no reference to social justifications for social mix and tenure ratios. This is not surprising given that the social rationales for social mix are often relegated during periods of economic uncertainty. During the global financial crisis in 2008, amendments were made to tenure mix ratios for Kensington and Carlton redevelopments to ensure financial return to the developer. Design features to facilitate social mix were reevaluated, resulting in segregated tenures, recreation and community spaces, different entrances and exits according to tenure (Levin et al., 2014) and a reduction in unit size resulting in fewer children who are catalysts for social encounter (Shaw et al., 2013). In the draft masterplans of Northcote and North Melbourne, there is also a segregation of tenures. This is particularly prominent at the Walker Street estate (see https://merrinorthcote.com.au/homes/), where social housing tenants will be clustered at the north-eastern corner of the site and closer to the busy street while the buildings with creek views are allocated to private housing. Given that waterside apartments are typically considered more desirable to tenants, it can be inferred that the layout of tenures is a result of real estate profitability rather than a desire to foster social integration.

Overall, we found that discourse was at times employed misleadingly to suggest that renewal was intrinsically good, as a triple bottom-line strategy to improve lives, urban esthetics and financial balance-sheets. For example, in their submission to a parliamentary inquiry, the government stated that Stage One of the PHRP is "expected to deliver 1,750 new public housing dwellings across the nine Melbourne sites it is funding (including an increase of 10% from existing levels)" (p. 25). The leading figure of 1,750 obscures the fact that as 1646 units will be demolished, the net increase will be only 104 units.

Further, the government (DHHS, 2018a, p. 42) state that the program "aims to maintain and sustainably increase public housing in inner city locations rather than displacing it." This statement appears to be misleading, given that the public housing at both sites will in fact be lost and replaced with social housing operated by a CHO. While "social" housing will not be displaced, people have been. The PHRP involves direct displacement where residents are required to relocate in order for their homes to be demolished. Any right to return to renewed estates cannot change the status of these residents as displacees and the impacts of their displacement. Further, social housing, while not displaced entirely, will be diluted due to the number of private dwellings that will be added to the site and neighborhood.

Measuring apparent and anticipated outcomes of renewal

To test this framing, we now step "inside the frame" advanced by social mix proponents to examine the actual or likely outcomes. To understand the existing social diversity in the terms cast by the renewal program of disadvantaged estates, we used secondary data to map the case study sites according to the Index of Relative Socio-economic Advantage and Disadvantage (IRSAD), which is a measure within SEIFA. Figures 2–5 demonstrate a significant spatial contrast of socioeconomic advantage and disadvantage between estates and their immediate surrounds and support the contention that Melbourne's inner-city public housing estates are islands of disadvantage located within affluent suburbs.

At Kensington (Figure 2) and Carlton (Figure 3), indicators of relative disadvantage on the estate are rated as mostly decile 1, despite their mixed-tenure renewals having been mostly completed at the 2016 census. Accordingly, when examining the distribution of relative advantage and disadvantage across the four maps, Kensington and Carlton are relatively disadvantaged compared to Northcote (Figure 4) and North Melbourne (Figure 5), where indexes tend toward upper deciles.

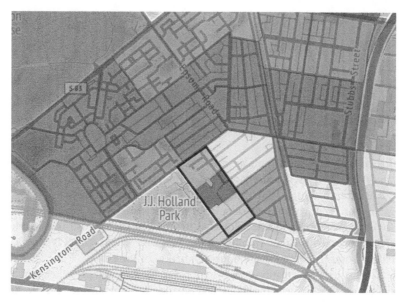

Figure 2. Kensington Estate IRSAD Maps – Post-renewal.

Figure 3. Carlton Estate IRSAD Maps – Post-renewal.

Figure 4. Northcote Estate IRSAD Maps – Pre-renewal Legend to maps.
Source: ABS (2016). Accessed using AURIN Portal (portal.aurin.org.au).[2]

The level of socioeconomic disadvantage of Melbourne's public housing tenants is confirmed in Map 3, where an SA1 is comprised entirely of the Carlton estate. The dark red shading indicates that the estate's residents are within the 10% of most disadvantaged across Australia.

The findings of our tenure mix data calculations are displayed in Table 1. The social-private housing ratio for each neighborhood was calculated by dividing the number of social housing dwellings in each neighborhood by the total number of dwellings for which tenure type was available. The remaining dwellings comprised the private housing portion of the ratio.

Table 1 depicts a post-renewal situation at Kensington and Carlton, and pre-renewal in both Northcote and North Melbourne. All four neighborhoods demonstrate a dominance of private housing tenure, particularly in Northcote and North Melbourne where the ratio is 11:89 social-private tenure. Considering

Figure 5. North Melbourne Estate IRSAD Maps − Pre-renewal Legend to maps.
Source: ABS (2016). Accessed using AURIN Portal (portal.aurin.org.au).[2]

Table 1. Tenure mix calculations, neighborhood scale, 2016.

	Kensington (post-renewal)	Carlton (post-renewal)	Northcote (pre-renewal)	North Melbourne (pre-renewal)
Number of SA1s constituting a neighborhood	8	11	10	9
Number of residents	4017	5829	4266	5075
Number of dwellings	2082	2978	2027	2603
With tenure type data available[4]	1706	2254	1656	2084
Social-private housing ratio	**21:79**	**34:66**	**11:89**	**11:89**

Source: ABS (2016). Compiled using ABS TableBuilder.

that social mix policy justifications target concentrations of disadvantaged tenure types, a neighborhood comprising 89% private housing does not present a compelling need for introducing more private housing. In Northcote and North Melbourne, social housing units would need to be added to achieve greater mix, rather than the current proposal to dilute public housing estates with private housing. Indeed, the public housing estates themselves provide the bulk of the tenure and social class diversity in these uniformly affluent neighborhoods. This counters the government's claim that the estates are a "concentration of sizeable disadvantaged groups in one location or neighbourhood."

The situated geography of all four estates within well-serviced inner-city neighborhoods suggests that opportunities for mixing within the wider community are present, both in pre- and post-renewal scenarios. Mixing between diverse groups is most likely to occur in shared public or community spaces, and less likely within precincts solely dedicated to residential uses (Barwick, 2018). Shops, parks, and other community facilities are typical urban spaces where strangers comingle and interact. Our descriptive statistical analysis demonstrates that in addition to the conditions that enable social *mixing*, such as shared public spaces, the tenure or socioeconomic diversity that provides the necessary precondition for any possible mixing is already present at the neighborhood scale in all four cases.

Table 2 compares tenure mix at the neighborhood and site scale, with the figures for Northcote and North Melbourne based on the proposals for redevelopment at each site (LSIC, 2018). The calculated neighborhood social mix ratios are vastly different to their site-specific counterparts, with the dominant form of housing flipped from social housing to private. At the site scale, the social-private ratios post-renewal will exceed the normative 30:70 so widely deployed in estate regeneration projects.

Table 2. Tenure mix comparison, neighborhood and site scales, 2016.

	Kensington	Carlton	Northcote *(proposed)*	North Melbourne *(proposed)*
Neighborhood scale social-private housing ratio	21:79	34:66	11:89	11:89
Site scale social-private housing ratio	48:52	24:76	43:57	37:63

However, this apparent gain is diminished when evaluated at the neighborhood scale, and with recognition that all of the public housing on these sites is lost through transfer to CHOs. The data suggests that the PHRP seeks to replicate the neighborhood-scale mix at the site scale.

Further, this calculation does not account for future uplift in private tenures over the 7 years that the government estimates redevelopment will take. These are areas of intensive large-scale apartment construction; residential development is forecast to increase private dwelling numbers in Northcote by around 1,239 dwellings, and 3,675 in North Melbourne (.id, 2019a, 2019b). This will further dilute the tenure mix composition in favor of private housing, resulting in a more homogenous neighborhood. These findings dispel key government claims about the creation of diverse communities.

Recent changes to allocation models for social housing are likely to further decrease social mix in the PHRP neighborhoods. Generally, almost all applicants that are successfully allocated public housing are drawn from the priority access portion of the waitlist.[3] Under recently designed arrangements, in new social housing units managed by a CHO only 75% must be allocated to people with priority needs. Given that all the new social housing on renewal sites will be managed by CHOs, at best only 75% of new dwellings will house priority applicants, compared to 100% if that housing remained public.

Further, CHOs are not compelled to allocate their 75% of units to priority access applicants on a site-by-site basis. Rather, that proportion is calculated across all of their properties, as confirmed by a 2017 update in the Victorian Housing Register (VHR):

> So long as a participating registered agency meets the policy objective of allocating the target number of Priority Access Group households in any given year, in principle it should not matter to which houses they are actually allocated. (VHR, 2017)

This means that any one PHRP site may plausibly house zero social housing residents from the priority access list.

CHOs have discretion to select tenants for properties who meet their organization's eligibility criteria. Eligibility can vary, but each CHO is required to provide their dwellings at a maximum of 74.9% of market rates, or risk losing their exemption from paying Goods and Services Tax. CHOs typically charge 30% household income in rent, widely recognized as the point at which housing stress starts. By contrast, public housing rental is set at 25% of household income. Simply put, the new allocation mechanisms, combined with the transfer of public housing to CHOs, will significantly shift the social make-up and tenancy profile. Thus, the public housing renewal agenda in Victoria should be understood as a reorganization of the geography of advantage and disadvantage across Melbourne, deepening a wholesale class restructuring of the inner-city.

Conclusion

This paper has examined the use of social mix as a policy rationale for public housing renewal in Melbourne, Australia. By interrogating the discursive framework used to advance the social mix rationale we found that public housing renewal in Victoria is principally motivated by economic viability rather than positive social outcomes. High-value inner-city public land is being sold and existing public housing stock transferred to non-government CHOs. The ratio of 30:70 has no basis other than real estate feasibility and commercial interests drive redevelopment designs. Social mix is deployed in a misleading way to conceal this privatization and the broader abandonment of government from its role in public housing. The discursive framing entrenches stereotypes about public housing estates and obscures government's long-term disinvestment from public housing.

Our quantitative analysis "stepped inside" this problematic social mix framing to model the actual outcomes of the stated policy intent. Our analysis shows that the claim that public housing renewal results in greater social mix is false. Indeed, social mix outcomes are worsened because renewal actually dilutes socioeconomic diversity. When public housing estates are viewed as vital components of dynamic, functioning neighborhoods, their "renewal" in the terms advanced through such policy frameworks will result in outcomes that directly contradict the purported intent. We have problematized social mix as a concept and policy discourse, but accepted the terms of the black letter policy for the purpose of examination in this paper. It is said in policy documentation and research that neighborhood scale is what matters, so we adopted this scale and stepped inside. Our findings demonstrate that when re-tested at the neighborhood scale, the PHRP's social mix approach fails to bring about more diverse communities or deconcentrate disadvantage. At site scale, the approach simply introduces middle-class tenures already dominant in the wider neighborhood, creating a homogenizing effect. At the scale of individual buildings, we see a concentration of disadvantage with residents segregated by tenure and real estate potential. At every scale, social mix dilutes, displaces and segregates socioeconomic difference. This analysis gives new weight to the current debates about social mix policies and their use in justifying the privatization of public housing and the further marginalization of precariously housed populations. By drawing attention to the question of scale in regard to social mix outcomes, the paper contributes valuable insight into how policymakers deploy research evidence to support policy dogmas. Social mix outcomes are rarely, if ever, assessed on the terms on which they are being advanced. We agree that crude categorizations of mix based on tenure are insufficient; yet they are the grounds on which substantial policy interventions are being made. These claims go largely un-evaluated. While our approach has limitations, the results suggest far greater attention needs to be given to the actual neighborhood structure that results, evidence that should be used to hold policymakers and governments to account in their deployment of such rationales.

Situated in a wider context of housing precarity and injustice, our analysis demonstrates that the rationale of social mix, deployed through estate renewal alongside other shifts in the provision and allocation of social housing, has the dual purpose of advancing state disinvestment from public housing and expanding private control of land and housing. The result is a deepening of the restructuring of housing advantage and disadvantage across inner and outer Melbourne.

Notes

1. The policy brief has since been updated (refer AHURI, 2020), and even more clearly advocates for social mix at the neighborhood scale.
2. Index scores are aggregated by deciles: in red, decile 1 represents statistical geographies within the 10% most disadvantaged relative to the rest of the Australian population, while decile 10, depicted in dark green, represents the 10% most advantaged. Boundaries of the housing estates are delineated in black.
3. Priority Access is for people who are: homeless and receiving support; escaping or have escaped family violence; have a disability or significant support needs; have special housing needs (Housing Victoria, 2020).
4. Tenure type data is not available for every dwelling as not all households completed the census.

Disclosure statement

No potential conflict of interest was reported by the author(s).

ORCID

Libby Porter http://orcid.org/0000-0001-7240-8206
David Kelly http://orcid.org/0000-0002-0285-2739

References

ABS. (2013). *IRSAD*. Retrieved May 28, 2019, from https://www.abs.gov.au/ausstats/abs@.nsf/Lookup/2033.0.55.001main+features100042011

ABS. (2016). *Statistical Area Level 1 (SA1)*. Retrieved May 17, 2019, from https://www.abs.gov.au/ausstats/abs@.nsf/Lookup/by%20Subject/1270.0.55.001~July%202016~Main%20Features~Statistical%20Area%20Level%201%20(SA1)~10013

Arbaci, S. (2007). Ethnic segregation, housing systems and welfare regimes in Europe. *European Journal of Housing Policy*, 7(4), 401–433. https://doi.org/10.1080/14616710701650443

Arthurson, K. (2010). Operationalising social mix: Spatial scale, lifestyle and stigma as mediating points in resident interaction. *Urban Policy and Research*, 28(1), 49–63. https://doi.org/10.1080/08111140903552696

Arthurson, K., Levin, I., & Ziersch, A. (2015). What is the meaning of 'Social Mix'? Shifting perspectives in planning and implementing public housing estate redevelopment. *Australian Geographer*, 46(4), 491–505. https://doi.org/10.1080/00049182.2015.1075270

Atkinson, R. (2005). *Occasional Paper 1: Neighbourhoods and the impacts of social mix: Crime, tenure diversification and assisted mobility*. University of Tasmania.

Atkinson, R. (2006). Padding the bunker: Strategies of middle class disaffiliation and colonisation in the city. *Urban Studies*, 43(4), 819–832. https://doi.org/10.1080/00420980600597806

Australian Housing and Urban Research Institute. (2017). *Public housing renewal and social mix: Policy brief*. At time of publishing, text has been superseded – refer to AHURI, 2020. Retrieved April 24, 2019, from https://www.ahuri.edu.au/policy/ahuri-briefs/public-housing-renewal-and-social-mix

Australian Housing and Urban Research Institute. (2020). *Public housing renewal and social mix: Policy brief*. Retrieved August 30, 2020, from https://www.ahuri.edu.au/policy/ahuri-briefs/public-housing-renewal-and-social-mix

Barwick, C. (2018). Social mix revisited: Within- and across-neighborhood ties between ethnic minorities of differing socioeconomic backgrounds. *Urban Geography*, 39(6), 916–934. https://doi.org/10.1080/02723638.2017.1405690

Bektaş, Y., & Taşan-Kok, T. (2020). Love thy neighbor? Remnants of the social-mix policy in the Kolenkit neighborhood, Amsterdam. *Journal of Housing and the Built Environment*, 35(4), 743–761. https://doi.org/10.1007/s10901-020-09729-5

Bolt, G., Phillips, D., & Van Kempen, R. (2010). Housing policy, (de)segregation and social mixing: An international perspective. *Housing Studies*, 25(2), 129–135. https://doi.org/10.1080/02673030903564838

Bricocoli, M., & Cucca, R. (2014). Social mix and housing policy: Local effects of a misleading rhetoric. The case of Milan. *Urban Studies*, 53(1), 77–91. https://doi.org/10.1177/0042098014560499

Bridge, G., Butler, T., & Lees, L. (2012). *Mixed communities: Gentrification by stealth?* Policy Press.

Costarello, I., Kleinhans, R., & Mugnano, S. (2019). Reframing social mix in affordable housing initiatives in Italy and in the Netherlands. Closing the gap between discourses and practices? *Cities*, 90(1), 131–140. https://doi.org/10.1016/j.cities.2019.01.033

Curley, A. M. (2010). Relocating the poor: Social capital and neighbourhood resources. *Journal of Urban Affairs*, 32(1), 79–103. https://doi.org/10.1111/j.1467-9906.2009.00475.x

DHHS. (2018a). *Submission to the Legal and Social Issues Committee inquiry into the Public Housing Renewal Program*. Victorian Government.

DHHS. (2018b). *Carlton estate housing redevelopment progress update*. Victorian Government.

Doney, R. H., McGuirk, P. M., & Mee, K. J. (2013). Social mix and the problematisation of social housing. *Australian Geographer*, 44(4), 401–418. https://doi.org/10.1080/00049182.2013.852500

Flanagan, K., Martin, C., Jacobs, K., & Lawson, J. (2019). *A conceptual analysis of social housing as infrastructure* (AHURI Final Report No. 309). Australian Housing and Urban Research Institute Limited.

Galster, G. (2013). Neighborhood social mix: Theory, evidence, and implications for policy and planning. In N. Carmon & S. S. Fainstein (Eds.), *Policy, planning, and people: Promoting justice in urban development* (pp. 307–336).

Galster, G., & Friedrichs, J. (2015). The dialectic of neighborhood social mix: Editors' introduction to the special issue. *Housing Studies, 30*(2), 175–191. https://doi.org/10.1080/02673037.2015.1035926

Goetz, E. (2013). *New Deal ruins: Race, economic justice and public housing policy*. Cornell University Press.

Graham, E., Manley, D., Hiscock, R., Boyle, P., & Doherty, J. (2009). Mixing housing tenures: Is it good for social well-being? *Urban Studies, 46*(1), 139–165. https://doi.org/10.1177/0042098008098640

Groenhart, L. E. (2013). Evaluating tenure mix interventions: A case study from Sydney, Australia. *Housing Studies, 28*(1), 95–115. https://doi.org/10.1080/02673037.2013.729268

Holmqvist, E., & Bergsten, Z. (2009). Swedish social mix policy: A general policy without an explicit ethnic focus. *Journal of Housing and the Built Environment, 24*(4), 477–490. https://doi.org/10.1007/s10901-009-9162-0

Housing Victoria. (2020), *Victorian housing register*. Retrieved September 4, 2020, from https://www.housing.vic.gov.au/victorian-housing-register

Hulse, K., Herbert, T., & Down, K. (2004). *Kensington estate redevelopment social impact study*. Swinburne University of Technology Institute for Social Research.

.id. (2019a). *City of Darebin: Residential development*. Retrieved August 30, 2020, from https://forecast.id.com.au/darebin/residential-development

.id. (2019b). *City of Melbourne: Residential development*. Retrieved August 30, 2020, from https://forecast.id.com.au/melbourne/residential-development

Jacobs, K., & Flanagan, K. (2013). Public housing and the politics of stigma. *Australian Journal of Social Issues, 48*(3), 319–337. https://doi.org/10.1002/j.1839-4655.2013.tb00285.x

Jama, A., & Shaw, K. (2017). *Why do we need social mix?* Retrieved March 15, 2020, from https://www.smh.com.au/cqstatic/gwsjcu/JamaAndShawReport.pdf

Johnston, B. (2017). *Discourse analysis* (3rd ed.). Wiley.

Kearns, A., & Mason, P. (2007). Mixed tenure communities and neighbourhood quality. *Housing Studies, 22*(5), 661–691. https://doi.org/10.1080/02673030701474628

Kearns, A., & Parkinson, M. (2001). The significance of neighbourhood. *Urban Studies, 38*(12), 2103–2110. https://doi.org/10.1080/00420980120087063

Kelly, D., & Porter, L. (2019). *Understanding the assumptions and impacts of the Public Housing Renewal Program, Centre for Urban Research*. RMIT University.

Kleinhans, R. (2004). Social implications of housing diversification in urban renewal: A review of recent literature. *Journal of Housing & Built Environment, 19*(1), 367–390. https://doi.org/10.1007/s10901-004-3041-5

Lees, L. (2008). Gentrification and social mixing: Towards an inclusive urban renaissance? *Urban Studies, 45*(12), 2449–2470. https://doi.org/10.1177/0042098008097099

Legal and Social Issues Committee. (2018). *Inquiry into the Public Housing Renewal Program*. Victorian Government Printer.

Levin, I., Arthurson, K., & Ziersch, A. (2014). Social mix and the role of design: Competing interests in the Carlton Public Housing Estate Redevelopment, Melbourne, Cities. *The International Journal of Urban Policy and Planning, 40*(1), 23–31. https://doi.org/10.1016/j.cities.2014.04.002

Lucio, J., Hand, L., & Marsiglia, F. (2014). Designing hope: Rationales of mixed-income housing policy. *Journal of Urban Affairs, 36*(5), 891–904. https://doi.org/10.1111/juaf.12090

Lupton, R., & Fuller, C. (2009). Mixed communities: A new approach to spatially concentrated poverty in England. *International Journal of Urban and Regional Research, 33*(1), 1014–1028. https://doi.org/10.1111/j.1468-2427.2009.00904.x

Manley, D. J., Van Ham, M., & Doherty, J. (2012). Social mixing as a cure for negative neighbourhood effects: Evidence based policy or urban myth? In G. Bridge, T. Butler, & L. Lees (Eds.), *Mixed communities: Gentrification by stealth?* (pp. 51–168). Policy Press.

Mele, C. (2019). The strategic uses of race to legitimize 'social mix' urban redevelopment. *Social Identities, 25*(1), 27–40. https://doi.org/10.1080/13504630.2017.1418603

Merri (n.d.), Merri Northcote Homes. https://merrinorthcote.com.au/homes/

Morris, A., Jamieson, M., & Patunly, R. (2012). Is social mixing of tenures a solution for public housing estates? *Evidence Base, 1*(1), 1–20. https://doi.org/10.21307/eb-2012-001

Münch, S. (2009). 'It's all in the mix': Constructing ethnic segregation as a social problem in Germany. *Journal of Housing and the Built Environment, 24*(1), 441–455. https://doi.org/10.1007/s10901-009-9160-2

Musterd, S., & Ostendorf, W. (2008). Integrated urban renewal in The Netherlands: A critical appraisal. *Urban Research & Practice, 1*(1), 78–92. https://doi.org/10.1080/17535060701795389

Pawson, H., & Pinnegar, S. (2018). Regenerating Australia's public housing estates. In K. Ruming (Ed.), *Urban regeneration in Australia: Policies, processes and projects of contemporary urban change* (pp. 311–332). Routledge.

Preiss, B. (2017). Social housing devalues private units nearby, developer says. *The Age*. Retrieved August 31, 2019, from https://www.theage.com.au/national/victoria/social-housing-devalues-private-units-nearby-developer-says-20171211-h02ki3.html

Productivity Commission. (2019). *Report on government services: Part G housing and homelessness*. Australian Government.
Raynor, K., Panza, L., Ordóñez, C., Adamovic, M., & Wheeler, M. A. (2020). Does social mix reduce stigma in public housing? A comparative analysis of two housing estates in Melbourne. *Cities, 96*, 102458. https://doi.org/10.1016/j.cities.2019.102458
Rose, D., Germain, A., Bacqué, M. H., Bridge, G., Fijalkow, Y., & Slater, T. (2013). 'Social mix' and neighbourhood revitalization in a transatlantic perspective: Comparing local policy discourses and expectations in Paris (France), Bristol (UK) and Montréal (Canada). *International Journal of Urban and Regional Research, 37*(2), 430–450. https://doi.org/10.1111/j.1468-2427.2012.01127.x
Ruiz-Tagle, J. (2016). The broken promises of social mix: The case of the Cabrini Green/Near North area in Chicago. *Urban Geography, 37*(3), 352–372. https://doi.org/10.1080/02723638.2015.1060697
Ruming, K. (2015). Everyday discourses of support and resistance: The case of the Australian Social Housing Initiative. *Housing, Theory and Society, 32*(4), 450–471. https://doi.org/10.1080/14036096.2015.1048896
Ruming, K. J., Mee, K. J., & McGuirk, P. (2004). Questioning the rhetoric of social mix: Courteous community or hidden hostility? *Australian Geographical Studies, 42*(2), 234–248. https://doi.org/10.1111/j.1467-8470.2004.00275.x
Sarkissian, W. (1976). The idea of social mix in town planning: An historical review. *Urban Studies, 13*(3), 231–246. https://doi.org/10.1080/00420987620080521
Schuermans, N., Meeus, B., & de Decker, P. (2016). Geographies of whiteness and wealth: White, middle class discourses on segregation and social mix in Flanders, Belgium. *Journal of Urban Affairs, 37*(4), 478–495. https://doi.org/10.1111/juaf.12155
Shaw, K., & Hagemans, I. (2015). 'Gentrification without displacement' and the consequent loss of place: The effects of class transition on low-income residents of secure housing in gentrifying areas. *International Journal of Urban and Regional Research, 39*(2), 323–431. https://doi.org/10.1111/1468-2427.12164
Shaw, K., Raisbeck, P., Chapline, C., & Huse, K. (2013). *Evaluation of the Kensington redevelopment and place management models: Final report*. University of Melbourne Faculty of Architecture Building and Planning.
Somerville, P., & Steele, A. (Eds.). (2002). *'Race,' housing and social exclusion*. Jessica Kingsley Publication.
Tach, L. M. (2009). More than bricks and mortar: Neighborhood frames, social processes, and the mixed-income redevelopment of a public housing project. *City & Community, 8*(3), 269–299. https://doi.org/10.1111/j.1540-6040.2009.01289.x
Tunstall, R., & Fenton, A. (2006). *In the mix: A review of mixed income, mixed tenure and mixed communities*. English Partnerships, Joseph Rowntree Foundation.
Tyler, I., & Slater, T. (2018). Rethinking the sociology of stigma. *The Sociological Review, 66*(4), 721–743. https://doi.org/10.1177/0038026118777425
VHHSBA. (2017). *Registration of capability: Public Housing Renewal Program stage one*. State of Victoria. Retrieved April 4, 2019, from http://www.theage.com.au/cqstatic/gwc77k/housing.pdf
VHHSBA. (2018). *North Melbourne, Northcote and Preston public housing redevelopment*. Retrieved March 4, 2019, from https://www.vhhsba.vic.gov.au/housing-and-infrastructure/north-melbourne-northcote-and-preston-public-housing-redevelopment
VHHSBA. (2019a). *Walker Street, Northcote*. Retrieved July 4, 2020, from https://www.vhhsba.vic.gov.au/housing-and-infrastructure/walker-street-northcote
VHHSBA. (2019b). *Abbotsford Street, North Melbourne*. Retrieved April 9, 2021, from https://www.vhhsba.vic.gov.au/housing-and-infrastructure/abbotsford-street-north-melbourne
VHR. (2017). *Victorian Housing Register Management Update #7*. Retrieved June 20, 2020, from https://chiavic.com.au/wp-content/uploads/2017/09/VHR-Management-Update-No-7-December-2017-CHIA-Vic-6.12.17-with-attachments-1.pdf
Victorian Auditor-General's Office. (2017). *Managing Victoria's Public Housing*.
Victorian Government. (2019). *Response to the Standing Committee on Legal and Social Issues Inquiry into the Public Housing Renewal Program*. Retrieved July 17, 2019, from https://www.parliament.vic.gov.au/images/stories/committees/SCLSI/Public_Housing_Renewal_Program/Government_Response_PHRP.pdf
Watt, P., & Smets, P. (2017). *Social housing and urban renewal: A cross-national perspective*. Emerald.
Wimark, T., Andersson, E. K., & Malmberg, B. (2020). Tenure type landscapes and housing market change: A geographical perspective on neo-liberalization in Sweden. *Housing Studies, 35*(2), 214–237. https://doi.org/10.1080/02673037.2019.1595535
Ziersch, A., Arthurson, K., & Levin, I. (2018). Support for tenure mix by residents local to the Carlton Housing Estate, Melbourne, Australia. *Housing Studies, 33*(1), 58–76. https://doi.org/10.1080/02673037.2017.1344201

Housing motivated youth in low-income neighborhoods: How practitioners shape conditions for encounters across diversity in 'intentional' social mix programs in Milan and Paris

Igor Costarelli and Talia Melic

ABSTRACT
The concept of social mix has been thoroughly examined in the housing literature. Research to date finds little evidence of encounters between socially diverse residents living in mixed settings. This paper provides comparative insights into new, socially mixed housing initiatives in Milan and Paris that have been conceived to promote encounters among diverse residents. Both initiatives, implemented by not-for-profit organizations, provide affordable housing for university students or young professionals in low-income social housing neighborhoods in exchange for their commitment to organize solidarity activities with and for their social housing neighbors. The paper examines how frameworks provided by housing practitioners for "intentional" encounters between motivated youth and low-income residents shape these encounters and considers the receptivity of the youth population to intentionally engage in common projects across diversity. It distils some core conditions within these programs that promote encounters among diverse residents.

Introduction

The idea that residential segregation erodes equality of opportunities and social mobility is at the basis of urban policies that promote social mix. Residential social mix has typically been pursued by increasing the share of private housing for middle income groups in areas with a high concentration of social housing and low-income groups (Kleinhans, 2004).

Many presumed benefits of social mix policies, such as increasing social capital, social networks, and cohesion, depend upon encounters taking place between residents from different tenures and social backgrounds, i.e. middle and low incomes (Bolt & Van Kempen, 2013). Researchers have also given attention to the potential for such encounters to reduce prejudice (Matejskova & Leitner, 2011; G. Valentine, 2008). While contested in the literature, the presumption that the lives of low-income residents can be improved by bringing in middle class residents to role model values, norms and behaviors for emulation continues to shape policymakers' discourse in justifying social mix as a desegregation measure. In addition to problematizing such claims, many researchers conclude that it is too simplistic to expect that social mix will automatically produce encounters and find that other factors, such as good planning and focused community development, come into play (Bolt & Van Kempen, 2013; Camina & Wood, 2009; Tunstall & Fenton, 2006). Indeed, a number of scholars call for further empirical enquiry into the conditions under which encounters across diversity occur (G. Valentine, 2008; Wilson & Darling, 2016; Wise, 2009). Discussions around poverty concentration and deconcentration measures, as addressed in this paper, are even more pertinent in times of increasing segregation along socioeconomic lines (Tammaru et al., 2016). Of particular note—

although poorly examined in the literature—is the role of housing organizations and other actors on the front line with residents, facilitating and supporting encounters within mixed residential settings (Camina & Wood, 2009; Chaskin & Joseph, 2011; Chaskin et al., 2013; Mugnano & Palvarini, 2013).

In recent framings of social mix in the social housing sphere in Italy and the Netherlands, housing practitioners create specific frameworks to promote habitual encounters "between people who would not otherwise meet" (Mugnano & Palvarini, 2013, p. 418). The aim of these encounters is to counteract social exclusion and social isolation, arising, for example, from a lack of relationships (Van Eijk, 2010). They take the form of common projects and regular, shared social activities among residents (Costarelli et al., 2019). As the site of such activities, the housing sphere can be included among what Amin (2012) denotes as a "micro-public," with the potential to produce new patterns of social interaction across diversity. Central to this framework is the creation and targeting of a specific category, "motivated youth." These "motivated youth" are willing to live side-by-side and proactively interact with their neighbors, who tend to be made up of specific populations such as the elderly, low-income tenants, refugees, or people experiencing homelessness.

The centering of motivation aims to sidestep barriers stemming from newcomer residents' unwillingness or indifference toward interacting with longstanding residents, which has proven to be a shortcoming of mainstream social mix policies (Bacqué et al., 2014; Rose et al., 2013). Therefore, bringing in new residents based on their willingness—or intention—to engage with longstanding residents qualifies these experiences as "intentional" social mix.

Whether or not practitioners' expectations of this new target group depart from or simply reproduce assumptions about role modeling rooted in culture of poverty theories (Lewis, 1966) merits consideration.

In assessing the effectiveness of social mix policy, Bolt and Van Kempen (2013) conclude that "what works in one place does not necessarily work in another place," (p. 3) suggesting the relevance of contextual factors and contingencies at both the program- and ground-level. In this regard, we consider the contextual conditions shaping encounters across diversity within a new framework of "intentional" social mix targeting motivated youth, in two case studies in Paris (France) and Milan (Italy). While the core mechanics of both programs are similar, several foundational differences underpin each case: their rationale, institutional settings, assumptions about youth and social housing tenants, the purpose and nature of intended encounters, and the envisaged role of housing practitioners in supporting this. We explore the implications of these differences in order to shed light on conditions that are conducive to encounters across diversity in mixed housing.

This paper discusses and compares housing practitioners' expectations of intentional social mix, the actions they take to fulfil these expectations, and the conditions shaping encounters across diversity based on an exploration of realities on the ground. The cases frame the benefits of these encounters in different ways. The French case seeks to go beyond the unidirectional role model theory, emphasizing instead an encounter that is mutually enriching—or *reciprocal*. The Italian case does tend to depict the youth as role models, but as models of resourcefulness rather than middle-class values and norms. In both cases, the newly created category of "motivated youth" are expected, through their civic engagement, to encourage residents to initiate collective actions and engage in civic participation, while also strengthening togetherness, social ties, and solidarity across diversity in their neighborhoods.

Finally, while at the level of program-design, the philosophies guiding the management of youth engagement differ (accompaniment in Paris in contrast to accountability and performance assessment in Milan), these approaches become somewhat blurred on the ground, where in both cases youth are situated, to some degree, as extensions of the state and not-for-profit actors in the housing and urban policy sector. This suggests that at the operational level, institutions shape young people's encounters across diversity in complex ways, neither completely top-down nor fully bottom up, but rather bottom-linked.

We begin by outlining the theoretical foundations of social mix and introducing the concept of "intentional" social mix as a new framing for encounters across diversity, while also probing and problematizing some of the assumptions that underpin traditional approaches to social mix and the categories adopted by policymakers in this regard (sections 1 and 2). Section three details the comparative framework employed in the paper before the two case studies are outlined in section four. Section five describes our approach to data collection and analysis. Section six presents and analyses the paper's findings along the three axes of what housing practitioners expect, what they do, and how this translates into reality. Finally, we draw some conclusions in section seven.

The theoretical roots of social mix

One of the most pervasive theories underpinning social mix policies is that middle class residents serve as role models to their poorer neighbors (Arthurson, 2012; August, 2019; Blokland, 2003). To a large degree, these assumptions have their roots in the culture of poverty and underclass theories that emerged in the 1960s in the context of poor, largely black American inner cities (Lewis, 1966). The culture of poverty thesis purported that the spatial concentration of poor, nonwhite populations had given rise to a distinctive way of life, characterized by norms and behaviors considered pathological and deviant in comparison to those of mainstream society (Arthurson, 2012; August, 2019; Blokland, 2003; Katz, 1993; C. A. Valentine, 1968). Wilson (1987) shifted the responsibility to the neighborhood as a space that structures and influences life opportunities, though acknowledged the role of structural changes (e.g., deindustrialization, racial segregation, middle-class outmigration) as the underlying cause of these effects. Though culture of poverty theories were heavily disputed even in those times (see Leacock, 1968; C. A. Valentine, 1968), and are still contested in all areas of social policy analysis, such ideas continue to shape the way poverty is framed and dealt with at the policy level, including in current social mix debates about the perceived benefits of middle-class role models for the poor (Arthurson, 2012). A core critique is that such assumptions effectively place the blame for poverty on individual behavior and the perceived moral failings of the poor (Arthurson, 2012; August, 2019; Blokland, 2003). The scope of policy intervention is thereby reduced to managing the behavior of people, and to the neighborhood or territory, often at the expense of treating the complex, structural root causes of poverty (Blokland, 2003).

Furthermore, expecting the middle class "to be forces of uplift and social good" (Lees, 2008, p. 2464) and placing their norms as the standard against which the lives of the poor are judged perpetuates deeply prejudiced conceptions of poor populations that reinforce antagonism and estrangement, and fuel discriminatory policy prescriptions (August, 2019; Katz, 1993; C. A. Valentine, 1968). In the European context, Blokland (2003) attributes the prevalence of social mix as a means to reduce the concentration of poverty to the underlying fear that a culture of poverty will emerge from an over-concentration of poor, unemployed, ethnic minorities in urban neighborhoods.

Another assumption of social mix policy that has been problematized is that residents can be clearly divided into binary categories—whether defined in terms of class, income levels, ethnicity, or housing tenure—that neatly correspond to specific lifestyles, values, behaviors, and preferences. Each category is expected to play a preconceived role, or *role inventory*, in the neighborhood. Social mix advocates often expect middle class residents to play a wide role inventory, strengthening community, cohesion, common bonds, togetherness, and solidarity in a given location (Blokland, 2003). However, research has found that the extent to which an individual or a group fulfills such prescribed roles within the neighborhood (neighborhood use) varies significantly according to their life stage and characteristics such as their age, gender, ethnicity, income, and educational level. Furthermore, across all categories, individual behaviors, choices, and initiatives are influenced by institutions. At the neighborhood level, institutions tend to be represented by street-level bureaucrats, but in areas that concentrate social housing, such roles are also assumed by social housing managers. As such, our focus on practitioners is paramount to better understanding a fundamental element of the conditions that promote encounters across diversity within intentional approaches to social mix.

"Intentional" social mix as a new framing for encounters across diversity in housing

Research into mainstream approaches to social mix, i.e., diversifying housing tenure within low-income neighborhoods to attract the middle-class, has not supported the assumption that diverse people living next to each other automatically engage in encounters across diversity (Arthurson et al., 2015; Blanc & Bidou-Zachariasen, 2010; Chamboredon & Lemaire, 1970; Chaskin & Joseph, 2011). In this context, a new framing of "intentional" social mix, introduced in reference to affordable housing programs in the Italian and Dutch contexts (Costarelli et al., 2019), emphasizes residents' motivation —or intention—to encounter their neighbors, rather than merely living side by side.

This framing gives rise to the new policy category, "motivated youth," conceived as vectors of social mix in place of the category of the middle class. Motivated youth who participate in such programs receive accommodation at below-market rates while being willing to contribute their time, energy and creativity to a common project that is anchored in a shared residential space. Examples of projects include shared meals, community gardens, or street parties. These actions, which take on varying levels of formality (e.g., inclusion in the rental agreement), are intended to facilitate encounters with social housing tenants who are predominantly low-income, based on the assumption that such interactions can strengthen solidarity, social ties and promote greater participation of underrepresented groups in civic life. In part, these objectives aim to mitigate the social isolation or exclusion of low-income residents, defined primarily in terms of lacking personal relationships within the estate, as can be the case of solitary elderly people, as well as relationships with more resource rich neighbors beyond the estate (Van Eijk, 2010). These objectives also point toward a vision of the neighborhood as the site where local dynamics, social relations and, to some extent, the use and distribution of resources, can be reshaped. Though, as with most area-based interventions, such approaches do not purport to directly address the deeper underlying structural causes of social inequality.

Within this framework, motivation is understood as that which drives youth to take action for the benefit of their neighborhood. Centering motivation is a way to overcome a key barrier to encounters across diversity in mainstream social mix approaches: newcomer residents' unwillingness or indifference to interacting with longstanding social tenants—largely because newcomers are not moving into these neighborhoods explicitly for this purpose (Bacqué et al., 2014; Rose et al., 2013).

"Intentional" social mix approaches also move away from the premise that the middle class should serve as role models. While some approaches abandon the role modeling ideal all together, in other cases, youth continue to be framed as role models for social housing residents, though now it is their resourcefulness that is being modeled, rather than middle class norms and practices. The idea of resourcefulness refers to having strong relational skills, being supportive, cooperative, and open-minded—virtues that, for policymakers, can be mobilized through youth action (Costarelli et al., 2020). Through the lens of Sen's (1992) theory of capabilities, resourcefulness can thus be understood as the capability of converting these skills and attitudes into valuable outcomes. In these cases, such outcomes include accessing affordable housing solutions, engaging in encounters across diversity, participating in civic life, and encouraging others to do so.

Another aspect of an intentional approach to social mix is the greater involvement of not-for-profit organizations and residents. This is possibly due to the smaller scale of these initiatives, in the form of individual projects and fine-grained social mix in specific cities and neighborhoods. This small-scale approach is a departure from the large-scale framework of state-led urban renewal policies, which have tended to demolish significant chunks of old social housing stock and replace it with mixed tenure developments. This shift raises questions about how the greater involvement of housing practitioners and managers in an intentional approach to social mix adds value through setting expectations, providing a clear framework, and in some cases concrete support for such encounters to occur

(Costarelli et al., 2019), which is the focus of this paper. Housing practitioners' roles in initiating and supporting encounters within mixed residential settings are particularly critical in three types of housing management activities (Priemus et al., 1999): selection of tenants, i.e. how professionals select suitable, motivated residents; allocation of dwellings, e.g., type of tenancy agreement, location of dwellings and intended scale of social mix; and stimulating resident participation, i.e. how practitioners support and encourage residents to participate by organizing (or co-organizing) and animating social activities.

Intentional social mix projects that target motivated youth have sprung up in both Milan (Italy) and Paris (France), as will be discussed in the following section.

Comparative framework

In assessing the effectiveness of social mix at the neighborhood level, Bolt and Van Kempen (2013) underline the relevance of contextual factors and contingencies at both the micro and macro level. On a macro scale, national and city level contextual factors influence policy approaches, discourses, and the values attached to the idea of social mix (Rose et al., 2013; Veldboer et al., 2002). This includes differences in planning cultures, in the role of the state and the market in housing and neighborhood development, and in commitment to multicultural policies (Fincher et al., 2014). On a micro scale, social mix outcomes can be shaped by the quality of the architecture; the state of maintenance of the dwellings and common areas; the presence of physical places within which encounters can occur (Van Eijk, 2010); the spatial configuration of different tenures (Kleinhans, 2004); and opportunities available to residents to organize and manage activities, or to participate in social programs (Tunstall & Fenton, 2006). Most importantly, the success of social mix depends on "the residents themselves, as they are the ones who contribute to neighborhood life through the ways they use the neighborhood and the way they choose to interact (or not) with others" (Bolt & Van Kempen, 2013, p. 5).

Since this paper aims to better understand the conditions that shape encounters across diversity within a new framing of intentional social mix, we believe Paris (France) and Milan (Italy) represent two pertinent research sites. In both cities, intentional social mix approaches have emerged despite divergent contextual factors, such as residential segregation dynamics, urban policy agendas, social housing systems, and relations between citizens and institutions. Unlike Italy, France has a tradition of urban policy that explicitly targets socio-spatial poverty through its national City Policy (*politique de la ville*), which has been in place since the early 1980s (Carpenter et al., 2020). Social mix via housing tenure diversification is a central objective of the policy, generally implemented in neighborhoods that concentrate public housing and poverty, through the demolition of older, high-rise social housing buildings and the construction of private dwellings intended to attract middle-class residents (Lelévrier, 2013). The official discourse on social mix aligns, in part, with the French Republican value of territorial equality, whereby area-based policies seek to reduce gaps between regions by reducing the spatial concentration of poverty (Raveaud & Zanten, 2007). Along with the emergence of this national urban policy came the definition of social exclusion and a lack of social ties as central problems to solve in such neighborhoods, paving the way for the kinds of actions that not-for-profit actors, like AFEV, undertake (Tissot, 2008). In Paris, social diversity is virtually synonymous with ethnic diversity (Préteceille, 2009). Thus, while social mix policies explicitly target socioeconomic diversity, they also de facto target ethnic diversity and the prevention of ethnic enclaves. The current City Policy, which runs from 2015 to 2022, designates approximately 1,500 priority neighborhoods, based on the proportion of residents that fall below a certain income threshold. Priority neighborhoods receive national and regional funding channeled through city contracts, which include provisions for housing and urban renewal programs (Ministry of Equality, Territory & Housing, 2015).

Unlike the French context, the ideal of social mix, though present, has never been a priority on the Italian urban housing agenda. The most relevant attempts to diversify the tenure and social composition of public housing neighborhoods can be traced back to the national urban renewal policy for disadvantaged neighborhoods (*Contratti di Quartiere*) of the late 1990s–early 2000s. In the framework of this area-based program, social mix via tenure diversification was intended to increase the share of low-middle income groups in public housing neighborhoods. Social animation activities were also implemented to promote social cohesion (Mugnano & Costarelli, 2015). The lack of emphasis on social mix policy in Italy compared to France can be partly explained by diverging realities and framing of urban segregation. The typical suburban landscape of France's largest cities, characterized by tower blocks of social housing estates that concentrate poor, ethnic minorities, is not the case for Italian cities. In Italy, a concentration of poverty exists in limited areas and tends to be scattered across its cities, including within central locations (Mugnano & Costarelli, 2015), making Wilson's (1987) neighborhood effects theory less relevant. Such differences are in turn connected to variations in the share, target, and spatial distribution of social housing. In line with a welfare regime that provides high levels of social protection, France adopts a universalist approach to the provision of social housing, which makes up fourteen percent of the overall housing stock and accommodates various income groups (OECD, 2018). In contrast, a residual approach—targeting only the most vulnerable and accounting for only four percent of the overall housing stock—prevails in the Mediterranean welfare context that characterizes Italy.

There are also differences in institutional frameworks. France has traditionally been a highly centralized state, with a strong sense of stateness that derives from its Republican values. The top-down approach that characterizes France subsequently leaves more room for non-governmental organizations to participate in the execution of policy-driven agendas, but less room for citizen participation to influence decision-making, including in urban policy (Desponds et al., 2014). Many so-called bottom-up initiatives end up falling under the framework of the City Policy. In contrast, Italy is a highly regionalized country and state intervention is highly fragmented, including in urban policy, which leaves more room for bottom up, though often patchy, interventions of other actors, in particular the third sector. While local devolution processes in Italy date back to the 1990s, decentralization has only started to become more prevalent in France in recent years (Carpenter et al., 2020), as reflected in the latest revision of its City Policy.

In the context of an exacerbating crisis of affordability in Italian cities, and in Milan in particular, nonprofit organizations have increasingly played a greater role in the provision of affordable housing for those who cannot keep up with the high costs of the private rental market, including university students and young workers. Public housing providers, i.e. not-for-profit organizations operating at the province-level, often enter into partnership with third-sector actors, including volunteer associations, foundations, cooperatives, or social enterprises. Through these partnerships, providers are able to restructure, allocate and manage unused dwellings. In this context, a new framing of social mix has emerged. A large part of this stock is located in neighborhoods that concentrate households with multiple vulnerabilities, such as low-income elderly people or people with a disability. Allocating units to youth who are motivated to start social activities with and for their neighbors is thus seen as a way of bringing in human and social capital to revitalize the urban and social environment of these estates, while broadening access to affordable housing.

In France, non-state actors have long played a role in implementing social and housing policies at the local level, partnering with municipalities and public landlords across cities such as Paris to pursue an agenda largely driven and influenced by the local council or the national City Policy (Nicholls, 2005). Social mix is a core feature of many such programs, a concept not only ingrained in the official policy framework, but also central to the driving aims and visions of many implementing, non-governmental organizations.

While such programs tend to be modest in scale, they are shaping alternative conceptions of social mix in practice: both in terms of its theoretical underpinnings and in approaches to implementation. A central innovation in these programs is the more hands-on role played by the housing organization and its personnel. Non-governmental organizations have the liberty to move away from the universalist approach enshrined in the French model to target specific groups, such as youth and, even more specifically, youth motivated by a social purpose. These alternative conceptions contribute new perspectives on social mix to the existing literature, which predominantly documents the lack of encounters across different residential tenure groups in socially mixed areas (Lelévrier, 2013; Rose et al., 2013). The case studies presented in the next section represent an example of such innovative programs.

Description of mixed housing programs

Ospitalità Solidale (Milan)

The project Ospitalità Solidale in Milan is an example of intentional social mix. It is the result of a public-private partnership, through which the city council has conferred housing cooperative DAR = Casa the right to renovate and manage 24 vacant social housing dwellings in two public housing neighborhoods, *Niguarda* and *Molise-Calvairate*. The renovation of the dwellings is financed by a national funding program under Italy's national youth policy. The renovated flats are small studios, about 25 square meters each, scattered throughout different housing estates and on different floors within each estate. Both neighborhoods are predominantly inhabited by large, migrant families with children, and solitary elderly people aged over 65. The project was launched in 2014, with short-term tenancies ranging from a minimum of 3 months up to 2 years. Dwellings are provided at below-market rent to 24 youth aged 18–30.

In addition to DAR = Casa, the socio-cultural association ARCI and the social cooperative Comunità Progetto help implement the social animation activities conducted in the neighborhoods. Youth who apply for this program are not only mobilized by the need to find an affordable home but are expected to interact with their neighbors through carrying out useful actions. Youth are thus granted access to affordable housing in exchange for committing time (10 hours per month) for social activities (e.g., gardening, convivial moments) as part of their rental agreement. This program provides opportunities for youth to live independently while creating a new way of living together in diversity, where youth purposefully contribute their resourcefulness to liven up disadvantaged neighborhoods and to interact with its residents, ultimately boosting opportunities for social inclusion. Their commitment to help develop community-oriented activities in the neighborhood in which they live also qualifies them as "resourceful." Their actual resourcefulness as well as suitability for this program is assessed by housing practitioners through interviews.

Kolocation à Projets Solidaire (Paris)

Kolocation à Projets Solidaire (KAPS or *home-sharing solidarity projects* in English) is a program for university students run by the non-governmental organization, Association de la Fondation Etudiante pour la Ville (AFEV). Established in 2010, the program now operates in 33 cities across France. It aims to promote encounters between residents of diverse socioeconomic backgrounds and to build capacity for civic engagement among university students who are motivated to advance social equality in their local neighborhoods. It does this by providing affordable, home-share accommodation in or next to City Policy priority neighborhoods to teams of five to six students, who commit to organizing solidarity activities with their social housing neighbors. Being an enrolled university student aged 18–30 is the only objective eligibility criteria for the program. Shifting the focus to capacity building in youth reflects an effort to overcome the culture of poverty paradigm, mobilizing an *education populaire* (popular education) approach which posits that all actors learn from engaging in activities with a social purpose. In practice, as we will later explore, this can come into tension with the expectations of other local actors, and also with deeply ingrained perceptions of the poor that alternative narratives and approaches must struggle to overcome.

Qualifying characteristics of youth who apply are discerned via collective and individual meetings and include the capacity to work in a team and to home-share, reliability, and whether an applicant's values and attitudes align with those of AFEV (e.g., solidarity, desire to overcome inequality). Tenancies last 1 year and are renewable, provided youth are still enrolled in study. In both Paris and Milan, practitioners offer youth short-term tenancies envisaging a temporary stay in target neighborhoods. As we will see further on, the transient nature of their stay can pose a challenge to efforts to achieve long-term outcomes. In the next two sections, we present our research methods and findings.

Data collection and analysis

This paper is based on original qualitative data collected under two separate, larger research projects. In Paris, research was conducted with students, AFEV practitioners, officials, and other local actors in relation to the Blémont social housing estate in Paris's 18th district. The Blémont estate is made up of eight blocks of a total of 760 units and 2,600 tenants. It is managed by public social landlord Paris Habitat which, together with the local council, is a core partner to AFEV in both the definition and management of the project. We collected eighteen in-depth, semi-structured interviews, including four students. Before a specific case study neighborhood had been identified, initially all six teams of KAPS students who were engaging across the 18th district at the time were invited via e-mail to participate in the research. Two teams who had large-scale projects underway (a street party and collective street fresco respectively) responded positively. Three teams responded negatively, either because they had already undertaken their core actions for the year or because the team had ceased to function well, and one team did not respond at all. Of the two teams who responded positively, research was initiated with both teams but continued into a second year with the team that was intervening in the *Blémont* neighborhood, as three of the original five students signed up for a second year, providing continuity. A final point is that only four of the five original students in the Blémont team agreed to find time to be interviewed, reflecting motivation dynamics within the team. It is thus important to note that the interview selection process of KAPS students favors teams that are functioning well and students that are motivated. As such, this case can be read as an exploration of the possibilities of the KAPS model when students are motivated by the social dimensions of the project (rather than a model that would function irrespective of student motivations), pointing to the need for robust recruitment processes (discussed later in the paper). One limitation to bear in mind then, is that our findings do not necessarily represent the varied experiences of KAPS students across the 18th district.

Our interviews also included two AFEV personnel (the coordinator of KAPS in the 18th district of Paris, and the staff member responsible for KAPS in AFEV's Ile-de-France headquarters) and three personnel from core partner organizations (public landlord Paris Habitat and the 18th district council's local development team), making up all the core institutional actors involved with the KAPS Blémont project. We also interviewed a former AFEV volunteer who had supported a KAPS team in the 18th district, a contact obtained through the AFEV coordinator. Three employees of local organizations and one resident who volunteered in a local association, all of whom collaborated with the KAPS students in the organization of the Blémont street party, were interviewed. We were able to identify them as the team's main collaborators on the ground by participating in meetings and actions organized in the lead up to the street party and in conversation with KAPS students. Finally, four social housing tenants were also interviewed. The tenants interviewed contributed to the Street Party in different ways and had multiple encounters with KAPS students, to the point of establishing social ties. They were identified with KAPS students. Interviews took place in 2018 over a 6-month period, averaging about 2 hours each.

In Milan, we collected thirteen interviews, including four in-depth interviews with young tenants of Ospitalità Solidale (two from each neighborhood in which the program is implemented as a means to attain some balance in presenting the realities of each targeted neighborhood). We also interviewed six practitioners from involved organizations (three practitioners from housing cooperative DAR = Casa, two practitioners from association Comunità Progetto and one from association ARCI). Three additional semi-structured interviews were held with local policymakers from the Department of Housing within both the city council and the Lombardy Region. These interviews were collected on an irregular basis, beginning in 2017 until February 2020. All local policymakers who took part in this study were directly contacted via e-mail and responded positively to the interview invitation.

As for the practitioners, the recruitment process followed a snowball approach. We first addressed practitioners from DAR = Casa, as this cooperative has major responsibilities for the whole project. Therefore, the proportion of practitioners from this cooperative we interviewed is higher than other categories of interviewees. These practitioners provided us with contacts of project managers responsible for the project in each neighborhood (ARCI association in the *Niguarda* neighborhood and Comunità Progetto in the *Molise-Calvairate* neighborhood). In both cases, there was only one person per organization responsible for the project in each neighborhood (in one case the project manager was accompanied by a project assistant who also took part in the interview). So, despite the limited numbers, all relevant people directly involved in this project took part in the study, providing valuable knowledge of all the main issues at stake. Practitioners also provided contacts for youth. This strategy for reaching youth has some potential implications for our findings, as the participating youth may reflect practitioners' preferences to select the most active and "reliable" tenants. Concentrating on this subsection of youth could bring about a social desirability bias, i.e. youth feeling "performance pressure" to only share positive experiences to avoid negative reactions from practitioners. However, as our findings demonstrate, this risk did not materialize, as respondents were open to discussing both the positive and negative aspects of their experiences. The spirit of their contributions did not reflect a relationship of being held to account by practitioners but suggested a collaborative relationship that more closely resembles the accompaniment approach envisaged in the French case. This is a point we return to later in the paper.

Another key point relates to the length of residence. Among the four youth interviewed in Milan (three workers and one student), two were more established residents of the neighborhood (having lived there for 1.5 and 2 years respectively) while two others had been living in the estates for a few months only (roughly 1–6 months). Combined with the more longstanding experiences reported by practitioners, the mix of young tenants with different lengths of residence provided a wider and balanced vision of the dynamics under investigation.

All interviews were recorded, transcribed, and analyzed to extract information on three specific subjects:

(1) Housing practitioners' expectations of "intentional" social mix: what do they expect to happen in the program?
(2) What practitioners do to realize such expectations: what actions do they take to help create and support encounters and a common project among diverse residents?
(3) The realities of "intentional" social mix: how do practitioners' expectations play out in practice? How do their discourse and actions shape these outcomes?

The next section presents our findings.

Findings

In this section we provide an overview of practitioners' expectations about encounters across diversity in these mixed housing programs; an exploration of their role in initiating and supporting encounters; and a discussion about the conditions on the ground that shape the nature and realities of encounters.

Housing practitioners' expectations

At the heart of both programs is the premise that youth who are motivated to participate in activities with a social purpose within socially mixed residential spaces can initiate or contribute to encounters across diversity. As noted, this "intentional" mix approach seeks to springboard off youth commitment to reach out across diversity in the local space, in contrast to the indifference that traditional approaches to social mix place on the motivations of the "middle class" when moving to a renewed neighborhood (Bacqué et al., 2014; Rose et al., 2013). Nevertheless, the expected benefits of mix remain similar: practitioners expect that regular encounters and dynamic activity among diverse neighbors can reduce the social isolation of a high proportion of solitary elderly tenants in these residences; break down barriers and micro-segregation across different strata of the population; and increase civic participation. In both programs, it is expected that youth can collaborate with and provide a boost to local initiatives that encourage social tenants to participate in neighborhood life and to connect to local services and associations. This is where efforts to address material deficit in these neighborhoods comes into play. In connecting social housing residents to local networks and opportunities, it is envisaged, for example, that they can dialogue about their needs in terms of resources and amenities both informally (e.g., through the council's local development officers) and formally (e.g., through participatory budgeting schemes); learn about grants for which they may be eligible; and, in the case of youth, receive support from local associations to find internships or training opportunities. This reflects a highly institutionalized approach to neighborhood development where neighborhood associations (and to some extent, youth themselves) effectively act as extensions of the State and implementers of its policies. In this way, motivated youth are as much effective agents of the State as they are vectors of social mix.

Notwithstanding such similar expectations, significant variations exist in the narratives that each program has about "motivated" youth and the social tenants with whom they interact. In Paris, AFEV's program is based on the premise that young people desire to feel "useful" to society and are searching to "broaden their horizons." AFEV is convinced that "youth want to invest in society, as long as they have the space to do so. They are looking for meaning, eager for solidarity, and in search of concrete action" (AFEV, 2020, p. 8; our translation).

This expected social motivation is markedly more ambitious than the diversity-seeking that Blokland and Van Eijk (2010) find fails to translate into the establishment of diverse social networks. Affordable housing is therefore not intended to motivate students to act, but rather to *enable* youth, who are taken to be self-motivated, to participate by freeing up their time. Given the high cost of housing in Paris, low rents are expected to relieve students of the need to take on part-time work. In Milan, a more explicit *quid pro quo* narrative underlies the program, offering below-market priced housing as an incentive for youth commitment to contribute to social cohesion, included as an explicit condition of their tenancy. These different framings of housing provision explain the distinct ways in which housing practitioners manage youth engagement, at least at the level of project design. In Milan, housing professionals adopt an accountability management approach, holding youth to account over their engagement and responsibilities toward self-organized activities. In contrast, in Paris, greater emphasis is placed from the outset on youth accompaniment and capacity building for civic engagement, through training as well as practical, step-by-step support. In practice, the boundaries between these two approaches can be somewhat blurred. In Milan, practitioners play a more hands-on role than initially anticipated, while in Paris, accountability does enter into AFEV's relationship with the KAPS students owing to targets set by external funding bodies (e.g., the social landlord). This is because such funding bodies have an obligation to ensure the program contributes to their own organizational goals.

Another difference relates to the expected beneficiaries of social mix. The Paris case promotes a bi-directional, or reciprocal, exchange embedded in AFEV's pedagogical approach of *education populaire* ("popular" education), whereby both students and social housing tenants have the potential to be resourceful and to benefit and learn from their encounters across diversity. In the Milan case, benefits are expected to flow mainly in one direction, from resourceful youth to social tenants, resembling more the traditional role model approach (see Kleinhans, 2004). This means that in Paris, unlike Milan, students are not expected to organize actions *for* but rather *with* their social housing neighbors, to tap into and boost existing local initiatives and to help identify resourceful people with whom the social housing landlord can liaise directly. In this way, AFEV attempts to depart from culture of poverty assumptions, reframing lower income residents as being resourceful and not simply recipients of the actions and example of the students. In the same way, KAPS students are not expected to come into the project as perfect models, as the middle class were treated in traditional social mix approaches, but rather as being able to learn from and grow through this experience. In the next subsection, we explain how professionals, as housing managers, play a critical role in promoting conditions for encounters across diversity and explore how these ideals translate into practice and challenges encountered on the ground.

Practitioners' actions to promote encounters

Practitioners' actions fall into four critical housing management activities (Priemus et al., 1999): the selection of neighborhoods, the allocation of dwellings, the recruitment of tenants, and the support and guidance provided to youth.

The institutional embeddedness of "intentional" social mix within France's official urban policy leads to a more structured program than that of Italy. This is clearly visible from the criteria used to select target neighborhoods or estates. In France, neighborhoods must fall under the City Policy "priority neighborhood" category, though neighborhoods that are considered too problematic or dangerous are increasingly excluded in an attempt to avoid exposing relatively inexperienced youth to difficult environments. How "problematic" neighborhoods are identified, and the extent to which doing so inadvertently stigmatizes these places, is a question that bears examination but is beyond the scope of this present paper.

In sharp contrast, in Italy, the logic underpinning both the selection of neighborhoods and the allocation of dwellings comes down to haphazardly "grabbing opportunities" wherever they arise. This can be explained by the absence of a well-structured urban agenda at the national scale comparable to that of France, which defines explicit criteria for implementing social mix. The project is in this case implemented through a partnership between local third sector organizations and the city council, which channels funding to refurbish the dwellings. These diverging strategies result in different local conditions shaping encounters across diversity. In Paris, the Blémont housing estate is located within a semi-gentrifying neighborhood, described as an "island" of low-income social housing within a more affluent, largely private tenured area. In contrast, the Milan project is located within a neighborhood that is considered deprived and composed predominantly of social housing.

As for the allocation of dwellings, at the time the research began, the Paris students lived in studio apartments in a student housing residence located within the same neighborhood as the Blémont estate (a five-minute walk), but not within the estate itself. They thus share many neighborhood spaces and amenities with Blémont residents, but not the living space itself. In September 2018, they moved into a purpose-built home-share residence for all KAPS students in the 18th district (within another priority neighborhood, slightly further away from the Blémont estate). In Milan, dwellings are assigned wherever a unit happens to become available. This has resulted in a pepper-potting social mixing approach, whereby some youth end up living in the same building as the social housing tenants with whom they are expected to interact, while others are scattered across different estates but also within the same neighborhood. As other studies have found (Arthurson, 2010; Jupp, 1999; Lelévrier, 2013), the distinct spatial configuration of social mix influences the extent to which residents—in this case youth—encounter and get to know their neighbors and one another. Across France, AFEV has also found that an "everyday" social mix is better facilitated in sites where students are housed within the social housing estates and share buildings with its residents, though collective initiative and action among students is reinforced in the student residence model (the case in Paris). This will be discussed later in the paper.

The quality of the housing and the surrounding neighborhood is another condition that is found to impact youth motivation. The studio flats in Paris are relatively new and the new residence is purposely built for groups of five to six students to live together, whereas in Milan the flats are one-person studios, refurbished but located within low-quality public housing complexes. In Milan, the lack of investment and dynamism in the neighborhood weakens youth commitment to the project and the time they desire to spend there, leading some youth to have the impression that "nothing happens here." This is in stark contrast to the KAPS students who are on the whole very satisfied with the quality of their apartments and, living in a bustling, semi-gentrified but nonetheless *"populaire"* (working class) neighborhood of the 18th district, are also motivated to spend their time locally alongside a range of residents including Blémont tenants. Unlike their French peers, Italian "resourceful" youth benefit from several on-site common rooms and a garden within which they can implement their activities.

The selection of youth is another central condition. In both cases, there is an effort to recruit youth who are motivated to contribute to the organizations' core social agenda. For practitioners in both Paris and Milan, motivation to take part in solidarity activities with neighbors is a key criterion to selecting suitable candidates, sought out through individual and/or collective meetings. As noted, this vetting procedure is a key departure from traditional social mix approaches. French practitioners target the student population specifically, who have in common the experience of being university students. Regarding social mix objectives of the program, there is an assumption that university students come predominantly from a middle-class background—according to AFEV officials, this is often, but not always, the case.

In contrast, Italian practitioners target both students and young workers who might consequently be at different life stages, with different priorities and time availability to dedicate to the project, leading to different neighborhood uses and role repertoires (Blokland, 2003).

Despite this difference, there is agreement across both cases that "it takes time" to feel at home and to establish a regular pattern of activity with residents, which can come into tension with the short-term duration of tenancy contacts and the turnover rate of youth. As one student in the Blémont neighborhood shares: "What is difficult is that it is extremely slow and often we leave after 1 year. One year is not very long to develop relationships." A high turnover of youth can also undermine the continuity of certain activities. The approach promoted in both cities to provide a "boost" to the existing activities of local organizations or resident groups, rather than initiating new projects, can go some length toward avoiding this challenge, but nevertheless needs to be complemented by longer periods living in the neighborhood. The student cited above ultimately chose (along with two other teammates) to stay on a second year. Further consideration could be given to encouraging such decisions which, in the program's current design, ultimately lie with the individual youth. In Milan, contract renewal is possible, but only if certain specified conditions (beyond the volition of youth) are in place, reflecting the *ex-post* conditionality mechanisms at work in the Italian program (Costarelli et al., 2020). One condition is the age of the youth. Another condition is that practitioners give a positive assessment of youth commitment, participation, contribution to activities, and suitability to the project. This approach to renewal demonstrates the extent to which, in the design of the program in Milan, accountability is intended to drive motivation within what is essentially envisaged as a contractual exchange (affordable housing in return for socially oriented activities).

Another key difference is that youth in Milan are not formally part of a team, as is the case in Paris, even though they do end up organizing actions collectively. In Paris, youth describe being in a team as "reassuring" and as a means to "count on others" as well as to fuel ideas and increase motivation. This collective momentum appears to be integral to the success of the program. However, the demonstrated value of formalizing groups of youth should not be seen as a panacea, particularly as the data suggests that the "group effect" cuts both ways: if a member of the group is less committed, this can undermine the motivation of the others, and youth appear to be particularly discouraged when they are let down by one another. Furthermore, by only including students in these teams (as opposed to including their social housing neighbors), an added layer of separation between the youth and their neighbors is introduced. In addition, while home-sharing in Paris can strengthen relationships within the group, it can pose potential challenges related to co-managing a household, which Italian youth do not have to deal with living alone in their single studios. As we will go on to explore, what seems to be important is that the glue that holds these teams together, when they function effectively, is a common social purpose and active commitment to the solidarity project, as well as bonds of friendship. It follows that in the Paris case, practitioners' care extends into the private dimension of students' lives, the home, where they mediate if needed to ensure a positive experience and to help sustain initiative within the neighborhood.

Another task of practitioners is supporting and guiding youth in their actions and progress. Despite diverging philosophies for managing youth (accompaniment in Paris versus accountable self-organization in Milan), in practice these approaches converge more than initially anticipated. In Paris, housing practitioners accompany students through various stages of planning, acting, reflecting, and reporting. They provide formal training which is both practical (e.g., neighborhood visits, project methodology, budgeting, poster design) as well as conceptual (e.g., on French urban policy, migration issues). They also provide morale-boosting encouragement. This approach to accompaniment stems from the expectation that students exit the program with enhanced capacity to arise as socially engaged citizens but that, as relatively inexperienced youth, they need support to learn to translate their aspirations into reality. Limited funding means that, in reality, AFEV personnel can be stretched too thinly across a growing number of KAPS teams to systematically deliver on this level of accompaniment. Nevertheless, from the perspective of AFEV's strategic partners and the students themselves, this only serves to underscore the need for such support.

In Milan, despite an initial expectation of relatively autonomous self-organization, practitioners ultimately step in to play a more hands-on role in response to what they perceive as a lack of self-regulation and fluctuating motivation. Like Paris, these actions consist of participating in meetings with youth to help them plan. However, they also go further by pre-organizing some activities themselves and inviting youth to participate, ultimately exercising power to shape youth behavior and increase opportunities for encounters. As one youth reports: "They put in front of you all the possibilities you have to participate, so you don't have to make too much effort, you can just join the activity." They also introduce tools intended to account for youth efforts, e.g., monthly self-registration of performed tasks. This unexpected shift brings the role of Italian practitioners closer to the accompaniment practiced by their French peers, though shows that Italian practitioners ultimately become significantly more interventionist than their French counterparts. This has potential implications for the extent to which youth are actually empowered to act resourcefully and appears to demonstrate a need for greater forethought about an accompaniment process that seeks to nurture and develop potential youth resourcefulness.

Italian practitioners also introduce a greater degree of flexibility than initially foreseen, which is characteristic of the French *modus operandi*. In Paris, though KAPS students are expected to devote 5 hours to the project each week, it is also expected that this number will fluctuate to accommodate the rhythm of student life: hours will inevitably drop during examination periods but hopefully rise when students are organizing major social activities. As such, practitioners do not monitor hours closely. This also reflects a spirit of seeing students as volunteers, and not as free laborers for AFEV or the public sector. Milan practitioners also show pragmatism based on the understanding that they have to be flexible to accommodate the unstable life plans of youth and their rapidly changing needs. However, this need for greater flexibility results in ambiguity and comes into tension with an accountability approach toward ensuring fulfillment of the 10 hour per month-volunteering quota, which is a formal condition of the tenancy agreement in Milan. We now focus on the realities of social mix on the ground.

Conditions for encounters on the ground

Our findings bring into focus three conditions as being particularly relevant for encounters across diversity in the context of intentional social mix programs: (i) a frequent and visible presence in the neighborhood/estate, facilitated by an on-site physical space for activities and related place-making processes; (ii) encounters that are characterized by openness and welcome; and (iii) the recruitment of receptive youth who proactively seek to encounter their neighbors across diversity. We explain this in detail.

In Paris, a frequent, visible everyday presence is found to be more conducive to creating repeated encounters and to mobilizing residents to engage in their neighborhood. This practice arose out of dissatisfaction with one-off events, which students find have little longer-term impact beyond a brief moment of conviviality. Thus, the Blémont street party, which the KAPS students are co-organizing with a collective of local actors and organizations, gives rise to a longer process of reaching out to social housing residents to elicit their participation. Every 1–2 weeks, they set up a stand offering beverages and snacks. Their focus on adjoining buildings facing a single courtyard enables repeat encounters and the building of rapport. The students do not hesitate to energetically chase after tenants coming back from work or school-runs to introduce themselves and encourage them to contribute to the organization of the street party. Though in small numbers, some residents hang around, chat with one another, and interact with the children playing ball in the courtyard. Another association joins the students from time to time to film tenants speaking about their neighborhood for a video that will be projected at the street party. This corresponds with Amin's (2012) vision of habitual encounters taking place through participation in common projects.

Furthermore, in talking to their neighbors about *contributing* to the organization of the party, the students' discourse reflects AFEV's narrative of framing both youth and social housing tenants as resourceful, as well as students' perceptions of their own role as opening up a space for Blémont residents to bring their neighbors together. One KAPS student explains how she was conscious of not seeing herself as a "savior" of this neighborhood, choosing instead to consider herself as just another resident who aspires "simply to give time to where I live, so that I also want to live here." This is also reflected in her efforts to get to know and converse with people "on an equal footing," not as residents of a social estate but as "whole people" with "a whole history behind them."

In this way, the students' actions do manage, at times, to transform what has been lived by many tenants as a place of passage into a moment of shared conviviality and encounters. Students do stress that an on-site room would significantly increase the potential of these encounters, particularly during the colder months. The students build ties with a small number of more engaged tenants, with whom they go for coffee, assist with errands, share holiday snaps, or visit at their homes, and some tenants also get to know one another better, "putting a name to a face" as some of them share.

Furthermore, a small number of Blémont social housing tenants contribute to the organization of a neighborhood street party, by organizing craft and dance workshops, participating in preparatory meetings, refereeing soccer games, donating and serving food, face-painting, setting up, or inviting other residents. A large number of social tenants attend the street party, and some report that the event contributes to more positive representations of the estate and of one another.

Yet despite youth intentions, in its first edition the street party largely remains something organized *for* the neighborhood, and not by them. The hope of local officials and organizations is that, going forward, social housing tenants gradually take greater ownership of its organization, so that the event will reflect their needs and aspirations. This will require learning to foster inclusive collective processes that can elicit much wider involvement and commitment leading up to the event. For example, consultative spaces would need to be created and mediated in ways that encourage a diversity of views to be expressed and valued, particularly the views of the AFEV students and, most importantly, Blémont tenants. In this respect, one particular challenge to overcome is that of groups of residents with more professional experience taking on the role of arbiters of what a successful event looks like. Avoiding this will require a conscious and sincere effort to ensure that *culture of poverty* assumptions do not color the perceptions that institutional actors and other residents have of social housing residents and their capacity to contribute to such processes. Ultimately, all residents must be recognized as having the potential to be resourceful, a capability that has already been demonstrated by a number of social tenants in the street party's first iteration. Finally, it seems necessary that any indicators of success for the event must include eliciting wide participation. In this way, the street party can go beyond a moment of conviviality, to become a common project, in which diverse residents of the neighborhood are engaged.

In Milan, spatial proximity is a condition for repeated encounters, but everyday encounters tend to be easier among young people living in the same building rather than *in situ* social tenants (e.g., the elderly and families). One youth shares, "we youth share a lot together, e.g., going out for dinner or dancing, especially if we live close to each other, so encounters are even more frequent." Youth find that they have more in common with each other including similar needs that lead them to exchange material help (e.g., sharing a Wi-Fi connection). There seems to be a gap in frequent encounters across diversity, with youth reporting that "the other families, although they're nice, have their own lives and it's more difficult to make connections." This finding appears to repeat shortcomings of traditional mix approaches, where social interaction is limited to instrumental exchanges largely among residents of similar social backgrounds (Chaskin & Joseph, 2011). Furthermore, interviewed youth in Milan claim that in some cases, encounters with *in situ* tenants "do not go beyond saying hello," and that their overall reactions to the activities triggered by the youth vary greatly, making it difficult to draw a univocal pattern. In some cases, it depends on the social group. Isolated elderly residents have more time to participate in convivial activities, such as dinners in the common rooms organized by the youth in collaboration with practitioners. In contrast, some of the migrant families are more hesitant to join and instead spend much of their time at home caring for their families—unless these families are mobilized to participate in purposeful activities. For example, an Italian language class for Arab mothers is considered to be a success of this program. This again further supports the value of common projects as a means to facilitate repeated encounters across diversity (Amin, 2012). "Parallel lives" continues to be the norm unless a common project, about which *in situ* residents feel concerned and involved in (though not obliged) exists (Mugnano & Palvarini, 2013). Again, this highlights the need for *in situ* residents to be seen as resourceful alongside the youth, and thus to be more actively included in the definition and design of such projects, rather than being treated as the recipients of these activities. The nature of the encounters that take place—i.e. what actually happens when youth interact with *in situ* tenants—is also fundamental. In some buildings in Milan, inter-generational conflicts occur between the newly arrived youth and their elderly neighbors, which can exacerbate the already difficult socioeconomic living conditions of some households. As one youth reported: "it's a fragile environment, so someone may welcome new activities and new people around their estate, while others are absolutely against them." This leads some youth to limit interactions to more formal greetings.

In Paris, despite mixed reactions from tenants (particularly when door knocking), it is the experiences of hospitality and encouragement from a number of social housing tenants—as well as the handful of tenants with whom they engage in repeated encounters and establish social ties—that appear to shape the students' overall impression of being warmly welcomed in the neighborhood.

Though marginal, other aspects of the French case correspond with practitioners' expectations of reduced isolation, particularly among solitary elderly tenants and shifting mutual perceptions. In Paris, an elderly resident shares how, in getting to know the KAPS students, she overcomes pre-conceptions that their university education would make them arrogant, stating: "I always said to myself, oh, they are doing long studies, they will have big heads, thinking to themselves: 'We study, we know things, we know many things they don't.' I thought they would judge us. Yet it's not at all the case." In another example, some local residents report that seeing Blémont (social tenant) youth volunteer to cook a barbeque at the street party changes their perceptions of them and helps to establish rapport, so that they begin to say hello to one another. These examples lend weight to the assumption that encounters across diversity facilitated through social mix can shift perceptions, as is presumed in much mainstream social mix theory (Kleinhans, 2004). At the same time, this also validates the premise that a reframing of social mix is needed for the intended encountering to materialize.

Discussion and conclusion

This paper compares recently emerged "intentional social mix" approaches in two mixed housing programs in Milan and Paris. Such approaches offer temporary affordable housing solutions for youth who commit to devoting time and energy to organizing social activities with social housing neighbors on a regular basis. Youth and social tenants embark on common projects, which offer opportunities for new encounters across diversity creating social mix through housing.

After outlining housing practitioners' expectations of "intentional social mix," we focused on the conditions that promote and sustain encounters across diversity, including the role of housing practitioners. At the program-level, these conditions relate to the criteria guiding the selection of neighborhoods, the allocation of dwellings, tenant recruitment, and a combination of accompaniment and accountability approaches to managing youth engagement by housing practitioners. At the ground-level, these conditions translate into frequent and visible presence of youth in the neighborhood, i.e. neighborhood use (Blokland, 2003); the nature of the encounters—that they are open and welcoming; and a high degree of cohesion among youth themselves that enables a constructive collective dynamic.

This paper demonstrates how this emerging reframing of social mix qualifies housing as a potential "micro-public," within which regular and shared social activities across diversity can take place in the way Amin (2012) envisages, producing patterns of social interaction that disrupt established cultural practices (and notably the practice of parallel lives). One way practitioners can strengthen this is to ensure that the common project—in these cases the social activities—is jointly defined with the local population, so that such activities are not being done to them, but rather are collectively conceived and owned. This also suggests that programs should be designed around the premise that resourcefulness can be an attribute of both social tenants and youth, with conscientious efforts made to counter the assumptions of deficit perpetuated by the culture of poverty theory: both in the design and objectives of the program, but also in the accompaniment and capacity building of youth.

This paper contributes to the literature by enriching the social mix debate on the limitations of role model theory and by proposing alternatives. It does this by drawing attention to two distinct approaches within intentional social mix projects. The first, exemplified through the Milan case, reframes *what* is being role modeled, moving away from the moral values and norms of the middle class, toward a modeling of the "resourcefulness" of youth. The second approach, exemplified through the Paris case, does away with the idea of role models all together, and promotes instead the mutual value of two-way, or reciprocal, encounters across diversity. In this approach, both students and social tenants are conceived as having the capacity to be resourceful and as potentially learning from these encounters. Despite these ideals and expectations, in practice, neither approach ultimately manages to include low-income groups as equal participants in the creation and implementation of social activities. This suggests that they have not managed to completely unroot deep-seated assumptions about low-income populations, and specifically social housing tenants, as lacking something and in need of outside assistance—in this case, the initiative to come together in solidarity, and the tools and connections to access key resources. While far from the U.S. context, this demonstrates the pervasiveness of culture of poverty theories even in Europe, and that untangling such ideas is a gradual process that must include low-income residents themselves.

This paper also contributes to the social mix debate by specifically considering the suitability of youth as social mix actors. Constructing and developing ways of engaging youth in structured activities is pivotal, with housing managers playing a key role in this (Chaskin et al., 2013). This study suggests that when carefully recruited and patiently accompanied by experienced housing practitioners, youth can tap into a reservoir of motivation and openness toward diversity to engage in encounters through common projects established with their neighbors. Yet, as with general experiences of social mix, their physical—and temporary—presence alone in mixed neighborhoods is insufficient to translate their aspirations into reality over the long-term. The risk of reproducing narratives of parallel lives with their new neighbors as described by Camina and Wood (2009) is indeed present, underscoring the importance of the above-mentioned conditions. Furthermore, while much effort is undertaken to build capacity in youth to participate in civic life, little attention is paid to building capacity of *in situ* residents. Extending "resourcefulness" as an attribute of all residents, that encounters across diversity can help to develop, necessitates further thought about how such resourcefulness can be tapped into among willing participants of the broader local population.

This paper also develops the idea of "motivated youth," whose social motivation goes much further than the diversity-seeking middle class of Blokland and Van Eijk (2010). Even with socially driven motivations, these youth do not act in a vacuum but are immersed in a network of local actors with their own intersecting and somewhat contradictory practices and discourses, who are in turn operating within a policy space that continues to be shaped by a continued pervasiveness of culture of poverty mind-sets. In addition, this motivation should be contextualized within the broader structural conditions of housing markets and the difficulty youth face accessing affordable solutions. From a youth's perspective, access to affordable housing is a legitimate need and can be seen as complementary to the social project, rather than undermining or discrediting it. Practitioners thus frame youth motivation as being twofold: both as the need for housing and the aspiration to be active in the local space—both motivations are present and are not in contradiction. Nevertheless, the challenge for practitioners in their recruitment processes is to discern that affordable housing is not the only motivation. This implies that practitioners need to learn how to tap into a deeper sense of purpose within youth and to create environments and collective dynamics that can further impulse their efforts. How to achieve this in practice is a question for further research.

Finally, while social mix approaches tend not to address the broader structural causes of the poverty that is concentrated in neighborhoods like those featured in this paper, bringing youth into these neighborhoods opens up interesting avenues of exploration concerning the potential longer-term, generational effects of such programs if implemented at a wider scale. That is to say, intentional social mix interventions involving youth may help build their capacity to contribute to broader structural shifts in society. Younger generations are increasingly at the forefront of conversations and movements relating to key societal challenges like ecological and environmental sustainability, planting seeds for marginal but growing shifts in industries ranging from food to fashion. What seeds might be planted by bringing youth who would otherwise live at a distance from lower-income neighborhoods into these places, in ways that enable them to get to know the dynamics of these places and the people who inhabit them?

A framework that promotes encounters across diversity, like that of these programs, could contribute to raising youth consciousness of the realities of those afflicted by poverty and other vulnerabilities, including consciousness of the capacities and resourcefulness of this population. Might this consciousness lead to shifts in future generational perspectives and choices about where to live, with whom to interact, what causes and visions of the future to support in their future careers and civic participation? Youth may also become more convinced of their own resourcefulness to contribute to lasting change in society that aligns with their values.

Of course, the small scale of these interventions, and the limited duration of this research, is much too insignificant to explore these questions in any meaningful way. But we conclude with them as important questions for future researchers, practitioners, and policymakers to consider, particularly in relation to the location and design of affordable housing for youth and students, and for how the period of university and youth more broadly is approached in relation to building capacity for civic participation. At the same time, care must be taken not to emphasize the potential changemaking role of youth to the detriment of the role of *in situ* residents of social housing estates who, as this paper argues, must also be seen and accompanied as resourceful actors in the reshaping of the neighborhood.

Acknowledgments

The authors would like to thank the editors and the anonymous reviewers, whose constructive comments and suggestions helped to improve earlier drafts of this manuscript. We are also grateful to all the professionals and residents who took part in the interviews, making this research possible.

Disclosure statement

No potential conflict of interest was reported by the author(s).

ORCID

Igor Costarelli ⓘ http://orcid.org/0000-0001-6746-4721
Talia Melic ⓘ http://orcid.org/0000-0003-3760-6471

References

AFEV. (2020). *Bilan d'activité 2019/2020. Plus que jamais, agir contre les inégalités et créer des liens solidaires* [Activity report 2019/2020. More than ever, take action against inequalities and create solidarity links]. https://afev.org/wp-content/uploads/2021/03/BILAN-ACTIVITE-19-20-web.pdf

Amin, A. (2012). *Land of strangers*. Polity Press.

Arthurson, K. (2010). Operationalizing social mix: Spatial scale, lifestyle and stigma as mediating points in resident interaction. *Urban Policy and Research, 28*(1), 49–63. https://doi.org/10.1080/08111140903552696

Arthurson, K. (2012). *Social mix and the city: Challenging the mixed communities consensus in housing and urban planning policies*. CSIRO Publishing.

Arthurson, K., Levin, I., & Ziersch, A. (2015). What is the meaning of 'social mix'? Shifting perspectives in planning and implementing public housing estate redevelopment. *Australian Geographer, 46*(4), 491–505. https://doi.org/10.1080/00049182.2015.1075270

August, M. (2019). Social mix and the death of public housing. In M. Moos (Ed.), *A research agenda for housing* (pp. 116–130). Edward Elgar Publishing.

Bacqué, M. H., Charmes, E., & Vermeersch, S. (2014). The middle class 'at home among the poor'—How social mix is lived in Parisian suburbs: Between local attachment and metropolitan practices. *International Journal of Urban and Regional Research, 38*(4), 1211–1233. https://doi.org/10.1111/1468-2427.12130

Blanc, M., & Bidou-Zachariasen, C. (2010). Paradoxes de la mixité sociale (éditorial) [Paradoxes of social diversity (editorial)]. *Espaces et sociétés, 140-141*(1), 7–20. https://doi.org/10.3917/esp.140.0007

Blokland, T. (2003). *Urban bonds*. Polity.

Blokland, T., & Van Eijk, G. (2010). Do people who like diversity practice diversity in neighbourhood life? Neighbourhood use and the social networks of 'diversity-seekers' in a mixed neighbourhood in the Netherlands. *Journal of Ethnic and Migration Studies, 36*(2), 313–332. https://doi.org/10.1080/13691830903387436

Bolt, G., & Van Kempen, R. (2013). Introduction special issue: Mixing neighborhoods: Success or failure? *Cities, 35*, 391–396. https://doi.org/10.1016/j.cities.2013.04.006

Camina, M. M., & Wood, M. J. (2009). Parallel lives: Towards a greater understanding of what mixed communities can offer. *Urban Studies, 46*(2), 459–480. https://doi.org/10.1177/0042098008099363

Carpenter, J., González Medina, M., Huete García, M. Á., & De Gregorio Hurtado, S. (2020). Variegated Europeanization and urban policy: Dynamics of policy transfer in France, Italy, Spain and the UK. *European Urban and Regional Studies, 27*(3), 227–245. https://doi.org/10.1177/0969776419898508

Chamboredon, J. C., & Lemaire, M. (1970). Proximité spatiale et distance sociale. Les grands ensembles et leur peuplement [Spatial proximity and social distance. Large complexes and their settlement]. *Revue française de sociologie, 11*(1), 3–33. https://doi.org/10.2307/3320131

Chaskin, R. J., & Joseph, M. L. (2011). Social interaction in mixed-income developments: Relational expectations and emerging reality. *Journal of Urban Affairs, 33*(2), 209–237. https://doi.org/10.1111/j.1467-9906.2010.00537.x

Chaskin, R. J., Sichling, F., & Joseph, M. L. (2013). Youth in mixed-income communities replacing public housing complexes: Context, dynamics and response. *Cities, 35*, 423–431. https://doi.org/10.1016/j.cities.2013.03.009

Costarelli, I., Kleinhans, R., & Mugnano, S. (2019). Reframing social mix in affordable housing initiatives in Italy and in the Netherlands. Closing the gap between discourses and practices? *Cities, 90*, 131–140. https://doi.org/10.1016/j.cities.2019.01.033

Costarelli, I., Kleinhans, R., & Mugnano, S. (2020). 'Active, young, and resourceful': Sorting the 'good' tenant through mechanisms of conditionality. *Housing Studies*. https://doi.org/10.1080/02673037.2020.1759789

Desponds, D., Auclair, E., Bergel, P., & Bertucci, M. M. (Eds). (2014). *Les habitants: Acteurs de la rénovation urbaine?* [The inhabitants: Actors of urban renewal?] PU.

Fincher, R., Iveson, K., Leitner, H., & Preston, V. (2014). Planning in the multicultural city: Celebrating diversity or reinforcing difference? *Progress in Planning*, 92, 1–55. https://doi.org/10.1016/j.progress.2013.04.001

Jupp, B. (1999). *Living together. Community life on mixed tenure estates*. Demos.

Katz, M. B. (1993). *The "underclass" debate: Views from history*. University Press.

Kleinhans, R. (2004). Social implications of housing diversification in urban renewal: A review of recent literature. *Journal of Housing and the Built Environment*, 19(4), 367–390. https://doi.org/10.1007/s10901-004-3041-5

Leacock, E. (1968). The concept of culture and its significance for school counselors. *The Personnel and Guidance Journal*, 46(9), 844–851. https://doi.org/10.1002/j.2164-4918.1968.tb03256.x

Lees, L. (2008). Gentrification and social mixing: Towards an inclusive urban renaissance? *Urban Studies*, 45(12), 2449–2470. https://doi.org/10.1177/0042098008097099

Lelévrier, C. (2013). Social mix neighbourhood policies and social interaction: The experience of newcomers in three new renewal developments in France. *Cities*, 35, 409–416. https://doi.org/10.1016/j.cities.2013.03.003

Lewis, O. (1966). *La vida: A Puerto Rican family in the culture of poverty—San Juan and New York*. Random House.

Matejskova, T., & Leitner, H. (2011). Urban encounters with difference: The contact hypothesis and immigrant integration projects in eastern Berlin. *Social & Cultural Geography*, 12(7), 717–741. https://doi.org/10.1080/14649365.2011.610234

Ministry of Equality, Territory and Housing. (2015). *Dossier de Presse: Sylvia Pinel présente 20 actions pour améliorer la mixité sociale dans le logement* [Press Kit: Sylvia Pinel presents 20 actions to improve the social diversity in housing].

Mugnano, S., & Costarelli, I. (2015). Il mix sociale nelle politiche di rigenerazione urbana dei grandi complessi residenziali a Milano [The social mix in the urban regeneration policies of large complexes residential buildings in Milan]. *Sociologia urbana e rurale*, 108, 86–100. doi:10.3280/SUR2015-108006.

Mugnano, S., & Palvarini, P. (2013). 'Sharing space without hanging together': A case study of social mix policy in Milan. *Cities*, 35, 417–422. https://doi.org/10.1016/j.cities.2013.03.008

Nicholls, W. J. (2005). Associationalism from above: Explaining failure through France's *Politique de la Ville*. *Urban Studies*, 43(10), 1779–1802. https://doi.org/10.1080/00420980600838135

OECD. (2018). *Compare your country: Affordable housing*. Social Housing. https://www1.compareyourcountry.org/housing/en/3/all/default

Préteceille, E. (2009). La ségrégation ethno-raciale a-t-elle augmenté dans la metropole parisienne? [Has ethno-racial segregation increased in the Paris metropolis?]. *Revue française de sociologie*, 50(3), 489–519. https://doi.org/10.3917/rfs.503.0489

Priemus, H., Dieleman, F., & Clapham, D. (1999). Current developments in social housing management. *Netherlands Journal of Housing and the Built Environment*, 14(3), 211–223. https://doi.org/10.1007/BF02496678

Raveaud, M., & Zanten, A. V. (2007). Choosing the local school: Middle class parents' values and social and ethnic mix in London and Paris. *Journal of Education Policy*, 22(1), 107–124. https://doi.org/10.1080/02680930601065817

Rose, D., Germain, A., Bacqué, M. H., Bridge, G., Fijalkow, Y., & Slater, T. (2013). Social mix and neighbourhood revitalization in a transatlantic perspective: Comparing local policy discourses and expectations in Paris (France), Bristol (UK) and Montreal (Canada). *International Journal of Urban and Regional Research*, 37(2), 430–450. https://doi.org/10.1111/j.1468-2427.2012.01127.x

Sen, A. (1992). *Inequality reexamined*. Russell Sage Foundation.

Tammaru, T., Van Ham, M., Marcińczak, S., & Musterd, S. (Eds.). (2016). *Socio-economic segregation in European capital cities: East meets West*. Routledge.

Tissot, S. (2008). "French suburbs": A new problem or a new approach to social exclusion? *Working Paper Series*, (160).

Tunstall, R., & Fenton, A. (2006). *In the mix. A review of mixed income, mixed tenure, mixed communities: What do we know?* Housing Corporation, Joseph Rowntree Foundation, English Partnerships.

Valentine, C. A. (1968). *Culture and poverty: Critique and counter-proposals*. University of Chicago Press.

Valentine, G. (2008). Living with difference: Reflections on geographies of encounter. *Progress in Human Geography*, 32(3), 323–337. https://doi.org/10.1177/0309133308089372

Van Eijk, G. (2010). Does living in a poor neighbourhood result in network poverty? A study on local networks, locality-based relationships and neighbourhood settings. *Journal of Housing and the Built Environment*, 25(4), 467–480. https://doi.org/10.1007/s10901-010-9198-1

Veldboer, L., Kleinhans, R., & Duyvendak, J. W. (2002). The diversified neighbourhood in Western Europe and the United States: How do countries deal with the spatial distribution of economic and cultural differences? *Journal of International Migration and Integration*, 3(1), 41–64. https://doi.org/10.1007/s12134-002-1002-y

Wilson, H. F., & Darling, J. (2016). The possibilities of encounter. In J. Darling & H. F. Wilson (Eds.), *Encountering the city: Urban encounters from Accra to New York* (pp. 97–110). Routledge.

Wilson, W. J. (1987). *The truly disadvantaged: The inner city, the underclass, and public policy*. University of Chicago Press.

Wise, A. (2009). Everyday multiculturalism: Transversal crossings and working class cosmopolitans. In A. Wise & S. Velayutham (Eds.), *Everyday multiculturalism* (pp. 21–45). Palgrave Macmillan.

Does pre-purchase counseling help low-income buyers choose and sustain homeownership in socially mixed destination neighborhoods?

Anna Maria Santiago and Joffré Leroux

ABSTRACT
For 3 decades, U.S. federal housing policies have sought to increase access to socially diverse and high opportunity neighborhoods and improve the quality of life for low-income families. Absent from current discussions of the costs and benefits of socially mixed communities is the potential value that they may have to low-income families seeking to purchase their own homes. In this paper, we examine the extent to which participation in homebuyer education and counseling programs supports sustainable low-income homeownership in socially mixed neighborhoods. Using quasi-experimental methodologies and longitudinal data from the Denver Housing Study for a sample of 533 low-income homebuyers, this study examines whether, compared with a comparison group of public housing residents who purchased homes on their own, participants in Denver Housing Authority's (DHA) homebuyer education and counseling program (HOP) were (1) more likely to purchase homes in socially mixed destination neighborhoods; and (2) sustain homeownership over time. Results show that low-income homebuyers purchased homes in destination neighborhoods characterized by considerable ethnic and income mix. When compared to non-HOP homebuyers, HOP homebuyers also were better off in terms of 2018 home value appreciation and fewer foreclosures, suggesting that homebuyer education and counseling improves long-term sustainability of homeownership.

Introduction

Since the mid-1960s, the U.S. federal government has supported numerous housing policy initiatives aimed at increasing the housing and economic opportunities available to low-income families (Galster & Santiago, 2008; Kleit & Galvez, 2011; Kneebone et al., 2019; Lucio et al., 2014; Oakley & Burchfield, 2009; Rohe & Watson, 2007; Shlay, 2006; Thomas et al., 2018). The underlying assumption scaffolding these initiatives maintains that expanding and improving housing and neighborhood options for low-income families enhances health and well-being, fosters economic and social mobility, and enables families to move from neighborhoods of concentrated disadvantage and social vulnerability to places of opportunity (see J. C. Fraser et al., 2013; Galster & Friedrichs, 2015; Wilson, 1987). For nearly 3 decades, U.S. federal housing policies have sought to transform low-income neighborhoods, increase access to diverse and high opportunity neighborhoods, and improve the quality of life for low-income families. These policy goals have been pursued through the desegregation of subsidized housing units, the use of Housing Choice Vouchers to increase access to private rental housing in a wide variety of neighborhoods, and at times, through the demolition of severely distressed public housing and its replacement with higher quality units in socially mixed communities—neighborhoods defined as those containing "diverse shares of social groups" (Galster & Friedrichs, 2015, p. 176). Socially mixed community development in the United States has been used to diversify the racial, ethnic and/or income composition of urban residential space, primarily at the neighborhood level, through redevelopment projects aimed at improving neighborhood housing stock and amenities in order to attract more affluent and often White residents (e.g., Chaskin et al., 2012).

Nonetheless, the value of socially mixed neighborhoods or communities to low-income families in the United States has been the subject of considerable scholarly and policy debate—a debate reinvigorated by the Great Recession (see Ellen & Dastrup, 2012; Saegert, 2015). Previous studies evaluating the outcomes associated with socially mixed housing in the United States report contradictory results: some suggest gains in housing quality and neighborhood resources (e.g., Brophy & Smith, 1997; Curley, 2010; Gress et al., 2016; Hyde & Fischer, 2021; Vesselinov et al., 2018) and neighborhood stability (G. Galster et al., 2005) while others note limited evidence of improvements in social mobility, social networks, and the interactions between lower income and more affluent neighbors (Buron et al., 2002; J. C. Fraser et al., 2013; Chaskin & Joseph, 2011; Clampet-Lundquist, 2004; J. Fraser et al., 2012; Oakley & Burchfield, 2009; Vale & Shamsuddin, 2015). These disparate findings on the benefits of and lingering concerns about social mix are replicated in studies across Europe, Australia, and Canada (see Arthurson, 2012; Arthurson et al., 2015; August & Walks, 2012; Bolt et al., 2010; Bucerius et al., 2017; Kleinhans & Varady, 2011).

Currently absent from this discussion of the costs and benefits of socially mixed communities is the potential value that they may have to low-income families seeking to purchase their own homes. Although both social mix and low-income homeownership could be conceivably intertwined theoretically and practically (e.g., promoting low-income homeownership in socially mixed neighborhoods), the potential intersection of these housing policy initiatives has not been fully explored in the U.S. context. Previous studies have noted that minority homebuyers prefer mixed neighborhoods (see review in Turner & Rawlings, 2009). Moreover, a recent benefit cost analysis of an innovative program for self-sufficiency and homeownership among low-income households receiving housing subsidies (Galster et al., 2019) suggests that program benefits accrued not only to program participants but also to their new (higher-income) neighbors and neighborhoods when low-income participants purchased homes (see p. 7).

Nonetheless, the extant literature underscores the risks associated with low-income homeownership. Previous studies suggest that low-income homebuyers, particularly minority homebuyers, make significant tradeoffs in terms of the sustainability of homeownership through constraints on residential location, equity building and heightened risks of foreclosures, predatory refinancing, and forced sales (see Garriga et al., 2017; Herbert et al., 2014; Herbert & Belsky, 2008; Hyra & Rugh, 2016; Lerman & Zhang, 2016; Lens, 2018; Mayock & Malacrida, 2018; Van Zandt & Rohe, 2011). In the aftermath of the Great Recession, policymakers have expressed renewed concerns about the value of owning a home for low-income families who may not have the financial means to purchase high quality homes in socially mixed, opportunity-rich neighborhoods or the ability to sustain homeownership over the long term[1] (Bostic & Lee, 2008; Clark, 2013; Goodman & Mayer, 2018; Mallach, 2011; Wainer & Zabel, 2020).

Proponents of low-income homeownership, however, point to the potential of pre- and/or post-homebuyer education and counseling as a tool that may mitigate these concerns (Ding et al., 2008; Myhre & Watson, 2017; Peck et al., 2019; Quercia et al., 2006; Quercia & Wachter, 1996; Rohe et al., 2002; Santiago et al., 2010a, 2010b, 2017). Moreover, as we argue here, such programs may provide a point of intersection between efforts to promote low-income homeownership and continued community investment in socially mixed neighborhood redevelopment. In this paper, we examine the extent to which participation in homebuyer education and counseling programs supports sustainable low-income homeownership in socially mixed neighborhoods. Using quasi-experimental methodologies and longitudinal data from the Denver Housing Study for a sample of 533 low-income homebuyers, this study examines whether, compared with a control group of public housing residents who purchased homes on their own, participants in Denver Housing Authority's (DHA) homebuyer education and counseling program (HOP) were (1) more likely to purchase homes in socially mixed destination neighborhoods; and (2) sustain homeownership over time.

The impact of homebuyer education and counseling programs

Homebuyer education and counseling is considered the bedrock that makes low-income homeownership feasible and sustainable. These programs provide prospective homebuyers with the requisite skills regarding budgeting and credit, knowledge about mortgages and the mortgage process, and facilitates access to sustainable mortgage credit (Argento et al., 2019). Long-standing interest in the effectiveness of pre-purchase homebuyer education and counseling programs has produced a rich and diverse literature focused primarily on the attainment of homeownership and short-term, post-purchase mortgage repayment behaviors (see reviews by Collins & O'Rourke, 2011; Mayer & Temkin, 2016; Myhre & Watson, 2017; Quercia & Wachter, 1996; Sackett, 2016). Previous studies have reported significantly lower rates of mortgage defaults and foreclosures for low-income homeowners who received homebuyer education and counseling compared to similar homeowners who did not (Agarwal et al., 2010; Avila et al., 2013; Ding et al., 2008; Hirad & Zorn, 2002; Mayer & Temkin, 2016; Myhre & Watson, 2017; Temkin et al., 2014). Nevertheless, others have reported no effect on the timeliness of mortgage payments or foreclosure prevention (Peck et al., 2019; Quercia & Spader, 2008; Smith et al., 2017; Theodos et al., 2015).

The variability in previous findings is associated with the range of existing homeowner education and counseling programs and the considerable variation in who they serve; what, when, where and how curricula are taught; and the duration of program participation (Fannie Mae, 2017). Additionally, few evaluations of homeowner education and counseling programs have utilized randomized control trials or other statistical techniques that make it possible to reliably estimate program effects and differences across program components. The 2015 study of financial coaching programs by Theodos et al. (2015) and the First-Time Homebuyer Education and Counseling Demonstration conducted by HUD that is currently in the field (see DeMarco et al., 2017; Peck et al., 2019) are notable exceptions. Moreover, given the relatively short periods of homeownership covered in existing post-purchase studies (e.g., 1–2 years, less than 4 years), we still have limited information about the role that homebuyer education and counseling plays in enhancing sustainability of homeownership over longer periods of time.

To our knowledge, no previous studies have examined how homebuyer education and counseling has played a role in the selection of destination neighborhoods, and particularly the choice of socially mixed neighborhoods. However, prior studies of mobility counseling programs for low-income, subsidized housing voucher recipients (Chetty et al., 2016; Cunningham et al., 2010; Darrah & DeLuca, 2014; Sard & Rice, 2016) suggest that such counseling, if incorporated as a component of homebuyer education, might be effective in promoting homeownership in more socially mixed neighborhoods. Additionally, little is known about the influence of homebuyer education and counseling on homeownership in the long term and other key indicators of sustainability. To address these gaps in the literature, this study examines the impact that pre- and post-homebuyer education and counseling has had on the selection and purchase of homes located in socially mixed neighborhoods and on five indicators of sustainable homeownership: homeownership rates, duration of homeownership tenure, subsequent home sales, foreclosures, and home value appreciation. To assess impact, these indicators were traced through the end of 2018 for a cohort of 533 former public housing residents who purchased their homes between 1995 and 2012; only 190 of whom had graduated from a homebuyer education and counseling program offered by the Denver Housing Authority to its residents.

The Denver Housing Authority's HomeOwnership Program

The Denver Housing Authority (DHA) launched its HomeOwnership Program (HOP) in 1994. All DHA public housing residents or Housing Choice Voucher holders are eligible to enroll in the program and remain in it as long as they live in DHA housing. In addition to being an early adopter of homebuyer education and counseling, DHA also has promoted subsidized housing residence in socially mixed neighborhoods for more than 50 years (see discussion in Galster et al., 2003; Santiago et al., 2001). Approximately two thirds of HOP residents live in some type of socially mixed neighborhood via dispersed housing, Housing Choice vouchers, or one of the HOPE VI developments. Many combine their participation in HOP with that of the Family Self-Sufficiency Program (see full description in Santiago et al., 2017). In collaboration with case management staff members, HOP participants design individualized plans outlining their human and financial capital asset development goals. Program participants are expected to complete financial assessments, review credit reports, money management counseling annually and participate in other activities (e.g., credit repair) as needed. HOP offers several classes each month on a wide range of financial capability topics (e.g., budgeting, debt reduction, saving, purchasing assets), and participants are eligible to enroll in Matched Savings Accounts, whereby DHA provides one to one matches of participant savings deposits up to US$1,500. In addition to the education, counseling, and supportive services provided by the HOP, Denver's program offered several financial incentive and assistance programs for tuition, books, transportation, or childcare that enable participants to acquire both financial and human capital assets until 2008. While there are no time limits for program participation, penalties for program noncompliance are extensive. Noncompliant HOP participants are terminated and lose the DHA match from their matched savings accounts or other escrow funds.

Two stages of program activities are associated with HOP. During the first stage, the focus is on activities leading to debt reduction, credit repair, savings accumulation and/or employment enhancement. Participants identified by program staff as being within a year of ability to purchase their own homes, which is minimally defined as being employed with the current employer for 1 year or more and having personal savings of at least US$500, move to the second stage of program activities. This second stage, known as the Home Buyers Club, provides participants with intensive real estate and finance training, presentations by housing industry representatives, peer support, and special benefits such as low mortgage interest rates, mortgage fee discounts, down payment and closing cost assistance and, when appropriate, second mortgage assistance (see discussion in Santiago et al., 2017).

Integrated into the homebuyer counseling sessions are discussions about what constitutes a sound home purchase including what to look for in both the house and the bundle of services and amenities that are tied to a home and neighborhood. These sessions include discussions about fair housing and lending practices. Home Buyers Club participants are expected to attend nine of the 12 classes offered monthly during the course of the year, complete the Colorado Housing Finance Authority home-ownership seminar, and pass a homeownership exam administered upon conclusion of the seminar. One-on-one meetings with case managers or other HOP staff members increase in frequency as participants move through the home contracting and mortgage process. Access to counseling does not end with home purchase. HOP graduates are welcome to seek counseling and assistance indefinitely from program staff. Post-purchase activities include seminars on home repair, and individual counseling aimed at loss mitigation, refinancing, loan modifications, delinquency, and foreclosure prevention. Following the Great Recession, the HOP Program was designated as a HUD-certified homebuyer counseling agency whose post-purchase services were made available to the general public as well.

In addition to HOP, there are several other programs within DHA that have expanded the housing and economic opportunities available to low-income families through the use of social mix. Beginning in the late 1960s, DHA purchased foreclosed homes or completed infill construction of new dwelling units in neighborhoods throughout the city and county of Denver. Known as the dispersed housing program, this initiative enabled subsidized housing families to live in neighborhoods in DHA-owned rentals alongside more affluent neighbors (see Galster et al., 2003). Currently, the DHA owns 1,500 of these dispersed units. Since the early 1990s, DHA has used mixed income housing redevelopment strategies to revitalize public housing units and stabilize neighborhoods through the completion of five HOPE VI development projects and one Choice Neighborhood project (the successor of HOPE VI). In total, these mixed income development initiatives have produced approximately 5,000 affordable housing units—representing one-quarter of all of the units available in the City and County of Denver (ChangeLab Solutions, 2018; Denver Housing Authority, n.d.; Jackson, 2018). Additionally, DHA manages approximately 6,000 Housing

Choice Vouchers. Thus, a significant fraction of DHA residents or Housing Choice Voucher holders have lived in socially mixed neighborhoods as subsidized housing tenants which, in turn, would be expected to influence potential destination neighborhoods when considering purchasing a home.

Measuring impacts from HOP participation

For this paper, quasi-experimental impact analyzes of the effects of homebuyer education and counseling were conducted on the selection of destination neighborhoods as well as a series of sustainable homeownership outcomes for two groups of Denver public housing residents who purchased homes between 1995 and 2012 (n = 533). The first group received pre-purchase homebuyer education and counseling through HOP (n = 190); many participated in post-purchase counseling activities as well. The second group of DHA residents purchased homes on their own foregoing any participation in HOP (n = 343). Please note that this was not a matter of random assignment into homebuyer education and counseling that might occur in a RCT study design. Rather, we identified these individuals from administrative data that documents exits from DHA and the reasons for those exits; thus, these low-income homebuyers became part of an extension to our larger *Denver Housing Study*. This group of homebuyers also purchased homes during the same time period as the HOP participants but made the decision not to participate in HOP when residing in DHA.

Data sources used in our analyses include: (a) unpublished DHA administrative data for the period between 1995 and 2012; (b) homeowner and dwelling data derived from the *Denver Housing Study*; (c) home transaction data in the public domain including home values, purchases, sales, and foreclosures from records archived in the Real Property Division and the Office of the Assessor for the various counties where our homeowners resided in the Denver metropolitan area. In order to estimate tract level indicators of neighborhood social mix, we used decennial Census data from 1990, 2000, and 2010 as well as data from the American Community Survey for the period between 2009 and 2018. For the period between 1990 and 2010, we used linear interpolation techniques to estimate annual indicators of neighborhood characteristics.

In this study, homeownership was identified using several indicators in DHA administrative databases identifying the housing tenure of residents when they moved out of public housing. The first looked at the "reason to vacate" field in the administrative database; exit for homeownership was flagged as an indicator of homeownership. A second item focused on the forwarding address for the homebuyer. Homebuyer names and addresses were matched with public domain information from the Real Property and Tax Assessors data files to verify ownership of the original home purchased and associated with their exit from DHA. These public databases were then used since time of purchase to track homeownership status through the end of 2018. The same databases also were used to identify whether the original homes were sold or went into foreclosure. Tax assessor data allowed the tracking of changes in home values since time of purchase until time of sale, foreclosure or December 2018, whichever was the latest point of homeownership.

Real Property data were used to identify the census tract location of each original home. Census data were employed to estimate two indicators of social mix within homebuyer destination neighborhoods in the Denver metropolitan area. We utilized two entropy-based measures of similarity to describe how evenly the different income and ethnic groups are distributed across Denver neighborhoods (e.g., Fischer, 2003). Entropy indices have the property of collapsing differences in group memberships for several groups into one single, unidimensional score.

Estimating neighborhood ethnic mix

Using U.S. Census nomenclature, we define four ethnic groups g: non-Hispanic White, non-Hispanic-Black, Hispanic, and other. The proportion of the population of census tract i in year t belonging to group g is labeled p_{git}. In each census tract, the ethnic entropy index for a given year is calculated as:

$$H_{it} = \frac{1}{\ln(4)} \sum_{g=1}^{4} p_{git} \ln\left(\frac{1}{p_{git}}\right)$$

Where dividing by ln(4) ensures that the resulting index is bounded between 0 and 1. A census tract in which all four groups are equally represented would have an index of 1, and a census tract in which only one group is present would have an index of 0.

For each census tract, ethnic entropy is calculated for years for the period from 1990 to 2018. For all years, 2010 census tract boundaries are used, with 1990 and 2000 data normalized to 2010 boundaries by the IPUMS National Geographic Information System (IPUMS NHGIS), see Manson et al. (2020). Entropy is calculated using decennial census data for years 2010 and before: for each tract-year, the proportion of each ethnic group is linearly interpolated from adjoining decennial censuses, and the entropy measure is calculated from those interpolated proportions. For years 2011–2018, data used are from the American Community Survey 3-year estimates and each year's measurement is used.

Estimating neighborhood income mix

The Theil index, or Theil's T, is a widely-used entropy-based measure of income spread (Organization for Economic Cooperation and Development [OECD], 2016; Semega et al., 2020). Unlike the ethnic entropy measure described above, the Theil index incorporates not only relative group size but also magnitude of income disparity.

In this study, the Theil index is calculated using American Community Survey data on mean household income by income quintile and mean household income by tract. For a given quintile g in census tract i in year t, the mean household income for that quintile is denoted k_{git} and the mean household income for that census tract is denoted μ_{it}.

In each census tract, the Theil index for a given year is calculated as

$$T_{it} = \frac{1}{\ln(5)} \sum_{g=1}^{5} 0.2 * \frac{k_{git}}{\mu_{it}} \ln\left(\frac{k_{git}}{\mu_{it}}\right)$$

where 0.2 is the share of households in each quintile.

Please note that this estimate of income entropy is an approximation—a "true" measure of entropy would sum over each household, not over each income quintile. This approximation simplifies reality by setting the income of each household in a quintile to the value of the mean income in that quintile. The index is calculated as if every household in the bottom quintile made the same amount of money, and every household in the second quintile made the same, and so on. Intra-quintile variation is flattened, but, nonetheless, the entropy measure captures whether the income quintiles are far away or close to each other. The Theil index is calculated only for the years 2009–2018 using the 5-year ACS ending that year. Unfortunately, as a result of changes in the income categories available in earlier releases of the ACS and the IPUMS NHGIS data, comparable income-quintile data are not available for the period prior to 2009.

Indicators of sustainable homeownership

Real Property data were used to derive five indicators of sustainable homeownership. The first was a dummy variable denoting ownership of the original home in 2018 (coded 1 = yes; 0 = no). The second was a measure indicating the duration of ownership of the original home in years from time of purchase through time of sale, foreclosure or current occupancy in 2018, whichever was latest. The third was a dummy variable denoting whether the original home was sold prior to 2019 (coded 1 = yes; 0 = no). The fourth was a dummy variable denoting whether the original home was foreclosed upon prior to 2019 (coded 1 = yes; 0 = no). Finally, real property and tax assessor data were employed to estimate the value of the original home at the last point of homeownership by our DHA

Table 1. Pre-matching descriptive statistics homeownership outcomes.

	HOP homebuyer			Non-HOP homebuyer		
Outcome	Mean	SD	n	Mean	SD	n
Total years of home ownership	11.75	5.84	190	10.67	6.78	333
Percent living in original home in 2019 (%)	50.0	50.1	190	39.0	48.9	333
Average purchase price of original home ($)	143,947	47,167	189	133,608	52,898	328
Average last home value recorded for original home ($)	257,947	106,989	178	216,407	107,537	311
Appreciation of original home ($)	115,745	100,929	177	81,405	107,029	307
Average annualized appreciation of original home ($)	8411	9540	177	3920	15,181	307
Average current value of original home in 2019 ($ if still homeowner)	328,464	73,155	95	317,395	63,380	129
Percent selling original home	30.0	45.9	190	32.4	46.9	333
Percent experiencing foreclosure on original home	20.00	40.10	190	28.80	45.36	333
Percent purchasing a second home	11.60	32.08	190	9.91	29.90	343
Percent purchasing a third home	2.11	14.39	190	2.04	14.16	343

homebuyers. This value was estimated at time of sale, foreclosure or current occupancy in 2018, whichever was latest and is presented as both the overall appreciation since time of purchase and the average annualized rate of home value appreciation. A summary of these outcomes prior to our matching techniques is presented in Table 1.

As shown in Table 1, half of the HOP homebuyers still owned their original homes in December 2018. On average, they had owned their homes for 11.75 years. The average appreciation of the original home over the course of homeownership was US$115,745; the average annualized rate of home value appreciation was US$8,411. The average last home value for all original homes (including values for homes at time of sale or foreclosure) was US$257,947. For homes that were still owned as of December 2018, the average home value was US$328,464. Nearly one out of three homeowners had sold their original homes with 11.6% going on to purchase a second home and another 2.1% purchasing a third home. One out of five HOP homebuyers had experienced a foreclosure with the first one occurring in 2004 and most occurring during the Great Recession. In contrast, fewer non-HOP homebuyers remained in their original homes by 2018 (39%). About one-third had sold their homes and nearly 29% had foreclosed. Average appreciation of the original home was US$81,405; the average annualized rate of home value appreciation was US$3,920. The last average value for all original homes was US$216,407; the current value for homes still owned by non-HOP homebuyers in 2019 was US$317,395.

Analytical approach

Propensity score analysis using one-to-one nearest neighbor matching with replacement was employed to match HOP homeowners and non-HOP homeowners on a common set of program characteristics (DHA housing program assignment, duration of residence in DHA subsidized housing) and participant characteristics (age, gender, educational attainment, immigrant status, single parent status, family size, earnings at time of home purchase; timing of home purchase). The characteristics of HOP homeowners and non-HOP homeowners prior to matching are summarized in Appendix A. These data suggest that HOP homebuyers were more likely to be female, older, U.S. born, African American, with larger families and have higher incomes at time of purchase than non-HOP homebuyers. Additionally, HOP homebuyers lived in DHA subsidized housing for longer periods of time than non-HOP homebuyers, were more likely to participate in the FSS Program, and more likely to purchase homes after the Great Recession. These observed differences between the two groups of homebuyers underscore the need for propensity score matching.

The impact parameter used is the average treatment effect on the treated (ATET), estimated by a difference in means across matched samples using *teffects psmatch* in Stata 14. The goal is to estimate the average treatment effect on the treated (ATET) of participating in the HOP program. For a given individual i and outcome Y, we label $Y_i(1)$ the value of that outcome for that individual if they had participated in the HOP program, and $Y_i(0)$ the value of that outcome if they had not. Only one of these two potential outcomes can be observed for each individual, and so the missing outcome has to be estimated. Propensity score matching was used to do so. First, the following logit regression is estimated using maximum likelihood:

$$\Pr[HOP_i = 1|x_i] = f(\beta x_i) + \eta_i$$

Where HOP_i is an indicator taking on the value 1 if a given observation (individual) participates in the HOP program, and x_i is a vector of observable characteristics for each household that help predict whether a given household participates in the HOP program or not. This matching strategy employs individual characteristics available in the DHA administrative data that are related to participation in HOP pre-purchase homebuyer education and counseling. Specifically, the observable characteristics employed are an indicator for whether an individual completed schooling beyond high school, the natural log of household income, duration of DHA residence in months, an indicator for whether the home was purchased prior to 2006 (the start of the Great Recession in Denver), an indicator for whether the homebuyer lived in a DHA development (instead of dispersed housing or holding an HCV voucher) while in DHA, and a set of demographic indicators for ethnicity, gender, immigrant status, single parent status and whether family size was four or greater.

Having estimated the logit regression, the fitted probabilities for each individual in the sample can be used. These fitted probabilities are the propensity score—the estimated probability that an individual with the same characteristics would have opted to enter the HOP program. A comparison group was then created using propensity score matching. For each HOP graduate, we selected the non-HOP homebuyer with the closest propensity score to the graduate. Please note, however, that if multiple non-treated observations are tied as the nearest neighbor for a treated observation, all are included in the comparison group but weighted such that the sum of the weights add to one. Thus, we have a weighted comparison group of the same size as the treatment group. The treatment group provide us the $Y_i(1)$ directly, and the matched comparison observation for each treatment provides us with $Y_i(0)$: the assumption is that the matched observation provides us with the unobserved potential outcome if that individual had not graduated from HOP.

Following Abadie and Imbens (2016), the necessary assumptions are (1) the conditional independence assumptions, $Y(1), Y(0) \perp HOP|x$, and (2) the common support assumption, $0 < p(x_i) < 1$. The conditional independence assumption states that, after controlling for the variables we select on, HOP participation status has no effect on the level of potential outcomes, and the common support assumption states that no individual in our sample will either surely choose HOP or surely not choose HOP based on their propensity score.

We can then easily compare the means of the treated and comparison groups to obtain the average treatment effect on the treated (ATET):

$$ATET = \frac{1}{N}(\bar{Y}_t - \bar{Y}_c)$$

Where $\bar{Y}_t$ is the outcome mean in the treated group, and $\bar{Y}_c$ the outcome mean in the matched control group.

Previous impact analyses (see Heckman et al., 1997, 1998; Heckman & Navarro-Lozano, 2004) have utilized this statistical matching of samples based on observed characteristics of treatment and comparison groups as a way of reducing selection bias. When a wide array of covariates are included in the matching process, these methods have been shown to approximate experimental results (Cook & Steiner, 2010; Shadish et al., 2008).

To ensure that the results are robust to different matching specifications (e.g., one-to-many matching and matching with a propensity score), the covariate balance for each outcome was assessed using standardized differences and variance ratios (Austin, 2009). The results of these analysis are presented in Appendix B. Most variables are closely balanced following matching, with standardized differences falling within the 0.1 to 0.2 range suggested by Stuart (2019) between the two groups after balancing. One variable does not: duration in DHA was longer for HOP graduates, a standardized difference of 0.28 and variance ratio of 1.02.

Results

The social mix of destination neighborhoods of low-income homebuyers

Figures 1a-c show the degree of ethnic mix within census tracts in the Denver metropolitan area during 2000, 2010, and 2018 as well as the destination neighborhoods of low-income homebuyers in the study. Census tract ethnic entropy scores approaching 0 reflect lower levels of ethnic mix while those approaching the 100th percentile reflect higher levels of ethnic mix. These maps suggest that study homebuyers typically purchased homes in ethnically diverse neighborhoods that remained diverse throughout the 2000–2018 period.

Figures 2a and b show the degree of income mix within the census tracts for 2010 and 2018. Please note that census tract income entropy scores are interpreted as follows: lower scores reflect less income inequality and greater income mix while higher scores reflect more income inequality and less income mix within the census tract. Again, these maps suggest that study homebuyers typically purchased homes in mixed income neighborhoods and that these neighborhoods generally did not experience increased segregation by income between 2010 and 2018.

Figure 1. (a). Ethnic entropy in the Denver metro area by census tract, 2000. (b). Ethnic entropy in the Denver metro area by census tract, 2010. (c). Ethnic entropy in the Denver metro area by census tract, 2018.

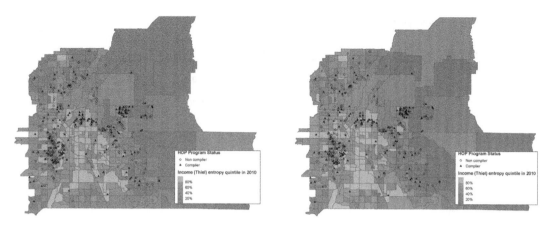

Figure 2. (a). Income (Thiel) entropy in the Denver metro area by census tract, 2010. (b). Income (Thiel) entropy in the Denver metro area by census tract, 2018.

Were HOP graduates more likely to purchase homes in more socially mixed neighborhoods than their non-HOP counterparts? To address this question, we conducted propensity score analyses to assess differences in destination neighborhood social mix between HOP and non-HOP homebuyers at time of move in and 2018 (see Table 2). Since the vast majority of the homebuyers purchased their homes by 2010, we also estimated OLS regression models using year of purchase fixed effects to predict destination neighborhood social mix at time of purchase and in 2010 given homebuyer and DHA program characteristics at time of move-in; these results are summarized in Table 3. Finally, to examine whether neighborhood characteristics, including social mix at time of home purchase, had any influence on neighborhood social mix post purchase, we estimated another set of OLS regression models using year of purchase fixed effects to predict ethnic and income entropy in 2018 (see Table 4).

Since HOP and non-HOP homebuyers differ on dimension that might also influence neighborhood choice, we used propensity score matching to match the two samples of homebuyers. Table 2 shows the average treatment effects reported as differences in means in ethnic and income entropy at time of move-in and 2018 between HOP and non-HOP homebuyers after propensity score matching. As we can see, both groups purchased homes in destination neighborhoods with high levels of social mix both in terms of ethnicity and income. HOP homebuyers purchased in destination neighborhoods with ethnic entropy scores that were higher by 0.03 at move in (.69 vs. .65, respectively) relative to the non-HOP comparison group. By 2018, neighborhood ethnic entropy averaged .71 in HOP graduate

Table 2. Propensity score analyses of ethnic and income entropy for destination neighborhoods of low-income homebuyers.

Entropy measures*	HOP	Non-HOP	Difference (ATET)	Standard Errors	N of Observations Treated	Control	Weighted Control*
Ethnic entropy in destination neighborhood in year moved in	0.686	0.654	0.032	0.022	169	190	169
Ethnic entropy in destination neighborhood in 2018	0.711	0.689	0.022	0.021	169	190	169
Thiel income entropy in destination neighborhood in 2018**	0.155	0.148	0.007	0.007	169	190	169
Differences in means significant at $p < .05$ are bolded							

*Propensity scores are matched one-to-one with the nearest neighbor. If multiple non-treated observations are the nearest neighbor for an observation, all are included in the control group but weighed such that the sum of weights add to one.
** Thiel income entropy scores could not be estimated for destination neighborhoods for year moved in for all homebuyers because data were not available prior to 2010.

Table 3. OLS regression models predicting social mix at time of move-in and 2010.

Selected Characteristics	Ethnic entropy of census tract, year moved in[a]		Ethnic entropy of census tract, 2010[a]		Theil index of census tract, 2010[b]	
Homebuyer characteristics						
HOP graduate	0.01	(0.02)	0.02	(0.02)	0.01	(0.01)
Age 40 or older	−0.02	(0.01)	−0.02*	(0.01)	0.01	(0.01)
Female	−0.01	(0.02)	0.00	(0.02)	−0.01*	(0.01)
Race/Ethnicity						
Latino	−0.11***	(0.02)	−0.16***	(0.02)	−0.01	(0.01)
Other than African-American or Hispanic	−0.12***	(0.03)	−0.14***	(0.03)	−0.01	(0.01)
Immigrant	0.00	(0.02)	0.02	(0.01)	−0.01	(0.01)
Educational attainment of HS degree or higher	−0.02	(0.02)	0.01	(0.02)	0.00	(0.01)
Household characteristics at time of move-in						
Single parent	−0.01	(0.02)	0.00	(0.02)	0.00	(0.01)
Family size ≥ 4	−0.02	(0.01)	0.01	(0.01)	−0.01	(0.01)
Household income (ln)	−0.02	(0.02)	0.00	(0.02)	0.00	(0.01)
DHA Program Characteristics						
Duration in DHA greater ≥ 6 years	0.00	(0.01)	0.01	(0.01)	−0.01	(0.01)
Lived in DHA dispersed housing	0.00	(0.02)	0.01	(0.01)	−0.01	(0.01)
Home Purchase						
Purchased house prior to Great Recession	−0.06	(0.06)	−0.16***	(0.06)	0.05***	(0.02)
Fixed effects for move-in year	YES		YES		YES	
N	445		445		445	
R^2	0.173		0.281		0.086	
Adjusted R^2	0.113		0.229		0.014	
F-statistic	2.966***		5.491***		1.202	

*p < .1; **p < .05; ***p < .01, based on robust standard errors.
[a]Greater ethnic mix is denoted by increases in ethnic entropy scores.
[b]Greater income mix is denoted by decreases in the Theil index.

destination neighborhoods as compared to .69 for the non-HOP comparison group. Neither of these differences in neighborhood ethnic mix were statistically significant. Additionally, the differences in means for income entropy between the two groups also were not statistically significant with both groups residing in destination neighborhoods averaging about 0.15 on the Theil index.

What predicts the level of destination neighborhood ethnic and income mix at time of move-in and in 2010? In Table 3, we present results from our OLS regression models with year of move in fixed effects predicting destination neighborhood ethnic and income entropy at time of move-in and in 2010. We see that the overall model Adjusted R^2 values ranged from .01 to .229 and the models were only statistically significant for predicting ethnic entropy. We note that participation in the HOP Program was not a significant predictor of residence in socially mixed neighborhoods at time of purchase or in 2010. However, other homebuyer and time of purchase characteristics appear to have marginally significant (p < .10) effects. Relative to African American homebuyers, homebuyers regardless of HOP program status who were Latino or "other" ethnicity (which in the Denver context is predominantly Vietnamese) moved to destination neighborhoods that had lower levels of ethnic mix. These neighborhoods also had lower levels of ethnic mix in 2010 suggesting some degree of ethnic enclave concentration in Denver although correlations (not shown here) between ethnic entropy and destination neighborhood of original home purchase suggest a random pattern. Older homebuyers purchased homes in destination neighborhoods that were slightly less ethnically diverse by 2010. However, female homebuyers purchased in destination neighborhoods that were more income diverse by 2010. Low-income homebuyers who purchased their homes prior to the Great Recession also resided in neighborhoods that were less ethnically and income diverse in 2010.

Table 4 summarizes the results that address a slightly different question: *Is destination neighborhood social mix in 2018 affected by the neighborhood characteristics present at time of home purchase?* We see that higher levels of neighborhood ethnic entropy at time of home purchase were significantly

Table 4. OLS regressions predicting ethnic and income entropy in 2018 by selected neighborhood characteristics at time of move-in.

	Ethnic entropy of census tract, 2018[a]		Theil income index of census tract, 2018[b]	
Neighborhood characteristics at time of move-in, unless noted				
Ethnic entropy	0.69***	(0.03)	−0.02*	(0.01)
Theil income index (2010)	0.43***	(0.11)	0.37***	(0.06)
Percent residents who moved in prior year	0.001**	(0.000)	−0.0004***	(0.0001)
Percent renters	0.00	(0.03)	−0.08***	(0.01)
Vacancy rate	0.00	(0.00)	−0.001	(0.001)
Percent of dwellings built prior to 1940	0.00	(0.00)	−0.0004***	(0.0001)
Neighborhood is surbuban	0.04***	(0.01)	−0.02***	(0.003)
Year moved fixed effects	YES		YES	
N	417		436	
R^2	.624		.537	
Adjusted R^2	.600		.509	
F-statistic	20.009***		12.562***	

*p < .1; **p < .05; ***p < .01, based on robust standard errors.
[a]Greater ethnic mix is denoted by increases in ethnic entropy scores.
[b]Greater income mix is denoted by decreases in the Theil index.

associated with increasing both ethnic and income mix in 2018. Additionally, while higher levels of neighborhood income mix in 2010 were associated with higher levels of ethnic mix in 2018, it also produced decreased income mix in 2018. Neighborhood residential instability and suburban location were also associated with significant increases in neighborhood ethnic and income mix in 2018. Finally, neighborhoods with higher shares of renters and older dwelling units at time of home purchase also experienced increased income mix in 2018.

These findings suggest that low-income homebuyers in our study sought out destination neighborhoods that were socially mixed although there is no evidence to support that participation in homebuyer education and counseling via the HOP Program per sé precipitated homebuyer location decisions. Additionally, it appears that neighborhood characteristics at time of home purchase had a significant influence on the social mix trajectory of destination neighborhoods, with most experiencing increasing ethnic and income mix by 2018. What the findings also suggest, however, is some degree of neighborhood selection by Latino and Vietnamese homebuyers in neighborhoods occupied by co-ethnics. Yet, the data also do not suggest patterns of residential turnover that produced high levels of ethnic or income segregation.

Sustainable homeownership outcomes

Did participation in the HOP Program support sustainable homeownership outcomes? Table 5 presents the results of the propensity score analyses on sustainable homeownership outcomes. Again, these results are presented as average treatment effects on the treated and reflect the differences in means between HOP graduates and a matched comparison group of non-HOP homebuyers. Homebuyers who purchased their homes after completing the HOP program exhibited statistically significant differences from their matched non-HOP counterparts on a variety of measures related to sustainable homeownership. These results suggest a positive impact from the HOP program participation that extends well beyond the early years of homeownership. The discussion below focuses on those results that were statistically significant for the two groups of low-income homebuyers.

Duration of homeownership

Since completing the program, HOP homebuyers, on average, accrued 2.8 more years of homeownership ($p = .001$) than non-HOP homebuyers—11.8 vs. 8.9 years, respectively. This could be driven by a few things. Though both groups are about as likely to have sold their first home, HOP homebuyers are significantly less likely to foreclose. They also have experienced greater appreciation in home value

Table 5. Sustainable homeownership outcomes for low-income homebuyers by HOP program status.

					N of Observations		
Outcome	HOP	Non-HOP	Difference (ATET)	Standard Errors	Treated	Control	Weighted Control*
Total years of home ownership	**11.8**	**8.9**	**2.8**	0.9	188	225	188
Percent residing in original home in 2019	50.0	45.6	4.4	8.3	188	223	188
Purchase price of original home ($)	143,422	147,924	−4,502	6,954	176	201	176
Last recorded home value for original home recorded while owned by homeowner ($)	**256,631**	**208,586**	**48,044**	17,902	175	198	175
Original home appreciation ($)	**115,002**	**54,541**	**60,461**	18,021	175	198	175
Annualized appreciation of original home ($)	**8,312**	**−1,784**	**10,096**	3,247	187	206	187
Current value of original home in 2018 ($ if homeowner)	328,129	287,223	40,906	17,090	94	99	94
Percent experiencing foreclosure of original home	**19.5**	**39.9**	**20.5**	8	164	174	164
Percent selling original home	29.8	19.3	10.5	7.0	188	223	188
Percent purchasing a second home	11.7	7.6	4.1	4.5	188	223	188
Percent purchasing a third home	2.1	2.9	−0.8	2.3	188	223	188
Differences in means significant at $p < .05$ are bolded							

*Propensity scores are matched one-to-one with the nearest neighbor. If multiple non-treated observations are the nearest neighbor for an observation, all are included in the control group but weighed such that the sum of weights add to one.

which may have led HOP homebuyers to hold on to their homes, especially during these post-Great Recession years of accelerated appreciation.

Home sales and subsequent home purchases

About 30% of HOP homebuyers and 20% of non-HOP homebuyers had sold their original homes by the end of 2018. Approximately one out of six homebuyers from both groups traded up, purchasing second and in some cases, third or fourth homes. There were no statistically significant differences in the sale and subsequent purchase of additional homes between the two groups of homebuyers, however.

Foreclosures

HOP homebuyers were approximately 20 percentage points less likely ($p = .021$) than non-HOP homebuyers to have experienced foreclosure on their first homes. Nearly 40% of the matched non-HOP homebuyers experienced foreclosure as compared to 20% of HOP homebuyers. The timing of original (first) home purchase influenced the likelihood of subsequent loss through foreclosure (see Figure 3). For both HOP and non-HOP homebuyers, buyers who purchased their homes prior to 2000 did not experience foreclosures until 2004/2005. The foreclosures during this period were generally the result of a significant shock to the household—the loss of the main financial provider because of job loss, health issues or death. Most of the foreclosures for low-income homebuyers occurred during the 2006–2011 period. The foreclosure crisis hit Denver in 2006 and lasted through 2010. A disproportionate share of foreclosures occurred with non-HOP homebuyers who were more likely to have experienced predatory lending either at time of original mortgage origination or as a result of predatory refinancing.

Appreciation in home value

The results in Table 5 also suggest positive long-term financial outcomes for the HOP homebuyers. Although there was no significant difference in original home purchase price between the two groups, the HOP homebuyers had significantly higher last recorded home values and original home value appreciation if we examine those indicators for all original homes. The average last recorded home value was 23% higher for HOP homebuyers than matched non-HOP homebuyers, US$256,631 vs. US$208,586, a US$48,044 ($p < .001$) difference. Conditional on still owning the original home in 2018, HOP homebuyers resided in home that were valued, on average US$40,906 more than their non-HOP counterparts—US$328,129 vs. US$287,223, respectively. In comparison, the median home value for the 7-county Denver metropolitan area was US$409,000. Appreciation of the original home was similarly

CREATING MIXED COMMUNITIES THROUGH HOUSING POLICIES 139

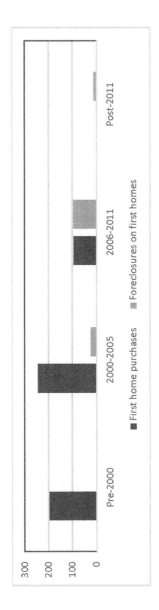

Year purchased	Total purchased	Never foreclosed	Foreclosure pre-2000	Foreclosure 2001-2005	Foreclosure 2006-2010	Foreclosure post 2010	% foreclosed
Pre 2000	199	165	0	6	19	5	15.4
2001-2005	244	155		18	57	14	36.5
2006-2010	92	67			11	14	27.2
Post-2010	2	2				0	0.0
Total	533	389	0	24	87	33	27.0

Figure 3. Timing of first home purchases and foreclosures.

different between the two groups, HOP homebuyers experiencing a US$60,461 ($p < .001$) higher original home appreciation than the matched non-HOP homebuyers. Moreover, annualized home appreciation was five times higher for HOP homebuyers: they experienced, on average, of US$8,312 while non-HOP homebuyers experienced an annual loss in home value of -US$1,784. Please note that the these estimated annualized losses for non-HOP homebuyers are primarily associated with steep drops in home values associated with short sales and foreclosures.

Influence of neighborhood social mix and other characteristics on homeownership

In Table 6, we assess the influence of destination neighborhood social mix and other selected neighborhood characteristics on the probability of homeownership in 2018 using OLS regression with year of purchase fixed effects and controls for homebuyer characteristics at time of purchase. We also include a dummy variable indicating whether the homebuyer was an HOP graduate or not. We find that being an HOP graduate was associated with an 11% higher probability of homeownership in 2018 after controlling for other characteristics of the neighborhood including social mix.

Conclusions and caveats

In this study, we examined the impact of a homebuyer education and counseling program offered to subsidized housing residents in Denver on the selection and purchase of homes located in socially mixed neighborhoods as well as on the sustainability of homeownership over time. Our findings suggest that low-income homebuyers in this study purchased homes in destination neighborhoods characterized by considerable ethnic and income mix at time of purchase that persisted through 2018. This is consistent to previous findings reported by Galster et al. (2005) and Turner and Rawlings (2009). While the evidence does not point to any causal link between HOP participation and selection of socially mixed neighborhoods, we also note that given DHA's longstanding dispersed housing program, larger Housing Choice Voucher program, and construction of multiple mixed-income developments, many DHA residents would have been exposed to such neighborhoods or had information about a range of neighborhoods which may have contributed to decisions about where to purchase homes. This is consistent with Cunningham et al. (2010) who reported that voucher participants remained in opportunity neighborhoods and Darrah and DeLuca (2014) who noted how access to information about other neighborhoods broadened the residential choice set for voucher recipients. We would expect that such exposure or access to information might be the case here.

Table 6. OLS regressions predicting ownership of original home in 2018[a].

	Ownership of Original Home in 2018	
	Coefficient	SE
HOP Program Graduate (1 = yes)	0.115*	(0.057)
Neighborhood characteristics at time of move-in, unless noted		
Ethnic entropy during move in year	−0.135	(0.200)
Theil income index (2010)	0.290	(0.788)
Percent residents who moved in prior year	−0.003	(0.002)
Percent renters	0.078	(0.184)
Vacancy rate	−0.006	(0.008)
Percent of dwellings built prior to 1940	−0.001	−0.002
Neighborhood is surbuban	0.027	0.057
Year moved fixed effects	YES	
N	427	
R^2	.121	
Adjusted R^2	.003	
F-statistic	1.445**	

*$p < .1$; **$p < .05$; ***$p < .01$, based on robust standard errors.
[a]Includes controls for homebuyer characteristics at time of purchase: age, gender, ethnicity, immigrant status, educational attainment, single parent status, family size, annual household income, duration in DHA, participation in dispersed housing, and home purchase prior to the Great Recession.

The results of this study show that a nontrivial number of low-income, former subsidized housing residents have been able to partially realize the American Dream of sustained homeownership in dwellings that have appreciated over time. Although the Great Recession produced significant losses of homes to foreclosure, post-Recession trends in home value appreciation have allowed homeowners to gain significant equity in their homes. While prior studies have underscored the losses experienced by low-income, minority homeowners during the Great Recession (see Garriga et al., 2017; Herbert et al., 2014; Hyra & Rugh, 2016; Lerman & Zhang, 2016), our findings suggest mixed evidence of strong post-Recession recovery for these low-income, predominantly minority homeowners in Denver. When compared to non-HOP homebuyers, HOP homebuyers were better off in terms of 2018 home value, home appreciation, and fewer foreclosures. The finding of fewer foreclosures among HOP homebuyers is consistent with previous research about the influence of homebuyer education and counseling on reducing defaults and foreclosures (see Ding et al., 2008; Myhre & Watson, 2017; Quercia et al., 2006; Sackett, 2016). The results from our study also suggest that participation in homebuyer education and counseling contributed to the sustainability of homeownership for HOP homebuyers—even many years after the original purchase. HUD's First Time Homebuyer Education and Counseling Demonstration Project that is currently in the field may be able to document these longer-term impacts for a large, national sample of low-income homebuyers.

There are a number of implications suggested by this study related to the sustainability of low-income homeownership. First, this study shows that low-income homeownership does not have to become the *American nightmare*. Low-income families can sustain homeownership and accrue home equity—a result that has been buoyed by sharply rising home values in the Denver metropolitan area over the past decade. These increased home values allowed Denver homeowners, especially low-income homeowners, to recover from the losses experienced during the Great Recession.

The data also suggest that intensive pre- and post-purchase homebuyer education and counseling improves long-term sustainability of homeownership. When this counseling occurs prior to purchase, it is most likely because of the assistance provided by program staff like those in HOP whose knowledge and skills about budgeting and money management helped low-income homebuyers secure homes they could afford and favorable mortgage products, terms and conditions at time of mortgage origination. Securing access to these types of programs may be difficult for low-income renters whether they receive housing assistance or not. Despite the growth of pre- and post-purchase counseling programs, especially since the Great Recession, there may be differentials in access—geographical or technological—making it more difficult for individuals to participate or for organizations to bring to scale. Yet, improving and increasing access to financial capability and asset building education and counseling services for public housing residents living in both traditional developments or socially mixed communities could enhance the economic well-being of these residents and facilitate the transfer of such skills to their children.

The findings also underscore the vulnerability of low-income homebuyers to major economic shocks like the Great Recession. Not only do these shocks increase the likelihood of foreclosures, they tend to tighten mortgage lending and access to credit. As these markets loosened over the past decade in Denver, the steep rise in home prices has furthered constrained the ability of lower-income families to even pursue homeownership as they have been priced out of the market. This is an area where public housing authorities and affordable housing developers may play a key role in expanding the number of affordable units available in socially mixed neighborhoods.

Given ongoing concerns with sustainability, there may be a need expand post-purchase counseling to support homeownership decisions related to refinancing and loan modifications particularly since low- to middle-income homeowners are particularly vulnerable to and targets of predatory lending activities that encourage vulnerable owners to sell their homes or extract equity. Recent deregulation of federal consumer financial protection laws may further exacerbate predation and exploitation of low-income homeowners.

Finally, as places like Denver continue to intentionally expand the footprint of mixed income developments in locations attractive to renters and owners alike, attention should be given to setting aside units targeted for low-income homeownership. As Gress et al. (2016) noted, about 10% of the HOPE VI public housing units developed nationwide were sold to low-income families; another 20% of the affordable units were sold to low- and moderate-income families. In places like Denver, the challenge would be to ensure expansion of both affordable renter and owner units for low-income families while not removing the total number of available units from the subsidized and affordable rental pools generated from mixed income revitalization projects.

This study has several important caveats. First, the program estimates employed here were produced by quasi-experimental methods, not through a random assignment experiment. Although this methodological approach is commonly used in program evaluation and has been shown to replicate experimental outcome measures (e.g., Cook & Steiner, 2010; Geyer et al., 2017; Shadish et al., 2008), propensity score matching cannot guarantee the elimination of unmeasured attributes of non-HOP homebuyers that differ systematically from our group of HOP homebuyers. For example, HOP homebuyers may be more conscientious and efficacious, increasing the likelihood of graduating from HOP as well as realizing more beneficial homeownership outcomes. Second, the findings from this study cannot necessarily be generalized beyond public housing residents who self-select into programs such as HOP. Since selection into the program is voluntary and there are hurdles to clear along the way to remain eligible, one might expect selection bias: actual participants in the program might be people or households who stood to particularly gain from the program whereas non-participants could be those who felt the program would not benefit them as much.

Third, the experience with HOP cannot necessarily be generalized to other homebuyer education and counseling programs operated by other housing authorities or agencies. The Denver Housing Authority is recognized as well-run and innovative with exceptional staff and has been designated as one of HUD's *high performer* public housing authorities for many years (U.S. Department of Housing and Urban Development, HA Profiles, n.d.). Finally, as with any study of programs that promote homeownership impacts on participants, the specter of economic shocks remain. In periods such as the current pandemic and economic recession, the ability to sustain homeownership is still precarious for all but the most affluent homeowners.

Note

1. The definition of *sustainable homeownership programs* in Quercia et al. (2006) is used in this study: "Sustainable homeownership programs help homeowners acquire the knowledge and skills they need to maintain and build the value of their housing investment. In addition to an asset-building focus, these programs help homeowners avoid problems and therefore have a preventive focus as well" (p. 310).

Acknowledgments

This research was supported by grants from the Ford Foundation and the John D. and Catherine T. MacArthur Foundation. The opinions expressed herein do not necessarily reflect those of our funders. The authors wish to thank Renee Nicolosi of the Denver Housing Authority for providing administrative data and unwavering support for our research spanning more than two decades. Special thanks to Iris Levin, Kathy Arthurson, George C. Galster, and two anonymous referees who offered valuable suggestions for clarifications and extensions of earlier drafts.

Disclosure statement

No potential conflict of interest was reported by the author(s).

Funding

This work was supported by the Ford Foundation [990-1387-1 and 990-1387-2] and the John D. and Catherine T. MacArthur Foundation [01-69251-HCD].

ORCID

Anna Maria Santiago http://orcid.org/0000-0003-1983-3937

References

Abadie, A., & Imbens, G. W. (2016). Matching on the estimated propensity score. *Econometrica*, *84*(2), 781–807. https://doi.org/10.3982/ECTA11293

Agarwal, S., Amromin, G., Ben-David, I., Chomsisengphet, S., & Evanoff, D. (2010). Learning to cope: Financial education and loan performance during a housing crisis. *American Economic Review*, *100*(2), 495–500. https://doi.org/10.1257/aer.100.2.495

Argento, R. B., Brown, L. M., Koulayev, S., Li, G., Myhre, M., Pafenberg, F., & Patrabansh, S. (2019). First-time homebuyer counseling and the mortgage selection experience in the United States. *Cityscape*, *21*(2), 51–74. https://doi.org/10.2307/26696376

Arthurson, K. (2012). *Social mix and the city*. CSIRO Publishing.

Arthurson, K., Levin, I., & Ziersch, A. (2015). Social mix, '[A] very, very good idea in a vacuum but you have to do it properly!' Exploring social mix in a right to the city framework. *International Journal of Housing Policy*, *15*(4), 418–435. https://doi.org/10.1080/14616718.2015.1093748

August, M., & Walks, A. (2012). From social mix to political marginalization? The redevelopment of Toronto's public housing and the dilution of tenant organizational power. In G. Bridge, T. Butler, & L. Lees (Eds.), *Mixed communities: Gentrification by stealth?* (pp. 273–298). The Policy Press.

Austin, P. C. (2009). Balance diagnostics for comparing the distribution of baseline covariates between treatment groups in propensity-score matched samples. *Statistics in Medicine*, *28*(25), 3083–3107. https://doi.org/10.1002/sim.3697

Avila, G., Nguyen, H., & Zorn, P. (2013, April). The benefits of pre-purchase homeownership counseling. *Working paper*. Freddie Mac. http://www.freddiemac.com/fmac-resources/perspectives/pdf/benefits_of_pre_purchase.pdf

Bolt, G., Phillips, D., & Van Kempen, R. (2010). Housing policy, (de)segregation and social mixing: An international perspective. *Housing Studies*, *25*(2), 129–135. https://doi.org/10.1080/02673030903564838

Bostic, R. W., & Lee, K. O. (2008). Mortgages, risk, and homeownership among low- and moderate-income families. *American Economic Review: Papers and Proceedings*, *98*(2), 310–314. https://doi.org/10.1257/aer.98.2.310

Brophy, P. C., & Smith, R. N. (1997). Mixed-income housing: Factors for success. *Cityscape*, *3*(2), 3–31. https://www.huduser.gov/periodicals/cityscpe/vol3num2/success.pdf

Bucerius, S. M., Thompson, S. K., & Berardi, L. (2017). 'They're colonizing my neighborhood': (Perceptions of) social mix in Canada. *City & Community*, *16*(4), 486–505. https://doi.org/10.1111/cico.12263

Buron, L., Popkin, S. J., Levy, D. K., Harris, L. E., & Khadduri, J. (2002, November). *The HOPE VI resident tracking study*. Urban Institute. https://www.urban.org/research/publication/hope-vi-resident-tracking-study

ChangeLab Solutions. (2018). *Denver Housing Authority: Case study*. Shttps://www.changelabsolutions.org/sites/default/files/HealthHousingStarterKit-CaseStudy-DenverHousingAuthority-FINAL-20180531.pdf

Chaskin, R., Khare, A., & Joseph, M. (2012). Participation, deliberation and decision making: The dynamics of inclusion and exclusion in mixed-income developments. *Urban Affairs Review*, *48*(6), 863–906. https://doi.org/10.1177/1078087412450151

Chaskin, R. J., & Joseph, M. L. (2011). Social interaction in mixed-income developments: Relational expectations and emerging reality. *Journal of Urban Affairs*, *33*(2), 209–237. https://doi.org/10.1111/j.1467-9906.2010.00537.x

Chetty, R., Hendren, N., & Katz, L. F. (2016). The effects of exposure to better neighborhoods on children: New evidence from the Moving to Opportunity experiment. *American Economic Review*, *106*(4), 855–902. https://doi.org/10.1257/aer.20150572

Clampet-Lundquist, S. (2004). HOPE VI relocation: Moving to new neighborhoods and building new ties. *Housing Policy Debate*, *15*(2), 415–447. https://doi.org/10.1080/10511482.2004.9521507

Clark, W. A. V. (2013). The aftermath of the General Financial Crisis for the ownership society: What happened to low-income homeowners in the US? *International Journal of Housing Policy, 13*(3), 227–246. https://doi.org/10.1080/14616718.2013.796811

Collins, J. M., & O'Rourke, C. (2011, April). *Homeownership education and counseling: Do we know what works?* Research Institute for Housing America, Research Paper No. 1102. https://www.hudexchange.info/resource/275/homeownership-education-and-counseling-do-we-know-what-works/

Cook, T., & Steiner, P. M. (2010). Case matching and the reduction of selection bias in quasi-experiments: The relative importance of pretest measures of outcomes, of unreliable measurement, and of mode of data analysis. *Psychological Methods, 15*(1), 56–68. https://doi.org/10.1037/a0018536

Cunningham, M., Scott, M., Narducci, C., Hall, S., Stanczyk, A., O'Neil, J., & Galvez, M. (2010, September). *Improving neighborhood location outcomes in the Housing Choice Voucher program: A scan of mobility assistance programs*. Urban Institute. https://www.urban.org/research/publication/improving-neighborhood-location-outcomes-housing-choice-voucher-program-scan-mobility-assistance-programs

Curley, A. M. (2010). Relocating the poor: Social capital and neighborhood resources. *Journal of Urban Affairs, 32*(1), 79–103. https://doi.org/10.1111/j.1467-9906.2009.00475

Darrah, J., & DeLuca, S. (2014). Living here has changed my whole perspective. *Journal of Policy Analysis and Management, 33*(2), 350–384. https://doi.org/10.1002/pam.21758

DeMarco, D., Fiore, N., Moulton, S., & Whitlow, S. (2017). *The first-time homebuyer education and counseling demonstration baseline report: Study design and implementation*. U.S. Department of Housing and Urban Development, Office of Policy Development and Research. https://www.huduser.gov/portal/publications/first-homebuyer-counseling.html

Denver Housing Authority. (n.d.). *DHA housing opportunities*. http://www.denverhousing.org/LWU/AffordableHousing/Pages/default.aspx

Ding, L., Quercia, R., & Ratcliffe, J. (2008). Post-purchase counseling and default resolutions among low- and moderate-income borrowers. *Journal of Real Estate Research (JRER), 30*(3), 315–344. https://doi.org/10.1080/10835547.2008.12091223

Ellen, I. G., & Dastrup, S. (2012, October). *Housing and the Great Recession*. Stanford Center on Poverty and Inequality. https://www.russellsage.org/research/reports/housing-great-recession

Fannie Mae. (2017, April). *Pre-purchase homeownership education qualitative research: Lower-income first-time homebuyers*. https://www.fanniemae.com/sites/g/files/koqyhd191/files/migrated-files/resources/file/research/housingsurvey/pdf/april2017-qualitative-research-homebuyer-education.pdf

Fischer, M. J. (2003). The relative importance of income and race in determining residential outcomes in U.S. urban areas, 1970-2000. *Urban Affairs Review, 38*(5), 669–696. https://doi.org/10.1177%2F1078087403038005003

Fraser, J., DeFilippis, J., & Bazuin, J. (2012). HOPE VI: Calling for modesty in its claims. In G. Bridge, T. Butler, & L. Lees (Eds.), *Mixed communities: Gentrification by stealth* (pp. 209–229). Policy Press.

Fraser, J. C., Oakley, D., & Levy, D. K. (2013). Guest editors' introduction: Policy assumptions and lived realities of mixed-income housing on both sides of the Atlantic. *Cityscape, 15*(2), 1–14. https://www.huduser.gov/periodicals/cityscpe/vol15num2/guest.pdf

Galster, G., Booza, J. C., Metzger, K., & Cutstinger, J. (2005). *An analysis and inventory of mixed-income/mixed-race neighborhoods*. Center for Urban Studies, Wayne State University.

Galster, G. C., & Friedrichs, J. (2015). The dialectic of neighborhood social mix: Editors' introduction to the special issue. *Housing Studies, 30*(2), 175–191. https://doi.org/10.1080/02673037.2015.1035926

Galster, G. C., & Santiago, A. M. (2008). Low-income homeownership as an asset-building tool: What can we tell policymakers? In H. Wolman & M. A. Turner (Eds.), *Urban and regional policy and its effects* (pp. 60–108). Brookings Institution Press.

Galster, G. C., Santiago, A. M., & Smith, R. (2019). Benefit-cost analysis of an innovative program for self-sufficiency and homeownership. *Evaluation Review, 43*(1–2), 3–40. https://doi.org/10.1177/0193841X19846697

Galster, G. C., Tatian, P. A., Santiago, A. M., Pettit, K. S., & Smith, R. E. (2003). *Why not in my backyard? Neighborhood impacts of deconcentrating assisted housing*. Rutgers/CUPR Press.

Garriga, C., Ricketts, L. R., & Schlagenhauf, D. E. (2017). The homeownership experience of minorities during the Great Recession. *Federal Reserve Bank of St. Louis Review, 99*, 139–167. https://files.stlouisfed.org/files/htdocs/publications/review/2017-02-15/the-homeownership-experience-of-minorities-during-the-great-recession.pdf

Geyer, J., Freiman, L., Lubell, J., & Villarreal, M. (2017). *Evaluation of the Compass Family Self-Sufficiency (FSS) Programs administered in partnership with public housing agencies in Lynn and Cambridge, Massachusetts*. Abt Associates. https://www.abtassociates.com/compassFSS

Goodman, L. S., & Mayer, C. (2018 Winter). Homeownership and the American Dream. *Journal of Economic Perspectives, 32*(1), 31–58. https://doi.org/10.1257/jep.32.1.31

Gress, T., Cho, S., & Joseph, M. (2016, September). *Hope VI data compilation and analysis*. National Initiative on Mixed Income Communities, Case Western Reserve University. https://papers.ssrn.com/sol3/papers.cfm?Abstract_id=3055254

Heckman, J., Ichimura, H., & Todd, P. E. (1997). Matching as an econometric evaluation estimator: Evidence from evaluating a job training programme. *Review of Economic Studies*, *64*(4), 605–654. https://doi.org/10.2307/2971733

Heckman, J., Ichimura, H., & Todd, P. E. (1998). Matching as an economic evaluation estimator. *Review of Economic Studies*, *65*(2), 261–294. https://doi.org/10.1111/1467-937X.00044

Heckman, J., & Navarro-Lozano, S. (2004). Using matching, instrumental variables, and control functions to estimate economic choice models. *The Review of Economics and Statistics*, *86*(1), 30–57. https://doi.org/10.1162/003465304323023660

Herbert, C. E., & Belsky, E. S. (2008). The homeownership experience of low-income and minority households: A review and synthesis of the literature. *Cityscape*, *10*(1), 7–9. https://www.jstor.org/stable/20868655

Herbert, C. E., McCue, D. T., & Sanchez-Moyano, R. (2014). Is homeownership still an effective means of building wealth for low-income and minority households? In E. Belsky, C. E. Herbert, & J. H. Molinsky (Eds.), *Homeownership built to last: Balancing access, affordability and risk after the housing crisis* (pp. 50–98). Brookings Institution Press.

Hirad, A., & Zorn, P. M. (2002). Prepurchase homeownership counseling: A little knowledge is a good thing. In N. P. Retsinas & E. S. Belsky (Eds.), *Low-income homeownership: Examining the unexamined goal* (pp. 146–174). Brookings Institution Press.

Hyde, A., & Fischer, M. J. (2021). New faces, new neighbors? How Latino population growth and lending expansion shapes the neighborhood racial and ethnic composition for White and Latino homebuyers. *City & Community*. https://doi.org/10.1177/1535684120981344

Hyra, D., & Rugh, J. S. (2016). The U.S. Great Recession: Exploring its association with Black neighborhood rise, decline and recovery. *Urban Geography*, *37*(5), 700–726. https://doi.org/10.1080/02723638.2015.1103994.

Jackson, M. (2018, December 18). Denver Housing Authority has lands of opportunity for developers. *Westword*. https://www.westword.com/news/denver-housing-authority-sells-land-where-it-could-build-affordable-housing-why-11065857

Kleinhans, R., & Varady, D. (2011). Moving out and going down? *International Journal of Housing Policy*, *11*(2), 155–174. https://doi.org/10.1080/14616718.2011.573205

Kleit, R. G., & Galvez, M. (2011). The relocation choices of public housing residents displaced by redevelopment: Market constraints, personal preferences or social information? *Journal of Urban Affairs*, *33*(4), 375–407. https://doi.org/10.1111/j.1467-9906.2011.00557.x

Kneebone, E., Reid, C., & Holmes, N. (2019, September 13). The geography of mixed-income neighborhoods. *Shelterforce*. https://shelterforce.org/2019/09/13/the-geography-of-mixed-income-neighborhoods/

Lens, M. C. (2018). Extremely low-income households, housing affordability and the Great Recession. *Urban Studies*, *55*(8), 1615–1635. https://doi.org/10.1177/0042098016686511

Lerman, R. I., & Zhang, S. (2016). *Coping with the Great Recession: Disparate impacts on economic well-being in poor neighborhoods*. Opportunity and Ownership Project, Report No. 6. The Urban Institute. https://www.urban.org/research/publication/coping-great-recession-disparate-impacts-economic-well-being-poor-neighborhoods

Lucio, J., Hand, L., & Marsiglia, F. (2014). Designing hope: Rationales of mixed income housing policy. *Journal of Urban Affairs*, *36*(5), 891–904. https://doi.org/10.1111/juaf.12090

Mallach, A. (2011). *Building sustainable ownership: Rethinking public policy toward lower-income homeownership*. Federal Reserve Bank of Philadelphia, Discussion Papers. https://www.philadelphiafed.org/-/media/community-development/publications/discussion-papers/discussion-paper_building-sustainable-ownership.pdf

Manson, S., Schroeder, J., Van Riper, D., Kugler, T., & Ruggles, S. (2020). *IPUMS national historical geographic information system: Version 15.0* [dataset]. IPUMS. https://doi.org/10.18128/D050.V15.0

Mayer, N. S., & Temkin, K. (2016). Prepurchase counseling effects on mortgage performance: Empirical analysis of NeighborWorks® America's experience. *Cityscape*, *18*(2), 73–98. https://www.huduser.gov/portal/periodicals/cityscpe/vol18num2/ch4.pdf

Mayock, T., & Malacrida, R. S. (2018). Socioeconomic and racial disparities in the financial returns to homeownership. *Regional Science and Urban Economics*, *70*(1), 80–96. https://doi.org/10.1016/j.regsciurbeco.2018.01.003

Myhre, M. L., & Watson, N. E. (2017, September). *Housing counseling works*. U.S. Department of Housing and Urban Development, Office of Policy Development and Research. https://www.huduser.gov/portal/publications/hsgfin/housing-counseling-works.html

Oakley, D., & Burchfield, K. (2009). Out of the projects, still in the hood: The spatial constraints on public-housing residents' relocation in Chicago. *Journal of Urban Affairs*, *31*(5), 598–614. https://doi.org/10.1111/j.1467-9906.2009.00454.x

Organization for Economic Cooperation and Development (OECD). (2016). Indexes and estimation techniques. In *OECD regions at a glance 2016*. OECD Publishing. https://www.oecd-ilibrary.org/governance/oecd-regions-at-a-glance-2016_reg_glance-2016-en

Peck, L., Moulton, S., Bocian, D. G., DeMarco, D., & Fiore, N. (2019). *Short-term impact report: The HUD first-time homebuyer education and counseling demonstration*. U.S. Department of Housing and Urban Development, Office of Policy Development and Research. https://www.huduser.gov/portal/sites/default/files/pdf/Short-Term-Impact-Report.pdf

Quercia, R., & Spader, K. (2008). Does homeownership counseling affect the prepayment and default behavior of affordable mortgage borrowers? *Journal of Policy Analysis and Management, 27*(2), 304–325. https://doi.org/10.1002/pam.20326

Quercia, R., & Wachter, S. (1996). Homeownership counseling performance: How can it be measured? *Housing Policy Debate, 7*(1), 175–200. https://doi.org/10.1080/10511482.1996.9521217

Quercia, R. G., Gorham, L. S., & Rohe, W. M. (2006). Sustaining homeownership: The promise of post-purchase services. *Housing Policy Debate, 17*(2), 309–339. https://doi.org/10.1080/10511482.2006.9521572

Rohe, W. M., Quercia, R. G., & Van Zandt, S. (2002). *Supporting the American Dream of homeownership: An assessment of Neighborhood Reinvestment's homeownership pilot program*. https://www.researchgate.net/publication/255610508_Supporting_the_American_dream_of_home_ownership_An_assessment_of_the_Neighborhood_Reinvestment's_Homeownership_Pilot_Program

Rohe, W. M., & Watson, H. L. (Eds.). (2007). *Chasing the American Dream: New perspectives on affordable homeownership*. Cornell University Press.

Sackett, C. (2016, Spring). *The evidence on homeownership education and counseling*. U.S. Department of Housing and Urban Development, Office of Policy Development and Research. https://www.huduser.gov/portal/periodicals/em/spring16/highlight2.html

Saegert, S. (2015, January). Interrupting inequality: Crisis and opportunity in low-income housing policy. *Metropolitics*. http://www.metropolitiques.eu/Interupting-Inequality-Crisis-and.html

Santiago, A. M., Galster, G. C., Kaiser, A. A., Santiago-San Roman, A. H., Grace, R. A., & Linn, A. T. H. (2010a). Low-income homeownership: Does it necessarily mean sacrificing neighborhood quality to buy a home?" *Journal of Urban Affairs, 32*(2), 171–198. https://doi.org/10.1111/j.1467-9906.2009.00478.x

Santiago, A. M., Galster, G. C., Santiago-San Roman, A. H., Tucker, C. M., Kaiser, A. A., Grace, R. A., & Linn, A. T. H. (2010b). Foreclosing on the American dream?: The financial consequences of low-income homeownership. *Housing Policy Debate, 20*(4), 707–742. https://doi.org/10.1080/10511482.2010.506194

Santiago, A. M., Galster, G. C., & Smith, R. (2017). Evaluating the impacts of an enhanced Family Self-Sufficiency program. *Housing Policy Debate, 27*(5), 772–788. https://doi.org/10.1080/10511482.2017.1295093.

Santiago, A. M., Galster, G. C., & Tatian, P. (2001). Assessing the property value impacts of the dispersed housing subsidy program in Denver. *Journal of Policy Analysis and Management, 20*(1), 65–88. https://doi.org/10.1002/1520-6688(200124)20:1%3C65::AID-PAM1004%3E3.0.CO;2-U

Sard, B., & Rice, D. (2016, January 12). *Realizing the Housing Choice Voucher program's potential to enable families to move to better neighborhoods*. Center for Budget and Policy Priorities. https://www.cbpp.org/research/housing/realizing-the-housing-voucher-programs-potential-to-enable-families-to-move-to.

Semega, J., Kollar, M., Shrider, E., & Creamer, J. (2020). *Income and poverty in the United States: 2019*. Current Population Reports, Bureau of the Census. https://www.census.gov/library/publications/2020/demo/p60-270.html#:~:text=The%202019%20poverty%20rate%20of,and%20Table%20B%2D1

Shadish, W., Clark, M. H., & Steiner, P. M. (2008). Can nonrandomized experiments yield accurate answers? A randomized experiment comparing random and nonrandom assignments. *Journal of the American Statistical Association, 103*(484), 1334–1356. https://doi.org/10.1198/016214508000000733

Shlay, A. B. (2006). Low-income homeownership: American dream or delusion? *Urban Studies, 43*(3), 511–531. https://doi.org/10.1080%2F00420980500452433

Smith, M. M., Hochberg, D., & Greene, W. H. (2017). The effectiveness of pre-purchase homeownership counseling: Evidence from a randomized study. *The Quarterly Review of Economics and Finance, 65*(1), 36–49. https://doi.org/10.1016/j.qref.2016.05.002

Stuart, E. A. (2019). Propensity scores and matching methods. In G. Hancock, L. M. Stapleton, & R. O. Mueller (Eds.), *The reviewers' guide to quantitative methods in the social sciences* (2nd ed., pp. 388–396). Routledge.

Temkin, K. M., Mayer, N. S., Calhoun, C. A., Tatian, P. A., & George, T. (2014). *National Foreclosure Mitigation Counseling program evaluation, final report, rounds 3 through 5*. https://www.neighborworks.org/Documents/HomeandFinance_Docs/Foreclosure_Docs/ForeclosureCounseling(NFMC)_Docs/2014_NFMC_UrbanInstituteReport.aspx

Theodos, B., Simms, M., Treskon, M., & Collazo, J. (2015). *An evaluation of the impacts and implementation approaches of financial coaching programs*. Urban Institute. https://www.urban.org/sites/default/files/publication/71806/2000448-An-Evaluation-of-the-Impacts-and-Implementation-Approaches-of-Financial-Coaching-Programs.pdf

Thomas, H., Mann, A., & Meschede, T. (2018). Race and location: The role neighborhoods play in family wealth and well-being. *American Journal of Economics and Sociology, 77*(3–4), 1077–1111. https://doi.org/10.1111/ajes.12239

Turner, M. A., & Rawlings, L. (2009, August). *Promoting neighborhood diversity: Benefits, barriers, and strategies*. Urban Institute. https://www.urban.org/sites/default/files/publication/30631/411955-Promoting-Neighborhood-Diversity-Benefits-Barriers-and-Strategies.PDF

U.S. Department of Housing and Urban Development. (n.d.). *HA profiles*. https://pic.hud.gov/pic/haprofiles/haprofiledetails.asp

Vale, L., & Shamsuddin, S. (2015, February 13). *In the US, mixed housing developments aren't working for low-income families*. https://www.citymetric.com/horizons/us-mixed-housing-developments-arent-working-low-income-families-698

Van Zandt, S., & Rohe, W. M. (2011). The sustainability of low-income homeownership: The incidence of unexpected costs and needed repairs among low-income home buyers. *Housing Policy Debate, 21*(2), 317–341. https://doi.org/10.1080/10511482.2011.576525

Vesselinov, E., Lennon, M. C., & Le Goix, R. (2018). Is it all in the eye of the beholder? Benefits of mixed-income neighborhoods in New York and Los Angeles. *Journal of Urban Affairs, 40*(2), 163–185. https://doi.org/10.1080/07352166.2017.1343633

Wainer, A., & Zabel, J. (2020). Homeownership and wealth accumulation for low-income households. *Journal of Housing Economics, 47*, Article 101624. https://doi.org/10.1016/j.jhe.2019.03.002.

Wilson, W. J. (1987). *The truly disadvantaged*. University of Chicago Press.

Appendix A. Characteristics of DHA residents who purchased homes by HOP participation status prematching (1994–2012 cohort)

Characteristics	HOP homebuyer	Non-HOP homebuyer
Number of participants	190	343
Percent age 34 years or older at time of purchase	70.0	21.8
Percent female	85.3	72.0
Ethnicity		
Percent African American	31.1	19.2
Percent Latino/Latina	50.0	61.5
Percent Other	19.0	19.2
Percent immigrant	28.4	45.5
Percent attaining education beyond high school	28.4	10.8
Percent single parent	59.5	61.5
Percent with families of 4+ members	52.1	24.6
Average yearly income ($)	34,904	24,270
Percent purchasing home prior to Great Recession	75.3	86.0
Percent residing in DHA development at time of purchase	26.3	24.6
Duration of residence in DHA subsidized housing		
Percent less than 12 months	0.0	5.5
Percent 12–23 months	5.3	12.5
Percent 24–35 months	10.0	14.6
Percent 36–47 months	10.0	13.4
Percent 48–59 months	11.6	11.1
Percent 60–71 months	8.4	9.6
Percent 72–83 months	8.4	8.5
Percent 84–95 months	11.6	6.7
Percent 96 months or more	34.7	18.1
In FSS Program	4.8	43.5

Appendix B. Covariance balance statistics for propensity score matching

	Standardized differences between treatment and control groups		Variance ratio	
	Raw	Matched	Raw	Matched
Percent age 40 years or older	0.08	0.10	1.02	1.03
Percent female	0.39	0.09	0.62	0.85
Ethnicity				
Percent Latino/Latina	−0.26	−0.08	1.07	1.00
Percent Black	0.25	0.11	1.38	1.12
Percent immigrant	−0.42	−0.01	0.82	0.99
Percent attained education beyond high school	0.40	0.00	2.28	1.00
Percent single parent	−0.06	−0.06	1.03	1.02
Percent family size 4+	−0.13	0.08	1.03	1.00
Natural log of yearly income	1.08	−0.21	0.54	0.86
Percent purchased home prior to 2006	−0.30	0.07	1.69	0.94
Percent residing in dispersed unit	0.41	0.00	1.09	1.00
Duration of residence in DHA	−0.36	0.28	0.99	1.02

Matching presented for annualized appreciation of original home

No. of observations: 470 raw, 373 matched

Treated observations: 175 raw, 175 matched

Control observations: 295 raw, 198 matched; ties are weighted to sum to 1 so the weighted control observations equal 175 matched

Index

Note: Figures are indicated by *italics*. Tables are indicated by **bold**. Endnotes are indicated by the page number followed by 'n' and the endnote number e.g., 20n1 refers to endnote 1 on page 20.

Abubakar, I. R. 5
Accra: exclusionary pathway 24–5, *25*; gentrification and displacement pressures in 20–1; geography of opportunity in 15–30; housing policy context in 19–21; inclusionary pathway 23–4, *24*; income mix in *18*; intriguing opportunity 16; residential segregation in 18; urban policy in 17–19, *18*, *19*
Activists 57
"adda (den) of pickpockets and thieves" 42
affordable housing 8, 26–8, 39, 42, 43, 46
Agonizers 57, 64
Agyei-Mensah, S. 20
Amaravati, comprehensive plan 43–4
American Community Survey 131
American nightmare 141
Amin, A. 108, 122
Andhra Pradesh Capital Region Development Authority Act 43
Andhra Pradesh Township and Industrial Development Corporation (APTIDCO) 42, 43
Arthurson, K. 2, 7, 54, 56, 73
Australia: case study 75–6, *76*; regeneration in 74–8, *76*, *77*, **78**; social mix in 93–4
Australian Urban Research Infrastructure Network (AURIN) 95
average treatment effect on the treated (ATET) 132, 133
Ayalim 54, 60, 62

Blokland, T. 116, 123
Boamah, E. F. 16
Bolt, G. 3, 108, 111
Bond, L. 3, 72
Bridge, G. 2, 3
British colonial government 19

Camina, M. M. 122
Cantonments 19
capacity building 27, 29
Capital Development Authority 43
Capp, R. 7
Carlton project 74, 75
Center for Transit Oriented Development 8
China, social mix in 4–5
Chu, C. 4
city-level initiative 44
City Policy 112
clustered 80
Cohen, R. 58
colonialism 5
community 10n1
community building 27, 29, 90
community housing organizations (CHOs) 94, 102
Community Liaison Committee (CLC) 81
COVID-19 21
cross-country analysis 73
crude quantitative indicators 95
Cunningham, M. 140

Darrah, J. 140
data collection methods 74
Dedoose software 40
Delgado, E. 56
DeLuca, S. 140
Denver Housing Authority (DHA) 127, 128–30; analytical approach 132–4; neighborhood ethnic mix estimate 130–1; neighborhood income mix estimate 131; quasi-experimental impact 130; sustainable homeownership indicators 131–2, **132**
desegregation policies 3
DHA *see* Denver Housing Authority (DHA)
di Mauro, Weder 9
diverse shares of social groups 127
Doan, P. R. 5

economic leverage 26, 28
economic return 98–9
education populaire 116
ethnic entropy index 130–1
ethno-national ideology 61
exclusionary pathway 24–5, *25*

Friedrichs, J. 1–3, 6

Galster, G. C. 1–3, 6, 15, 84, 140
Garin Torani 54, 58, 60

gentrification 56, 66
geography of opportunity 15
Ghanaian housing policy 16
"ghettoization" 36
Global East 4–6, 10n2
globalization forces 35
Global South 4–6
Government of Ghana's National Housing Policy 16
Grammenos, D. 56
Grant, R. 20
Greater Accra Metropolitan Area 16
Great Recession 127, 133, 141
Green Ono project 74, 76–7, *77*, 78
Gress, T. 142

homebuyer education and counseling program (HOP) 127–8; duration of homeownership 137, 138; foreclosures 138; home sales and subsequent home purchases 138; home value appreciation 138, *139*, 140; impact 128; sustainable homeownership outcomes 137, **138**
Housing Authority of the City and County of Denver, 8
Housing Choice Vouchers 126
housing colonies 46
Housing Development Bank 6
housing ownership 53
housing regeneration programs 8, 71–2; physical and social outcomes 72–3; similarities and differences 77–8
Hsiao, H. 5

incentives and influence 26, 27
inclusionary housing policies 37, 40–1, *41*, 45
inclusionary pathway 23, *23*, 24
inclusionary policy 25–7, *26*
inclusionary zoning stipulations, actual implementation of 41
inclusive governance 26, 28
Index of Relative Socioeconomic Advantage and Disadvantage (IRSAD) 95, 99
India: comprehensive plan 36, 44–5; federal housing programs 38; federal mixed-income housing policies 36; federal policies and local low-income housing initiatives 44–7; inclusionary housing policies 45; inclusive development policies 36; integrated urban and housing development 37–8, 47; large-scale low-income public housing projects 46–7; low-income housing policies 35; multi-level approach 47–8; national housing programs 35; national policies, for low-income housing 38–9; private developer participation 45–6; social integration and affordable production 36; socioeconomic segregation 36–7; spatial segregation 35; state-sponsored segregation 35–6
integration 16, 97
intentional social mix 108–11, 122; *see also* social mix
International Monetary Fund 19
intolerance and insularity 16

Israel: case study 76–7, *77*; NGO in 54; price of redevelopment 64–5, *66*; privatization 54, 57–8; privatizing public housing to NGOs in 58–9; regeneration projects in **78**; settling public housing in 59–60; social involvement, population diversity, and alienation 62–4, *63*; social order, urban redevelopment, and social justice 61–2; space judaization and NPM 60–1

Jakkampudi JNNURM colony 42, 47
Jakkampudi land pooling scheme 41–2
Japan, social mix in 5
Jawaharlal Nehru National Urban Renewal Mission 35, 38, 39, 40, 43

Kaddar, M. 56
Kainer Persov, N. 7
Kelly, D. 7
Killen, S. 15
Kolocation à Projets Solidaire (Paris) 113–14

land shortage 38
land use planning 36, 48
large-scale low-income public housing provision 46–7
Lees, L. 56, 63
Lelévrier, C. 73
Leroux, J. 7
Levin, I. 7
local town planners 44
logit regression 133
low-income homeownership 127
low-income housing enabling mechanisms 48
Low-Income Housing Tax Credits (LIHTC) 8

Manson, S. 131
manual content analysis 39–40
McGranaham, G. 18
"mezzo-level" construct 2
micro-public 108, 122
mixed income developments 9
mixed-income housing initiatives 37
Mohanty, P. K. 42
Mosselson, A. 5
motivated youth 108, 110

National Housing Policy 27
National Urban Policy Framework 16, 20
neighborhood effects 72
Netanyahu, Benjamin 60
New Amidar 58, 61
New Public Management (NPM) 54
"no neighborhood left behind" 9
non-governmental organizations (NGO) 54, 112

Ohana, T. 62
Ospitalità Solidale (Milan) 113
Otiso, K. 16
Owusu, G. 16, 20

"peripheral towns" 57
PHRP *see* Public Housing Renewal Program (PHRP)
"population dispersal" policy 57
Porter, L. 7
Posthumus, H. 73
practitioners' actions 117–19
practitioners' expectations 115–17
Pradhan Mantri Awas Yojana 38, 39, 41–3, 46
privatization 53, 54
proactive leadership 26, 27
propensity score analysis 132–3
public housing 90
The Public-Housing Act of 1998 58
Public-Housing Forum (PHF) 58
Public Housing Renewal Program (PHRP) 91, 93, 94, 98
public housing tenants 64–5, *66*
public-private partnership (PPP) projects: Jakkampudi funded under 42–3; private developer participation 45–6

qualitative examinations 10
quasi-experimental methodologies 127

racial segregation 16
Rajiv Awas Yojana 35, 38, 39, 40
rapid urbanization 16, 35
Rawlings, L. 140
real property data 130
redevelopment project 61
regeneration housing programs 7
research methodology, mixed-income housing models 39–40
research projects 73, **74**
residential segregation 15

Santiago, A. M. 7
Sassen, S. 19
segregated 80
segregationist policies 5
Seixas, V. B. 73
Shruggers 57
Singapore, social mix in 6
Sinxadi, L. 5
60:40 land-sharing model 41, 42
slum 38, 39, 42, 45, 46, 49n2
slums 36
small-scale mixed-income initiatives 44, 48
social animation activities 112
social cohesion 72, 82–3
social contact 56
social forces 94
social inclusion project 2
social inequality 15
social mix 78, 90; apparent and anticipated outcomes measure 99–102, *99*, *100*, *101*, **101**, **102**; in Australia 93–4; benefits 3, 73, 85, 107; Carlton study 73–4; in China 4–5; community housing 90; comparative studies 73; conditions 119–21; data collection and analysis 114–15; definition 2, 55–6; disadvantaged communities in 1; discursive framing 96–102; economic return and social trade-offs 98–9; effectiveness 108; in Global East and Global South 4–6; goal of 1; housing models 38; and housing programs 85–6; ideas of 7; influence 9–10, 140, **140**; integration 97–8; intentional 108, 109, 110–11; interaction 97–8; international 73; in Israel 54; in Japan 5; link between physical design 84–5; low-income homebuyers 134–7, *134–5*, **135–7**; mechanism 1–2; mediating factors 3; mid-nineteenth century 71; neighborhoods 126, 127; perspectives 2; physical outcomes 79–81, *79*, **79**; in planning and housing policy 1; policymakers 53; positive and negative side effects of 2–3; prime locations in cities 2; privatization 53, 54; public housing 90; residential 107; roots and contours 91–3; in Singapore 6; social outcomes 81–3; in South Korea 5; in Sub-Saharan Africa 5; theoretical roots 109–10; unexpected outcomes 56–7; unintended consequence 84; urban process 56; use of 2
social mix version 2.0 1, 6–9; developmental issues 7; learnings from the global east and global south 9; question of intentionality 7–8; transit-oriented design 8
Social Security and National Insurance Trust 20
Songsore, J. 18
South Korea, social mix in 5
Sowah, M. A. 21
spatial logic of exclusion 16
State Housing Corporation 19
"state-led ethno-gentrification" 62
state-led gentrification project 2
state-led regeneration 71
Statistical Area Level 1s (SA1s) 95–6
Statistics' Socio-Economic Index for Areas (SEIFA) 95
Stuart, E. A. 133
Sub-Saharan Africa, social mix in 5
sustainable homeownership programs 142n1
Swanson, K. 56

Tach, L. M. 36
Tema Development Corporation 19
Tetteh, K. 16
Theil index 131
Theodos, B. 128
thick descriptions 40
Tian, Y. 4
TI8 software 59
TOD *see* transit-oriented design (TOD)
transit-oriented design (TOD) 8
Turner, M. A. 140
2015 Housing Plan 17

United Nations's Sustainable Development Goal 11 4
United States: poverty deconcentration policy 15, 16; poverty deconcentration theory, policy and results in 21–3; urban policy in 17–19, *18*, *19*
Upgraders 57, 64
urban expansion areas 49n1

Vandepuije, A. O. 21
Van Eijk, G. 116, 123
van Kempen, R. 3, 108, 111
Victorian Auditor-General's Office (VAGO) 94
Victorian Housing Register (VHR) 102
Vijayawada: federal housing programs 38; greenfield city—Amaravati 43–4; inclusionary housing efforts 40–1, *41*; Jawaharlal Nehru National Urban Renewal Mission 41–2; mixed-income housing efforts 40–4, *41*; Pradhan Mantri Awas Yojana-affordable housing in partnership 42–3

Vijayawada Municipal Corporation 40, 42
vote-bank politics 46

Wilson, D. 56
Wilson, W. J. 112
Wood, M. J. 122
World Bank 19

Yang, S. 5
Yankson, P. 20

Ziersch, A. 7

For Product Safety Concerns and Information please contact our EU representative GPSR@taylorandfrancis.com Taylor & Francis Verlag GmbH, Kaufingerstraße 24, 80331 München, Germany

Printed and bound by CPI Group (UK) Ltd, Croydon, CR0 4YY

17/12/2024

01807709-0019